IMAGES
of America

BLOWING ROCK

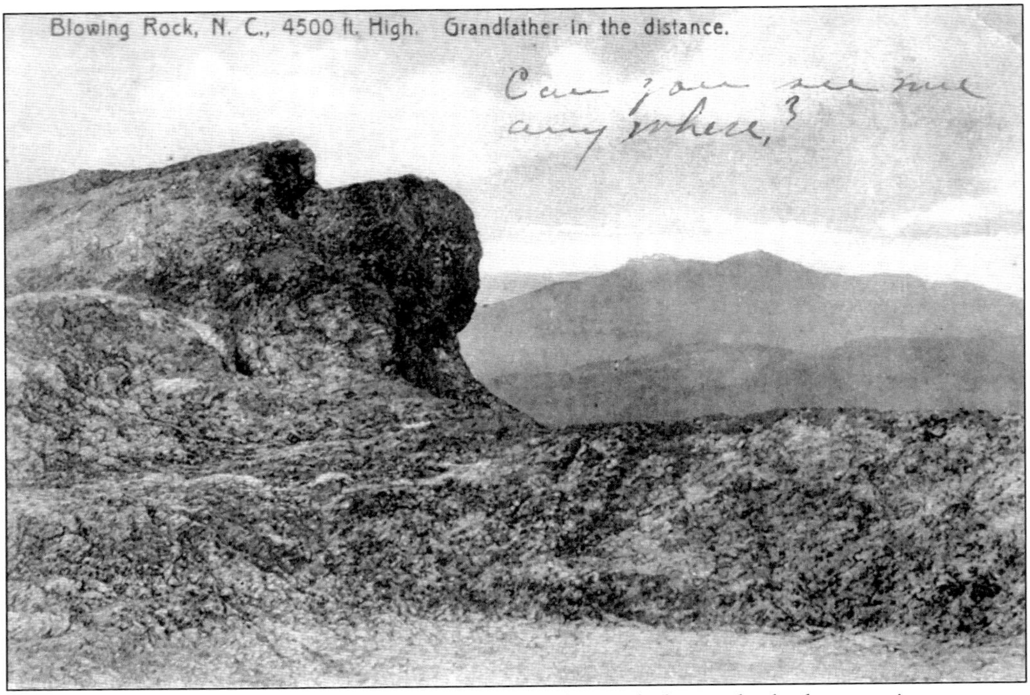

THE BLOWING ROCK. This early postcard shows the rock from which the town's name was taken. Known as North Carolina's first tourist attraction, this overlook has been a favorite sight for visitors since the late 1800s. *Ripley's Believe it or Not* listed it as the only place it snowed upside down. Because of the sweeping winds from the gorge below, light objects that are thrown from the rock will sometimes be blown back up. (Courtesy of Watauga County Library.)

IMAGES
of America

BLOWING ROCK

Donna Akers Warmuth

ARCADIA
PUBLISHING

ISBN 978-0-7385-1647-9

Published by Arcadia Publishing
Charleston, South Carolina

Printed in the United States of America

Library of Congress Catalog Card Number: 2004102351

For all general information contact Arcadia Publishing at:
Telephone 843-853-2070
Fax 843-853-0044
E-mail sales@arcadiapublishing.com
For customer service and orders:
Toll-Free 1-888-313-2665

Visit us on the Internet at www.arcadiapublishing.com

Contents

ACKNOWLEDGMENTS

This collection of photographs and postcards of Blowing Rock, North Carolina, shows the development of the town from an agricultural settlement in the lost provinces to the cosmopolitan, arts, and unique retail center of today. While the year-round population only numbers 1,500, the summer and fall seasonal residents swell that number to 6,500. Yet somehow the town retains its atmosphere of a quaint small town where neighbors greet each other by name.

By no means is this volume intended to be a formal, thorough history of the town, since books such as *A Village Tapestry* are available. Rather, this volume stands as a documentation of a sampling of the places, people, and things of Blowing Rock's past. Unfortunately, significant people and places may not have been included in this book due to lack of photographs and space limitations.

This book would not have been possible without the assistance and generosity of many people in the community, especially Jerry Burns, editor of *The Blowing Rocket*, who allowed the author unlimited access to his large collection of images and information; Ginny Stevens, past president of the Blowing Rock Historical Society, who shared the wealth of the historical society's photographs, postcards, and research; and Barbara Lentz Wright, board member of the Blowing Rock Historical Society, who provided contacts within the community, advice on the project, and a vital link to the local families. These three individuals provided me with photographs, postcards, historical information, and a plethora of contacts in the community; without their kind assistance, the book could not have come together. Citizens such as these fine folks are part of what makes the town so special.

The Blowing Rock Historical Society, who published a beautiful postcard book, *Post Cards of Historic Blowing Rock*, was very supportive of another publication of images and allowed the author to borrow images from their collection. A portion of the proceeds from this volume will be donated to the historical society to continue their worthy endeavors. Several of the photographs included were taken by local photographers, such as Worrell Photography and Palmer Blair, so the author would like to credit their work.

Many thanks and much appreciation to the following individuals and groups who shared photographs, postcards, and information about Blowing Rock: Web Alexander, Blowing Rock Historical Society, *The Blowing Rocket* and Jerry Burns, Blowing Rock Fire Department, Blowing Rock Police Department, Gracie Bradshaw, Susan Bratton, Janie Robbins Campbell, Joe Dulaney, Stella Greer Dobbins, Heidi Ellis, Pug Greene, David Harwood, Janice Coffey Herblin, Willie May Query Jewell, Ann Allison Kincaid, LaVaughn Klutz, Brian Lambeth, Ralph E. Lentz II, Carolyn Greene Robbins, Sarah Blair Spencer, Ginny Stevens, Cullie Tarleton, Richard Trexler, Watauga County Public Library, Barbara Lentz Wright, and Emma Jean Bowman Wynn. The assistance, patience, and advice of Maggie Tiller, with Arcadia Publishing, have also been essential for successfully completing this project.

A portion of the author's royalties from sales of this book will be donated to the Blowing Rock Historical Society to assist in their important work to preserve the history of this unique village.

INTRODUCTION

The village of Blowing Rock sits on the Eastern Continental Divide at an elevation of approximately 4,000 feet. Its location near the Blue Ridge Parkway is fortunate and provides additional recreational amenities. Unique restaurants, mountain inns, and fascinating shops offer a myriad of opportunities to visitors. Ordinary visitors have also been joined by many famous visitors to the town, including Dwight Eisenhower, Pearl Buck, Annie Oakley, Richard Nixon, Margaret Mitchell, Eleanor Roosevelt, Calvin Coolidge, and Herbert Hoover. This collection of images reflects the real lives of the people who lived here. Stereotypes of the ignorant and poor Appalachian mountaineer are challenged by these images of residents who dressed in the styles of the day and who valued education and hard work.

The first travelers near the Blowing Rock region were Native Americans traveling on the Nickajack Trail, which ran from today's Hickory, through Lenoir, past Blowing Rock, to Linville, and on into Tennessee. In 1752, Bishop August Spangenberg, the earliest documented explorer, passed through the area and wrote about how his party crawled on hands and knees and dragged their supplies and saddles up the mountains, since their horses were in danger of falling backward. Due to the harsh topography and cold winter conditions, the bishop decided instead to settle near Winston-Salem at Bethabara.

It was not until the 1790s that the pioneering Greene family became the earliest settlers in the area. Life was harsh here, and self-sufficiency and fortitude were necessary for survival. Other early settlers included the following family names, descendents of which are still here today: Hayes, Storie, Estes, Bolick, and Coffey. These early settlers began to transport goods such as cabbage, hay, and livestock south from the mountains to Lenoir to trade and sell. Herders from the Lenoir area brought their livestock to the mountain for grazing, and they were soon followed by eager tourists looking for cooler summer weather. The first tourists stayed in residents' houses as boarders or camped out. By the mid-1800s, the village was a busy town of 100 persons, who seemed already to be aware of the appeal of their mountain town.

As transportation became more important, the Lenoir–Blowing Rock Turnpike was incorporated in 1845 and construction of this steep road soon began. It took hundreds of workers, both slave and free, to carve the winding road up the mountain. This route made Blowing Rock only a long day's journey from Lenoir and more attractive as a summer resort. During the Civil War, families from the Piedmont sent their women and children up to the safety of the mountains. After the war, many of the husbands joined their families and decided to make permanent homes here.

Only in the late 1800s did boarding houses, hotels, and inns begin to spring up to meet the demands of the tourists. The first resort opened in Blowing Rock in 1875, when William Morris began taking summer boarders. Other inns followed, and in 1884 the Watauga Hotel was opened. It was reported in local newspapers that Blowing Rock was the south's leading resort in the late 1800s and early 1900s, rivaled only by the developing Miami Beach area. Visitors and seasonal residents were welcomed by the locals, since they provided another market for agricultural goods, and a service industry developed. By 1894, the population of the village was 400, counting visitors. Drug stores, livery stables, churches, stores, a post office, and bowling alleys soon followed. W.L. Holshouser was the first to open a store in 1893; it sold everything from caskets to automobiles. According to John Preston Arthur in *A History of Watauga County*, "Blowing Rock is established beyond question as one of the finest and most popular pleasure resorts of the South."

The extension of the East Tennessee & Western North Carolina Railroad line to Boone in 1918 also helped to connect Blowing Rock with the rest of the world. Visitors from afar would ride a train to Lenoir and travel by surrey or stagecoach up to Blowing Rock. In 1900, tolls on the turnpike were 25¢ for a two-horse wagon, 20¢ for a one-horse wagon, 10¢ for a horseback rider, and pedestrians (brave and hardy souls) were free. Later, autos were charged a $1 toll.

All of the residents and visitors have contributed much to the town and helped to create its unique allure and success. Some of the more notable people who made Blowing Rock their seasonal home contributed to worthy causes such as schools, healthcare, education, libraries, and churches. These prominent families include the following: Stringfellow, Snyder, Daingerfield, Cones, Price, Cannon, Mebane, and Broyhill. Local families adapted to the new economic opportunities that tourism provided and sold produce, livestock, and crafts to seasonal residents. Locals opened hotels, motels, inns, stores, restaurants, and gas stations to accommodate the increasing numbers of tourists. Although several fires have occurred downtown, many historic buildings remain and the town has grown up through the 20th century with a healthy economy and an emphasis on preserving its heritage.

References

Altmayer, Bud. *A Family History of Watauga County*. Boone, NC: Minor's Printing Company, 1994.

Arthur, John Preston. *A History of Watauga County, North Carolina*. Johnson City, TN: The Overmountain Press, 1915, reprint 1992.

Bate, Ginger Smith. *Walking Around the Lake: Memories of Childhood in Blowing Rock*. San Jose, CA: Ginger Smith Bate, 1999.

Blowing Rock Historical Society. *Post Cards of Historic Blowing Rock*. Boone, NC: Parkway Publishers, 2002.

Buxton, Barry M. *A Village Tapestry: The History of Blowing Rock*. Boone, NC: Appalachian Consortium Press, 1989.

Lentz, Ralph E. II. *W.R. Trivett, Appalachian Pictureman*. Jefferson, NC: McFarland and Company, Inc. Publishers, 2001.

Noblitt, Philip T. *A Mansion in the Mountains: The Story of Moses & Bertha Cone & Their Blowing Rock Manor*. Boone, NC: Parkway Publishers, 1996.

One

Downtown

Once called "America's Switzerland," the village of Blowing Rock is located at approximately 4,000 feet in elevation. Not until after the Revolutionary War did a settlement begin to grow in the area. The early settlers included family names such as Greene, Hayes, Storie, Estes, Bolick, and Coffey. These families were subsistence farmers who farmed the land here. The locals transported agricultural goods by wagon south to Lenoir. The Lenoir–Blowing Rock Turnpike project developed after 1845 and improved the accessibility to the village. The 1880 census lists 62 households in the town, with heads of households in 47 of these identified as farmers or farm laborers. The town was incorporated in 1889. The tourism trade began to take off after the Civil War. The first summer visitors would camp or stay in the local people's houses as boarders. Later, they built large summer homes which they referred to as "cottages." The tourism and summer residents have greatly improved the economic diversity of the area. The first mayor was Joseph Bogle Clark, who was a colorful character. Early downtown included residences, stores, churches, blacksmith shops, livery stables, hotels, and drug stores. Several fires have occurred downtown and destroyed the earliest frame structures. As more affluent tourists and summer visitors came, the social gaps between these people and the local population grew. However, many of the "cottagers" gave back to the community and established libraries, scholarships, healthcare, education, and other opportunities for locals. The downtown area today retains the charm and peacefulness that early postcards and photographs reflect.

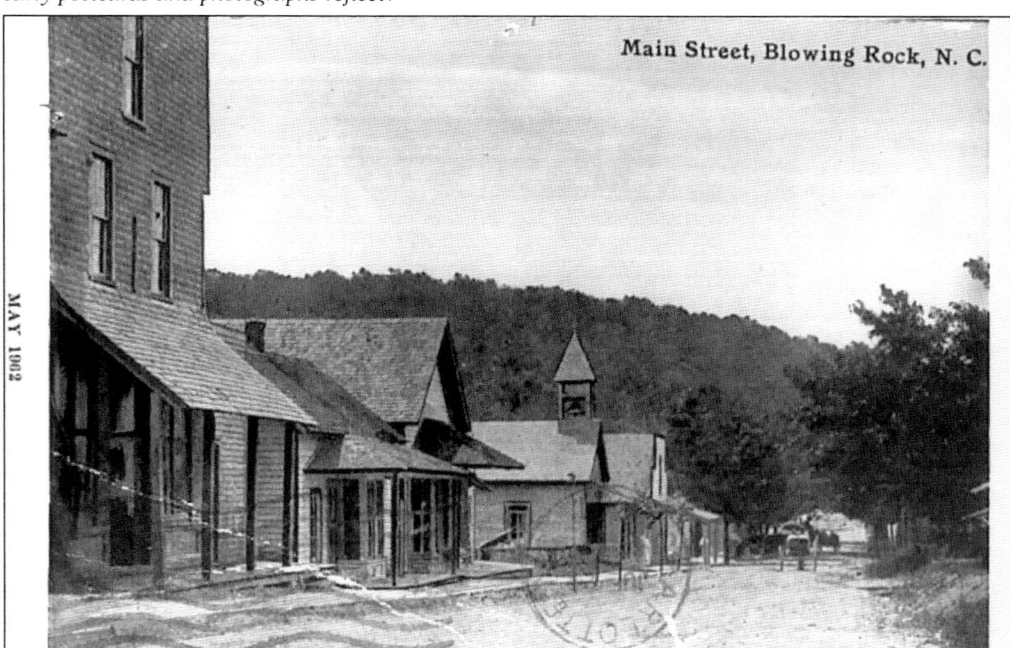

MAIN STREET, C. 1905. Pictured in this southern view along Main Street are, from left to right, the Mercantile Company of Thomas Coffey, the Photography Shop (owned by Wiley Vannoy), Dr. Rabey's Drug Store, the first Episcopal Church and Reading Room (with bell tower), and H.C. Hayes General Store. (Courtesy of *The Blowing Rocket.*)

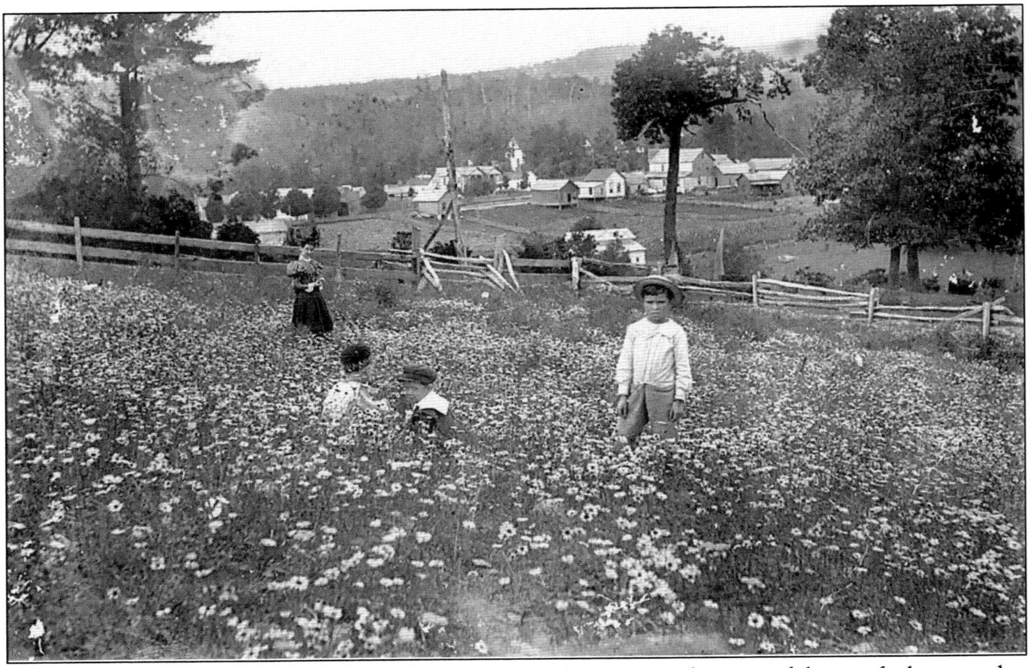

AT PLAY IN FLOWER FIELDS. This quaint photograph captures the peacefulness of a bygone day in this view of downtown from Boyden Hill. These folks seem to be contemplating the beauty of the outdoors. The village lies below them. (Courtesy of *The Blowing Rocket*.)

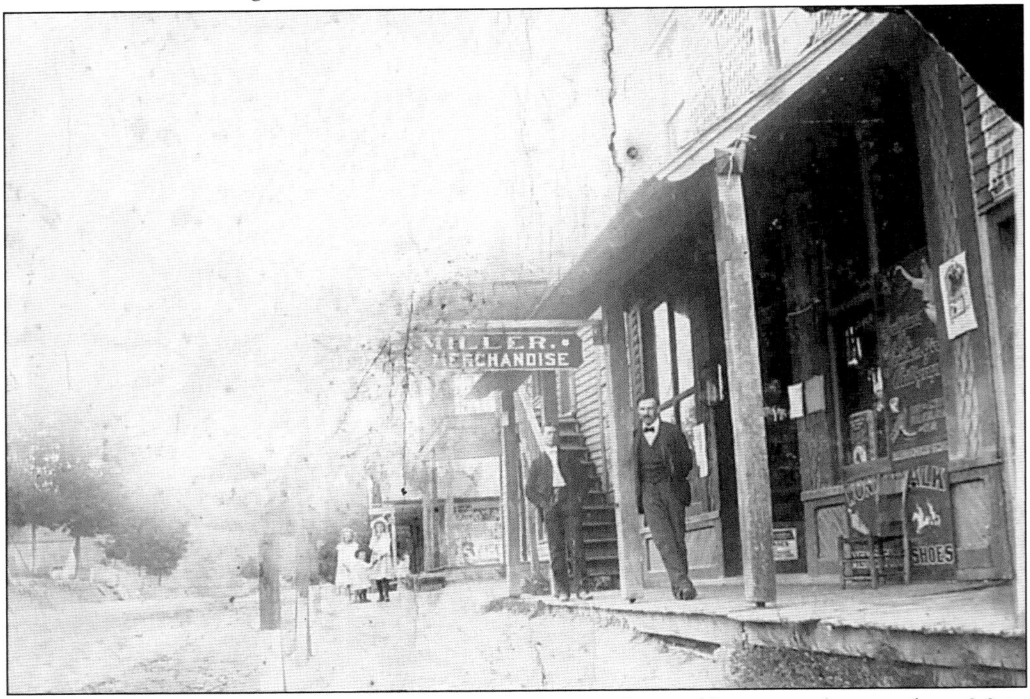

MILLER GENERAL STORE. Cicero Miller is standing in front of his general store along Main Street. Three children can barely be seen along the street, which appears to be dirt at this time. Street trees have been planted on the opposite side of the road. (Courtesy of *The Blowing Rocket*.)

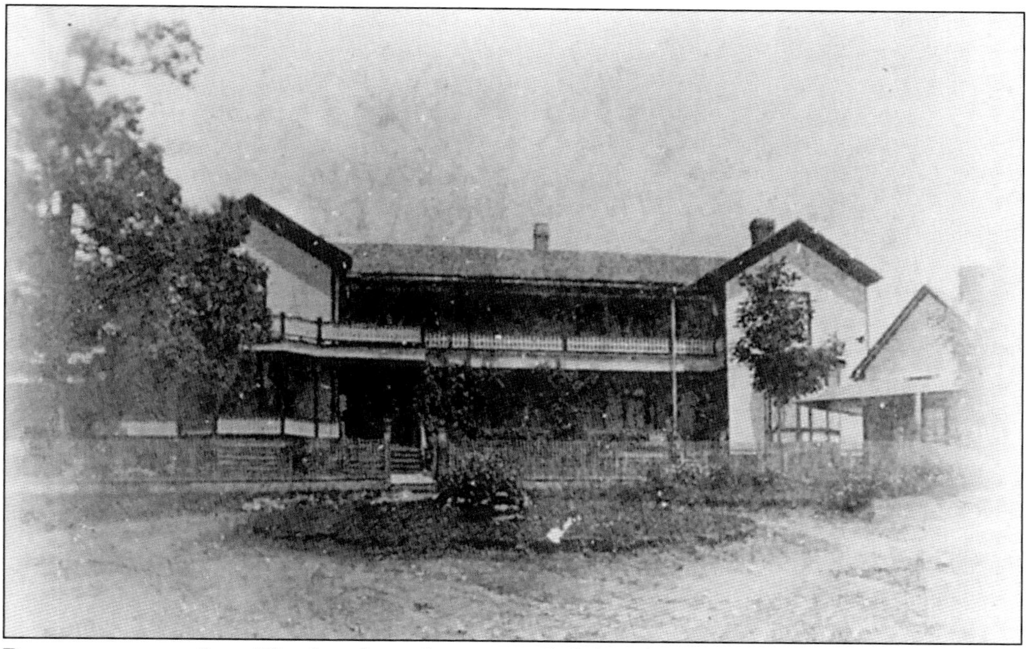

RHODODENDRON INN. This hotel may have preceded the Blowing Rock Hotel and was located near the same site. The inn was operated by Mrs. Hempshire Stringfellow. The building burned in 1902 or 1903. The Rhododendron Inn was one of the early inns catering to visitors and travelers. (Courtesy of *The Blowing Rocket.*)

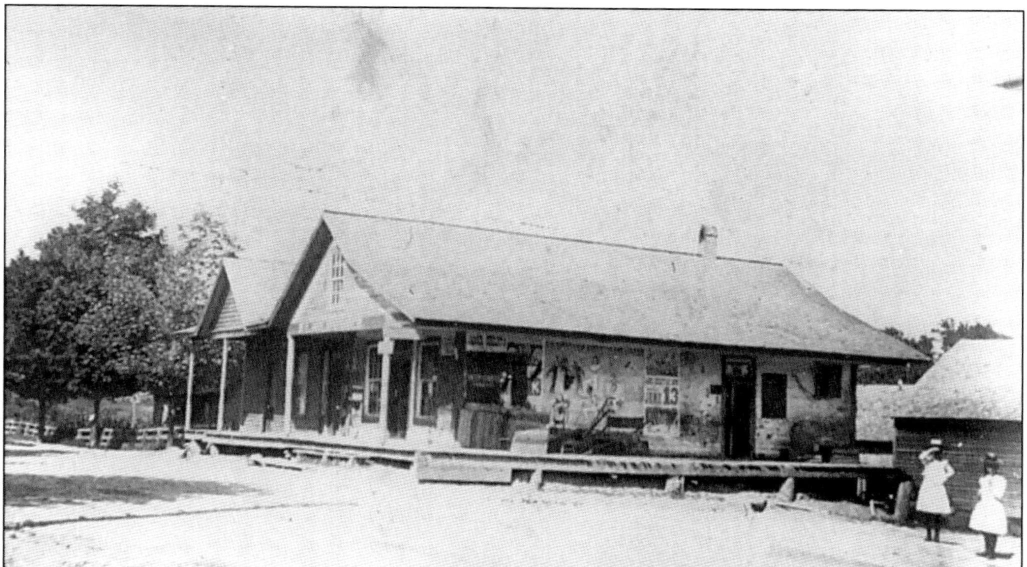

HOLSHOUSER STORE, C. 1895. This was the first store of W.L. "Will" Holshouser, located at the corner of Main Street and Sunset Drive, where the Wachovia Bank currently stands. The building burned in the 1923 fire. (Courtesy of *The Blowing Rocket.*)

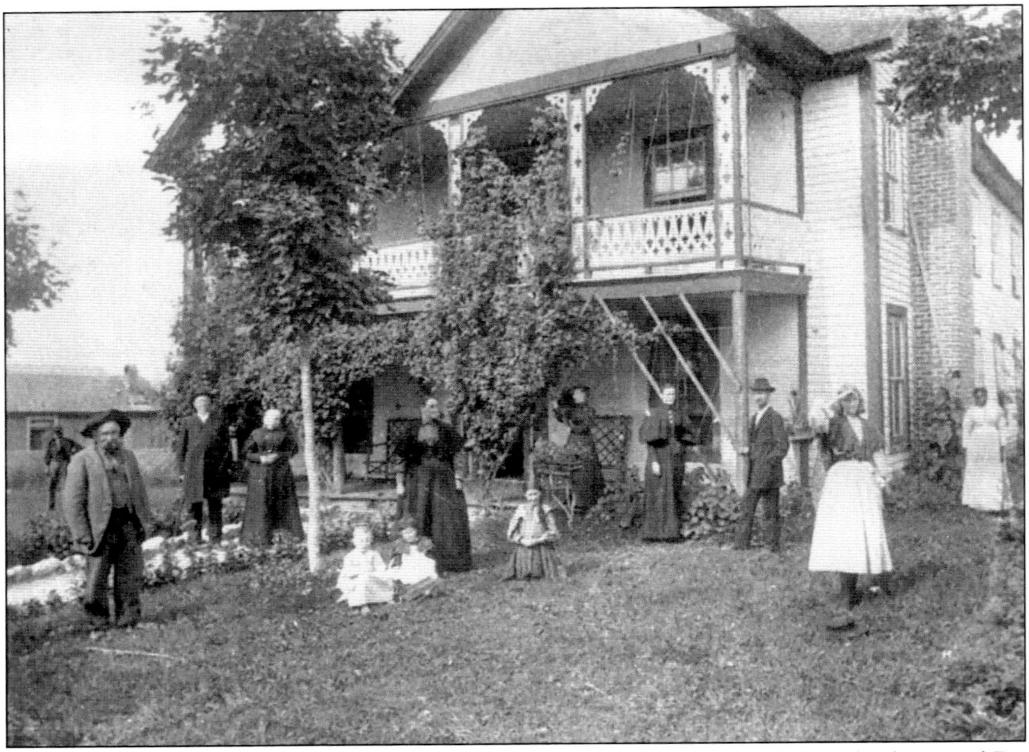

Dr. Reeves's House. This photograph is identified as the Reeves House, the home of Dr. Letcher C. Reeves. Dr. Reeves was the second doctor in Blowing Rock and operated a drug store on Main Street. He was from Alleghany County and in the 1890s moved from Boone to Blowing Rock to practice medicine. Unfortunately, he died from a ruptured appendix in 1899. His wife, Sallie Council Reeves, and daughter operated a gift shop in the town for several years. This house is thought to have been located behind Dr. Reeves's drug store on Main Street. The drug store was a social gathering place, especially in the evenings, with Saturday night dances. The decorative detailing along the porch columns and balustrade reflects a more affluent household. Note that most of the people in the photograph are well dressed in the latest styles of the day. Early photographs such as these can help dispel the myth of the "poor, ignorant Appalachian." (Courtesy of *The Blowing Rocket*.)

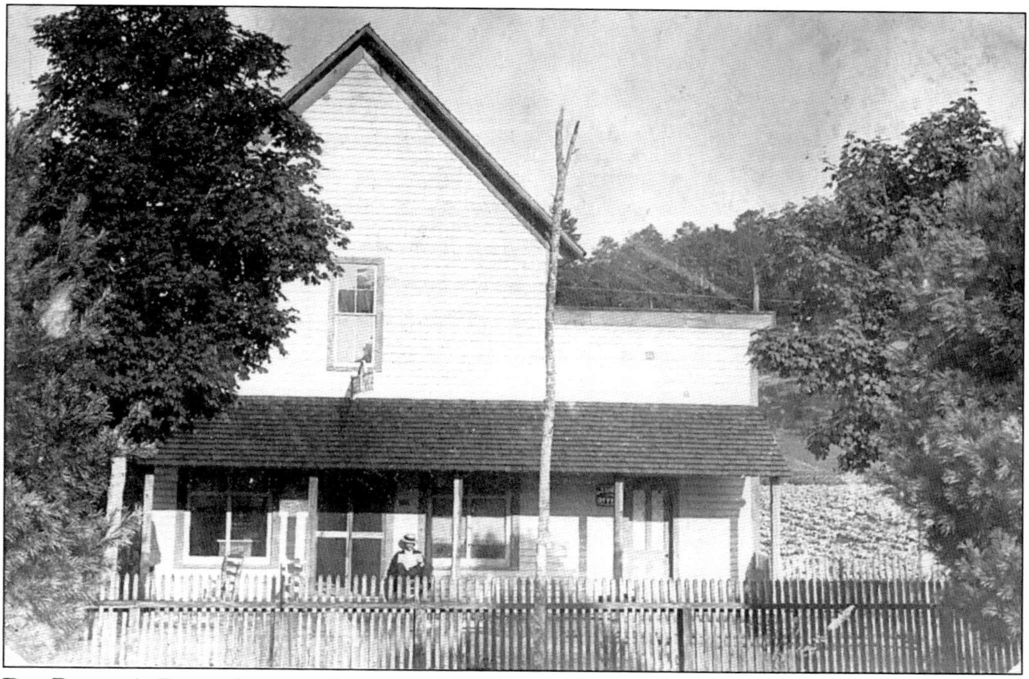

DR. REEVES'S DRUG STORE. This is a *c.* 1898 view of Dr. Letcher Reeves's drug store, which was located on Main Street. The store was a community gathering place in the evenings with dances and music. The previous photograph shows Dr. Reeves's house. (Courtesy of *The Blowing Rocket.*)

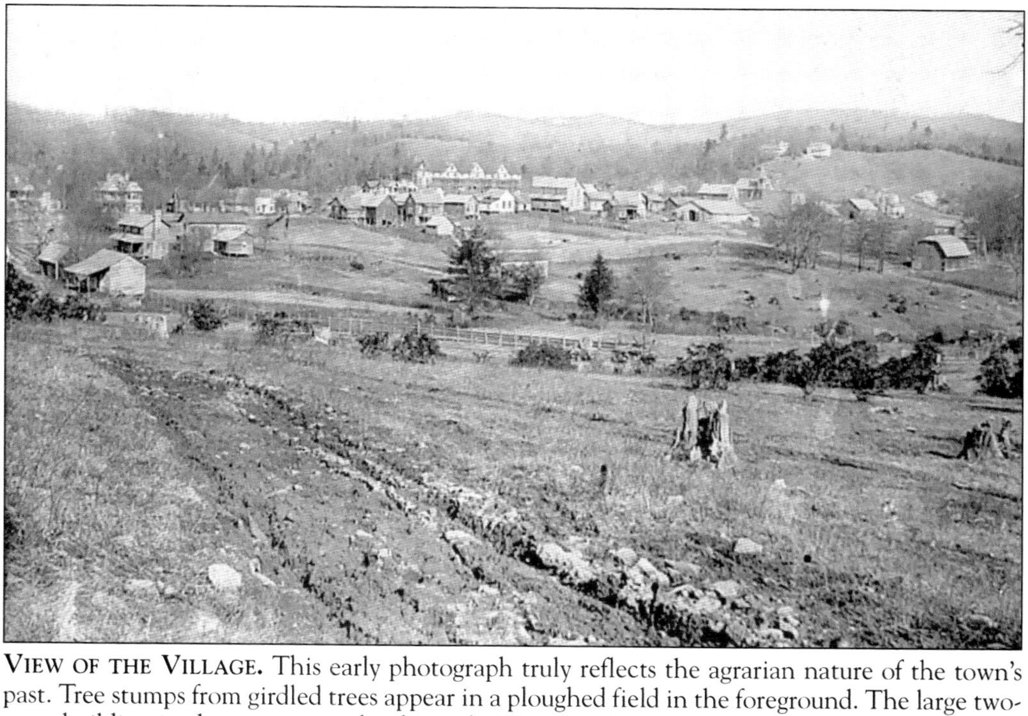

VIEW OF THE VILLAGE. This early photograph truly reflects the agrarian nature of the town's past. Tree stumps from girdled trees appear in a ploughed field in the foreground. The large two-story building in the center may be the early Watauga Hotel, and the Cone Mansion is barely visible on the top center ridge. (Courtesy of *The Blowing Rocket.*)

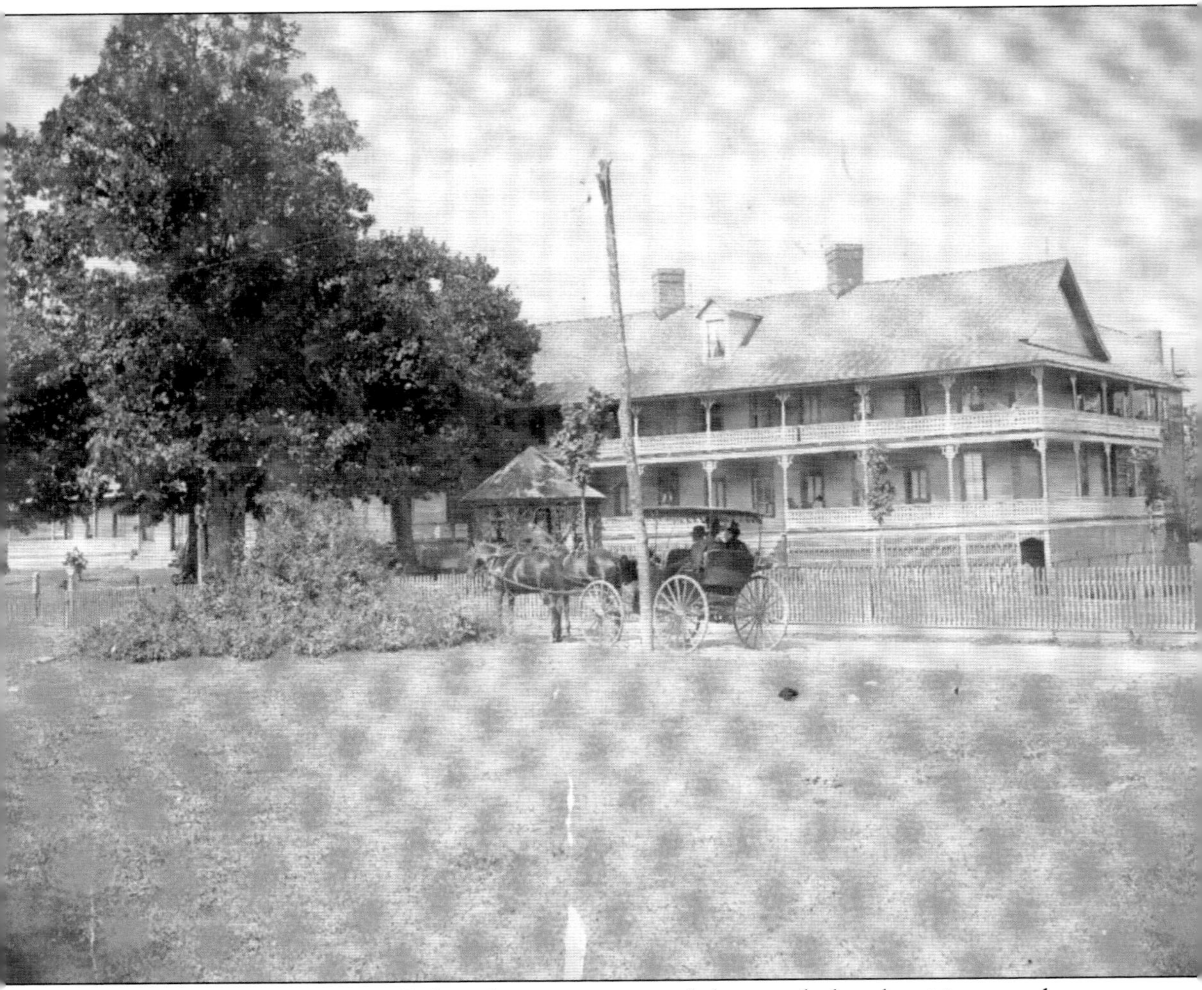

Blowing Rock Hotel. Before the construction of these early hotels, visitors to the town would either camp out or stay in small boarding houses. This large hotel was built by Col. Robert H. Gray and John King in 1888. The site had been previously used as a stockade during the Civil War. This large hotel was located near the intersection of 321 Business and Chestnut Drive. Guest cottages on the property were also available. A few of the cottages remain near Chestnut and Main Street and are used as residences. Dances and various social events were held at the hotel, as well as at the Green Park Hotel and Watauga Hotel, and offered entertainment to attract summer visitors. Livery stables were located near the hotel. The hotel became modernized in the 1930s when the 36 rooms were equipped with hot and cold running water and private baths. In 1939, the hotel celebrated its 50th anniversary and claimed the honor of being the oldest resort in the nation still owned and operated by the same family. (Courtesy of *The Blowing Rocket.*)

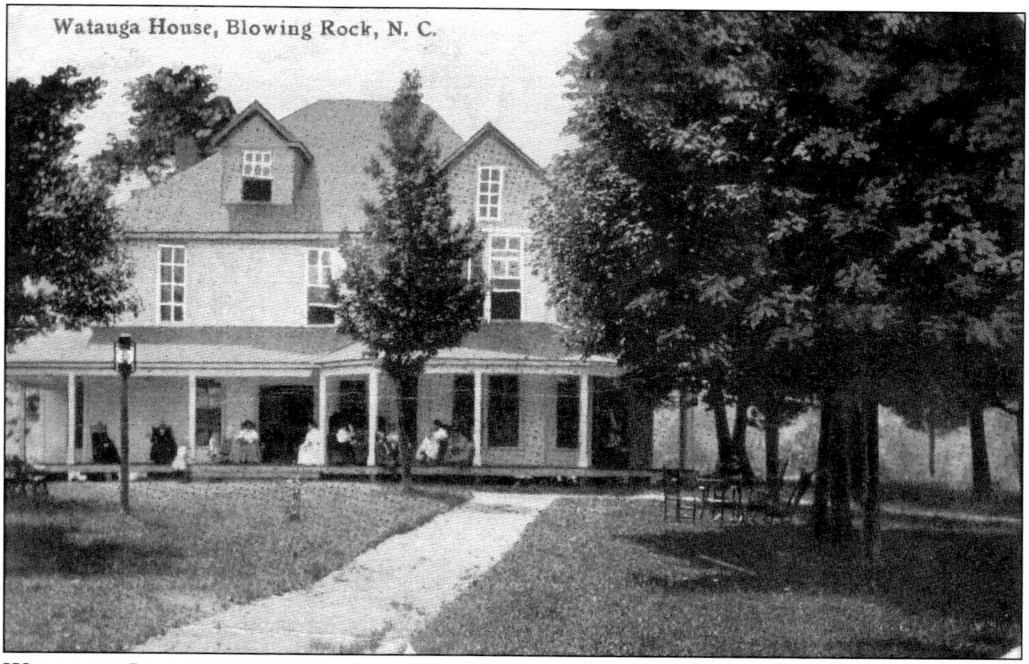

WATAUGA INN, C. 1912. The Watauga Hotel was first built on this site in 1888 and was one of the earliest hotels in town. Several cottages were added to the property, one of which now houses the Blowing Rock Museum. Fire destroyed the hotel in the early 1900s, and the Watauga Inn, shown in this photograph, was built on the property. Another fire in 1926 burned this building, and the land eventually became a park for the town. (Courtesy of Stella Greer Dobbins.)

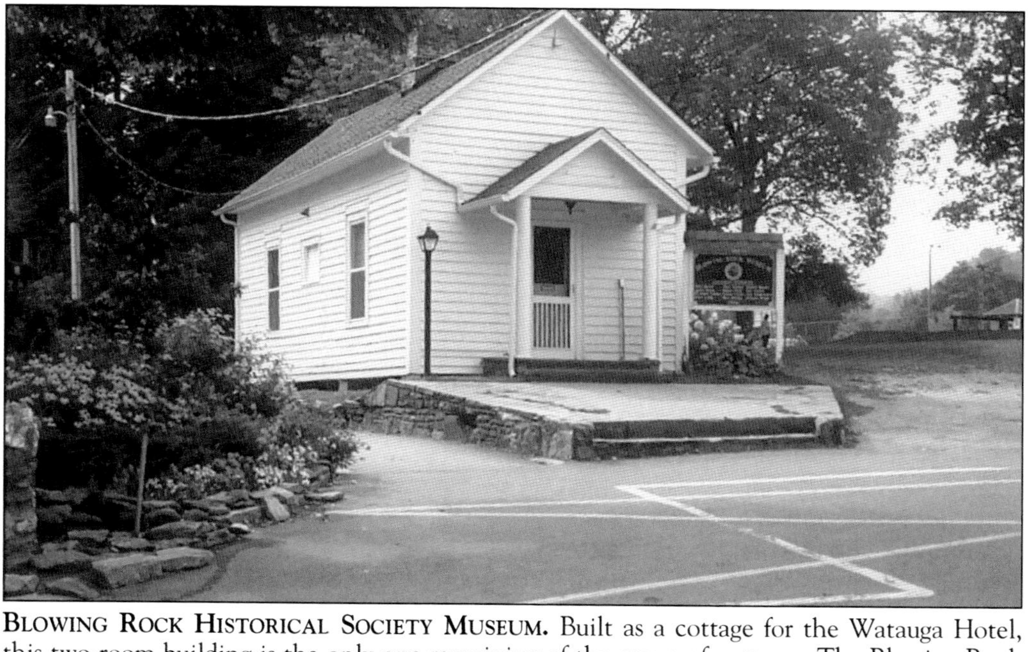

BLOWING ROCK HISTORICAL SOCIETY MUSEUM. Built as a cottage for the Watauga Hotel, this two-room building is the only one remaining of the group of cottages. The Blowing Rock Historical Society now operates a fascinating museum featuring the town's history in the building. (Courtesy of Ginny Stevens.)

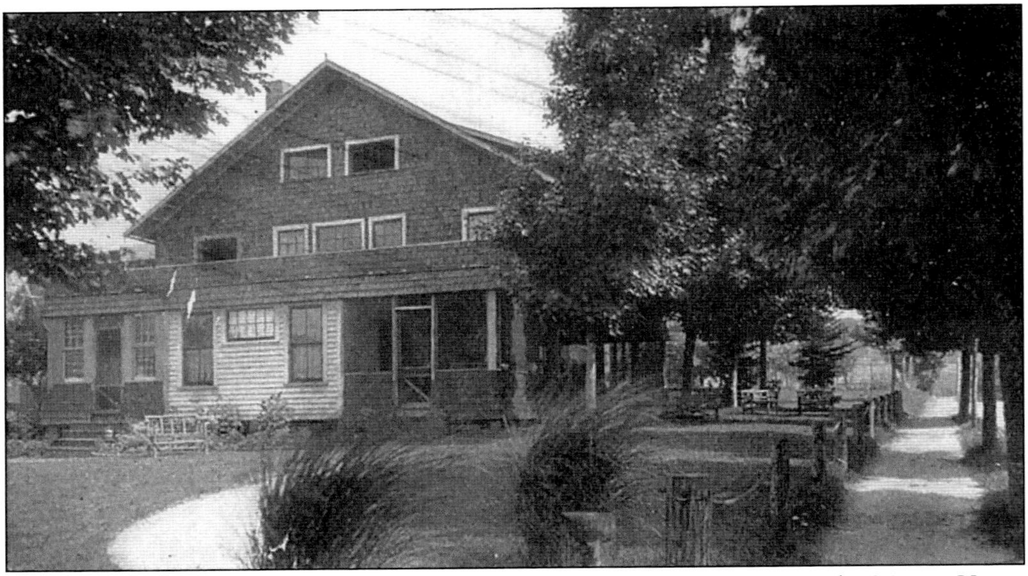

Martin Cottage. Although built in 1870 along Main Street as a home, the Martin House soon began to take in summer boarders, with the catchy slogan, "not a hotel, but a home." The Martin House is one of the village's identifiable landmarks. Today, the building houses several retail stores, and additions have been constructed. (Courtesy of *The Blowing Rocket*.)

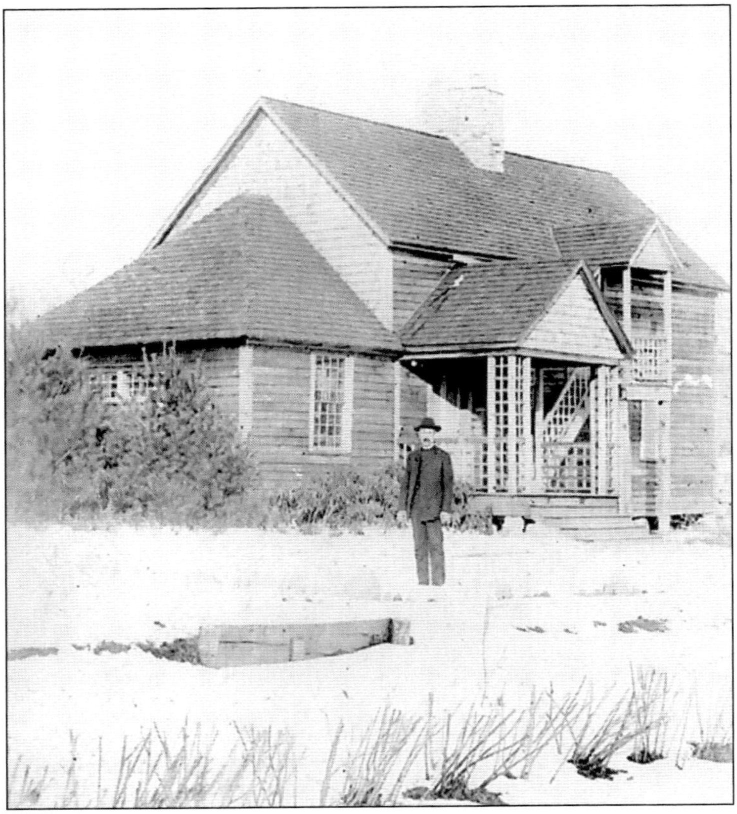

Reverend Savage and Randall Memorial Workshop. Rev. William Savage, Episcopal minister from 1902 to 1917, helped organize this craft center in 1907. The workshop had equipment for weaving, spinning, basketry, and woodwork for locals to develop crafts. (Courtesy of *The Blowing Rocket*.)

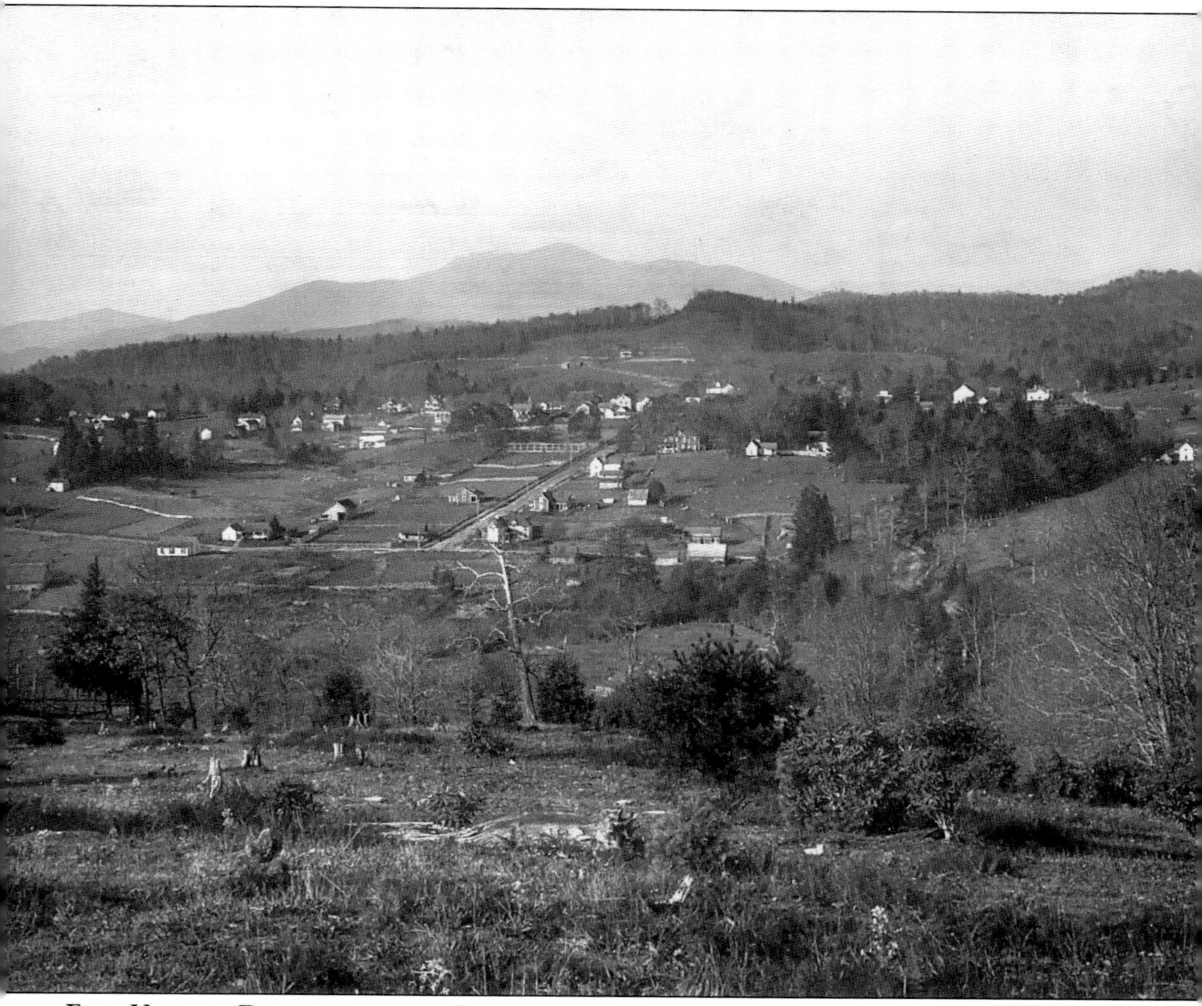

FAIR VIEW OF DOWNTOWN AND GRANDFATHER MOUNTAIN. This early photograph, taken with a view to the west, shows the cleared ridges around the town and the agricultural basis of the economy. Tree stumps and mountain laurel can be seen in the foreground. The small houses and barns reflect the simple lives of the local population prior to the summer tourist boom. The peacefulness and small town flavor of the village, which it has managed to maintain, is apparent in this image. Sunset Drive is running up the center of the photograph and Ransom Street is shown along the bottom edge of the town. The Hayes house can be seen along Main Street in the background. Grandfather Mountain appears in profile in the background. (Courtesy of *The Blowing Rocket.*)

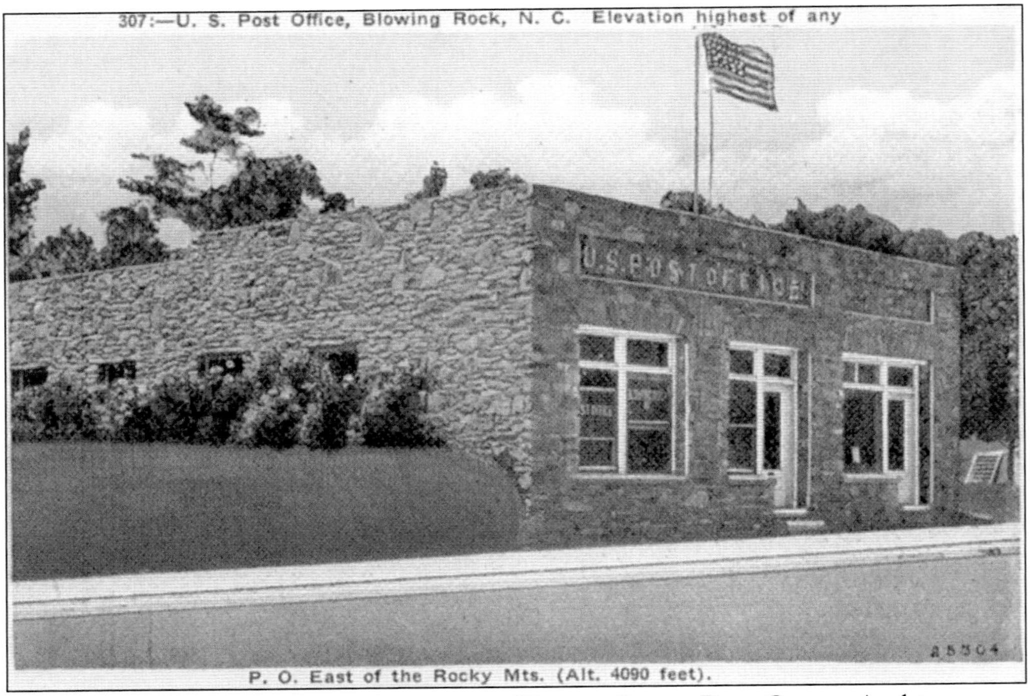

UNITED STATES POST OFFICE. As this postcard proclaims, the town had the post office at the highest elevation of any east of the Rocky Mountains. Located at the corner of Main Street and U.S. 221, this rustic building was built about 1924 of native stone. It later became the Parkway Hotel and now houses Mountain View Realty. (Courtesy of *The Blowing Rocket.*)

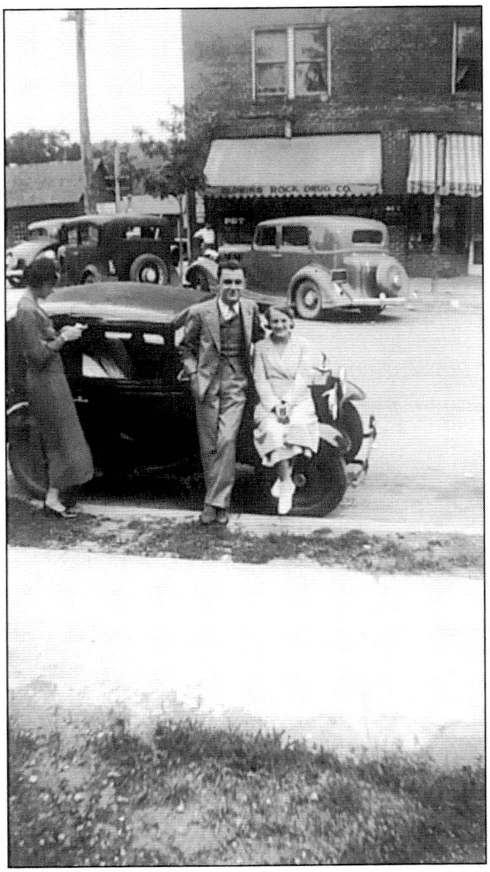

DEE CANNON AND DORIS GREENE. The Blowing Rock Drug Company is located in the background of this 1934 photograph of the downtown area. Dee Cannon and Doris Greene are posed leaning on their automobile. (Courtesy of *The Blowing Rocket.*)

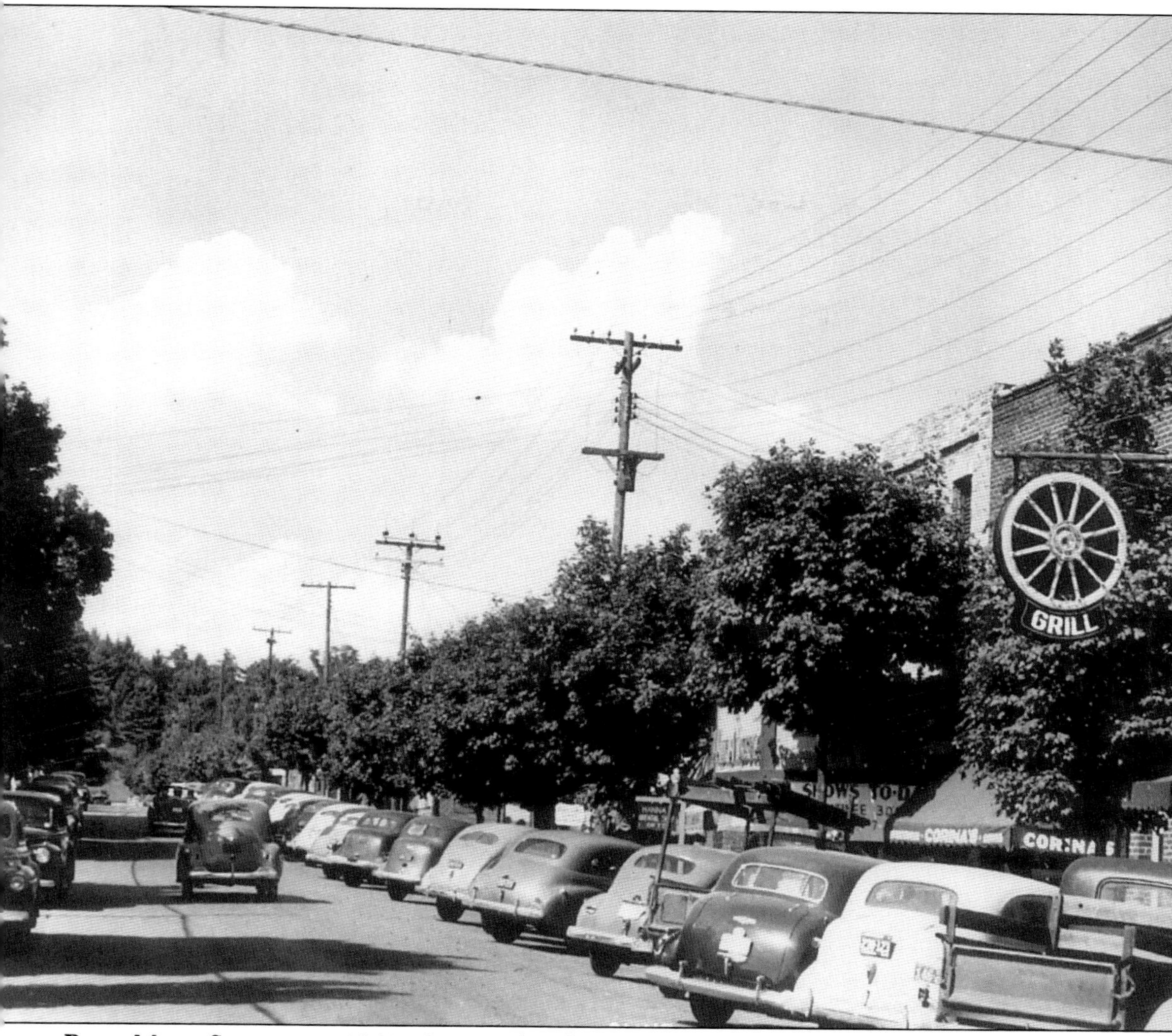

BUSY MAIN STREET, C. 1940. Cars are lined up on a busy downtown shopping day. This northern view of Main Street shows the Wagonwheel Grill, Corina's dress store, the Yonahlossee Movie Theatre, Hanna's Oriental Rug Shop, and Fincke Gallery. Not visible in the photograph but located up the street from the Wagonwheel Grill were Boot Black's Shop (shoe repair), Craig's Grocery (run by Gene Craig and Perry Lentz), and the Women's Exchange (run by Miss Lena Reeves). The Wagonwheel Grill was a very popular eatery known for its delicious strawberry shortcake. In these days, downtown functioned not only to provide goods and services but also served as a meeting and greeting place. (Courtesy of *The Blowing Rocket*.)

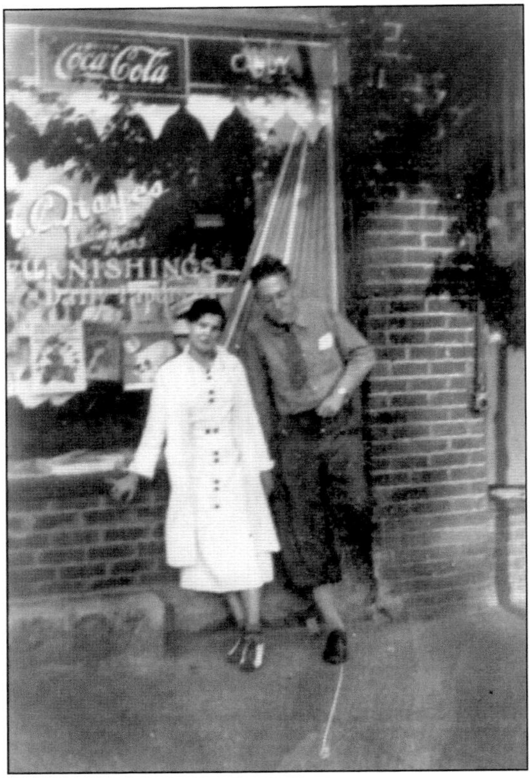

Stella Greer and Billy Mack Hardin, 1936. These young people are standing in front of H.C. Hayes Ladies' and Men's Furnishings, where they were employed. Owned by Henry C. and Lucinda Hayes, the store was located next to present-day Sonny's Grill. The building is still standing and is used as a restaurant. (Courtesy of Stella Greer Dobbins.)

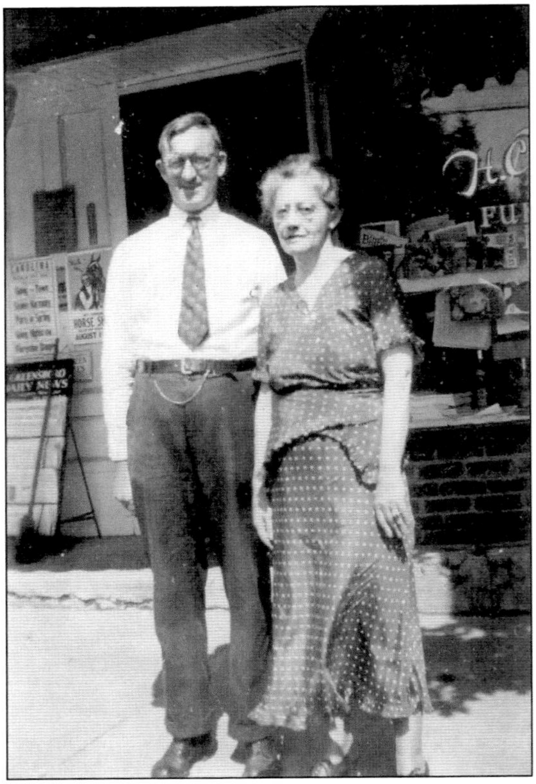

Henry C. and Lucinda Hayes, c. 1930. Mr. and Mrs. Hayes were business owners in downtown Blowing Rock. They owned the H.C. Hayes Ladies' and Men's Furnishings store (pictured behind them), the Razooks building, and the Hayes house, which was located downtown but was recently moved to U.S. 221. (Courtesy of Stella Greer Dobbins.)

CLARA JOHNSON AND BILLY MACK HARDIN AT RAZOOK'S. In this c. 1930 photograph, Clara Johnson and Bill Mack Hardin pose in front of Razook's Women's Sportswear. The store sold upscale ladies' clothing. The building is still located downtown and is used for retail purposes. (Courtesy of Stella Greer Dobbins.)

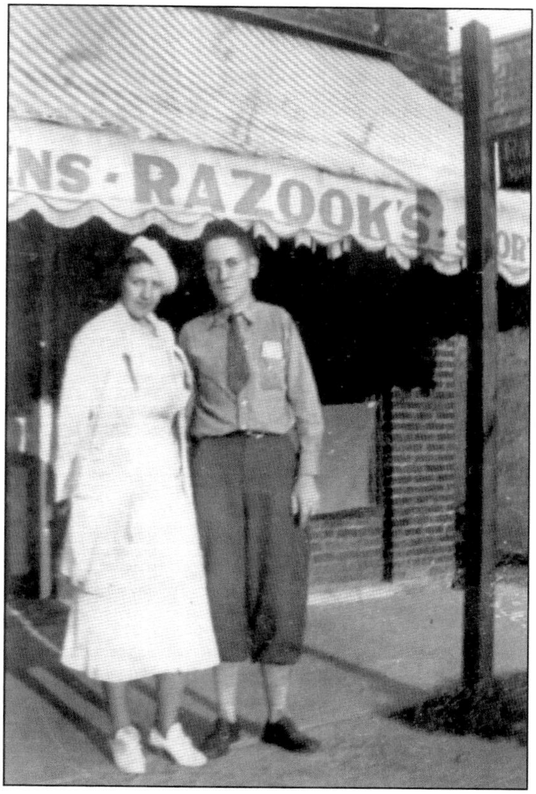

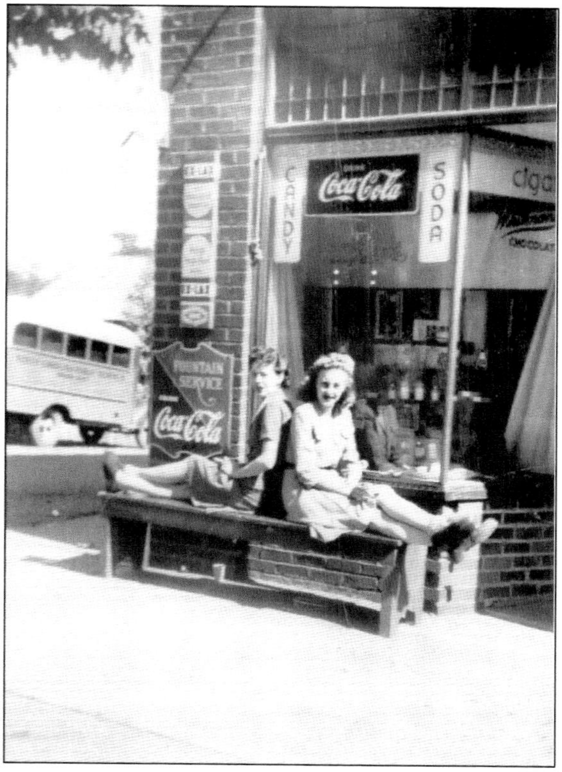

TWO YOUNG LADIES HANGING OUT AT THE DRUG STORE. These young ladies seem to be enjoying a lazy afternoon at a downtown drug store. The store was located on the corner of Sunset and Main, and the building now houses a retail store. (Courtesy of Emma Jean Bowman Wynn.)

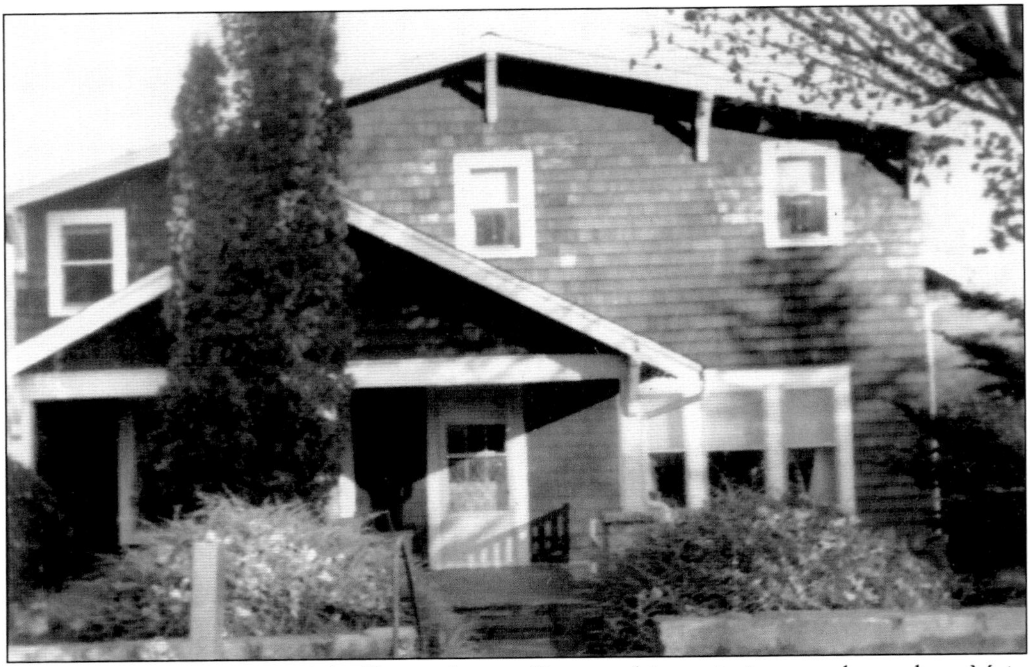

GREENE INN. Built in 1923 by Emma Austin Greene, this rustic inn was located on Main Street beside the present First Citizens Bank. In the early 1930s, the house became the Greene Inn, providing board and three delicious meals for boarders and the public until the late 1950s. (Courtesy of Emma Jean Bowman Wynn.)

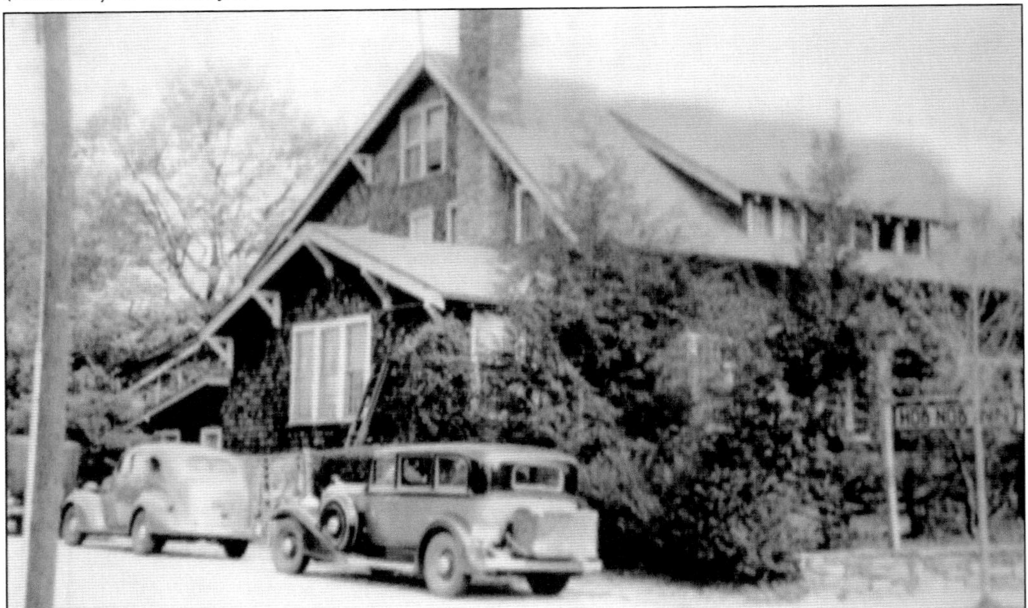

HOB NOB INN. This early inn was in business about 1934 at the corner of Main Street and Park Avenue. The inn later became the New Watauga Inn. Unfortunately, it burned in 1946, and since this was the third hotel named "Watauga" to be destroyed by fires, the namesake of "Watauga" was never again used for an inn or hotel. (Courtesy of Blowing Rock Historical Society.)

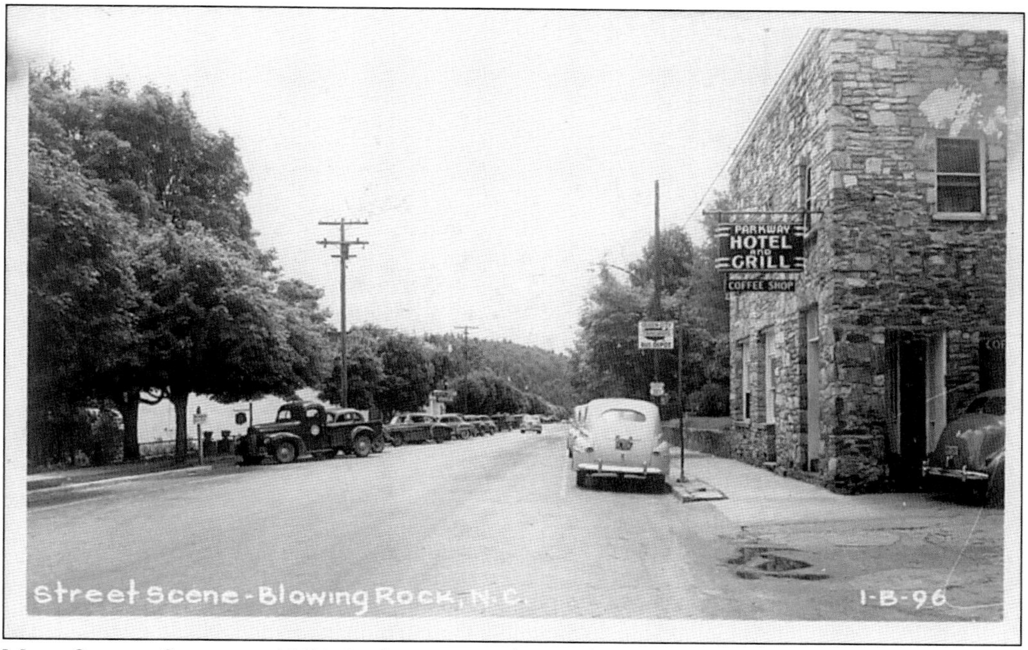

Main Street Scene, c. 1950. In this view to the south of Main Street, the Parkway Hotel and Grill is visible. This restaurant was popular with locals and tourists for many years. The stone building is still standing and houses offices. (Courtesy of Ginny Stevens.)

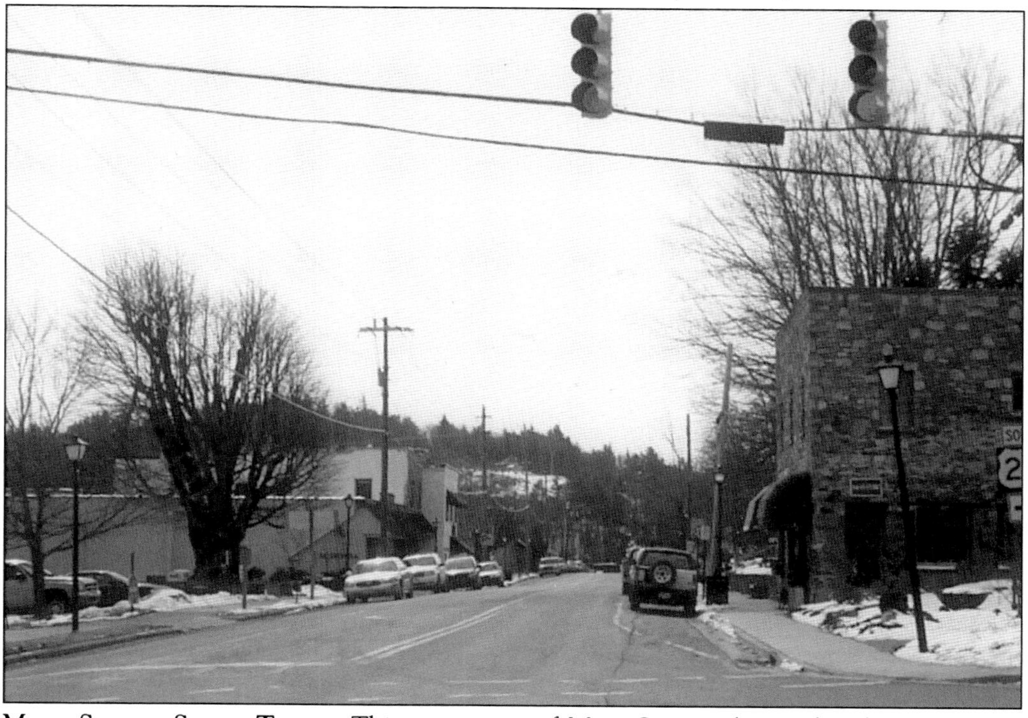

Main Street Scene Today. This same view of Main Street taken today shows how the streetscape and buildings of yesterday have not changed much. The gray stone building on the right, once the post office and then the Parkway Hotel and Grill, now houses an art gallery and offices.

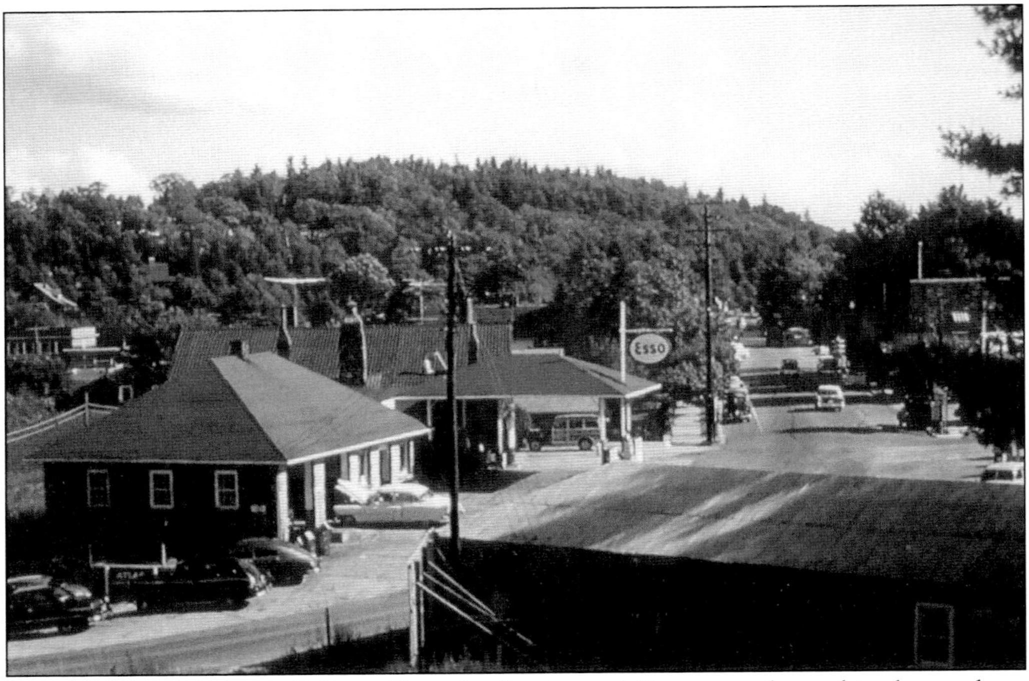

ESSO STATION. Shown *c.* 1956, an Esso Gas Station and Garage was located in the northern end of town. Bill Lentz was the owner of the station. The buildings remain and are used for various retail stores. The building in the foreground has been demolished, and the lot is now a parking lot. (Courtesy of Pug Greene.)

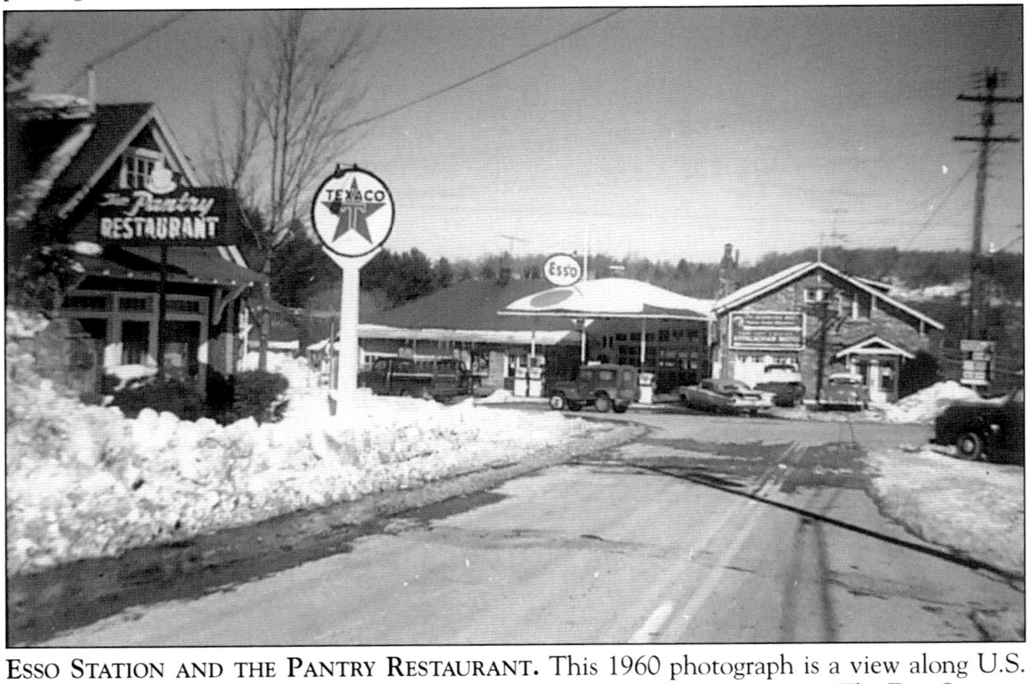

ESSO STATION AND THE PANTRY RESTAURANT. This 1960 photograph is a view along U.S. 221 of the Pantry Restaurant (now the Speckled Trout) and a Texaco station. The Esso Station, owned and operated by Bill Lentz, was across Main Street, and in the rock building to its right were the bus station and freight station. (Courtesy of Barbara Lentz Wright.)

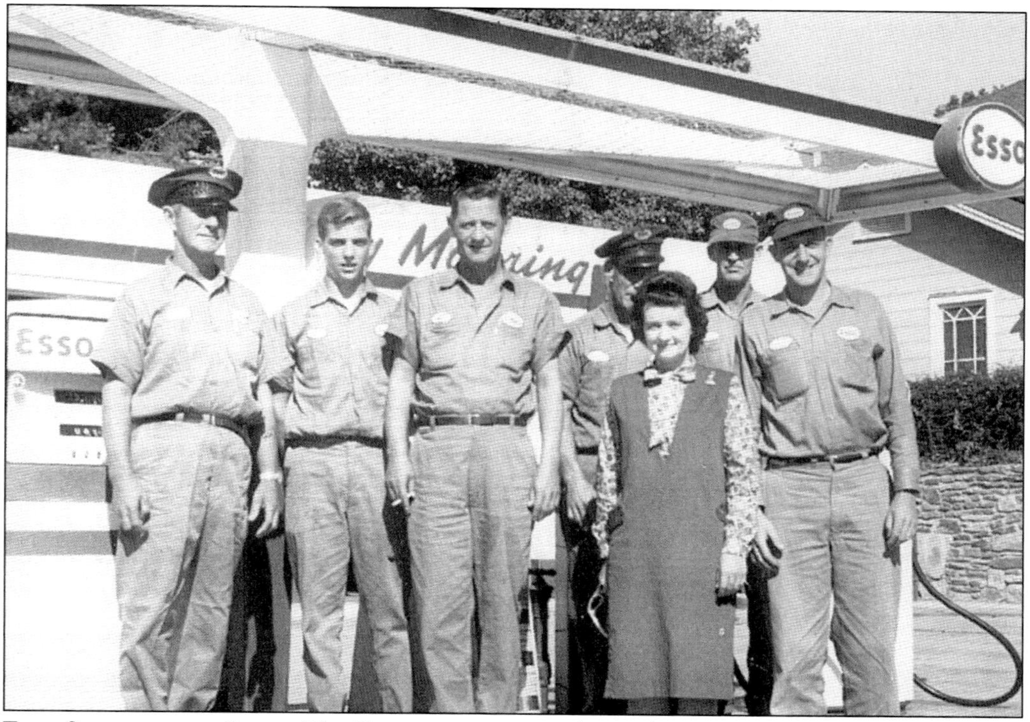

ESSO STATION AND STAFF. The Esso service station, located on the corner of Main Street and Park Avenue, was a presence in downtown for many years. Pictured from left to right are (front row) Betty and Hayden Pitts (owners); (back row) Doss Keller, John Cook, Jack Greene, Boyd Cook, and Stewart Bolick. (Courtesy of *The Blowing Rocket*.)

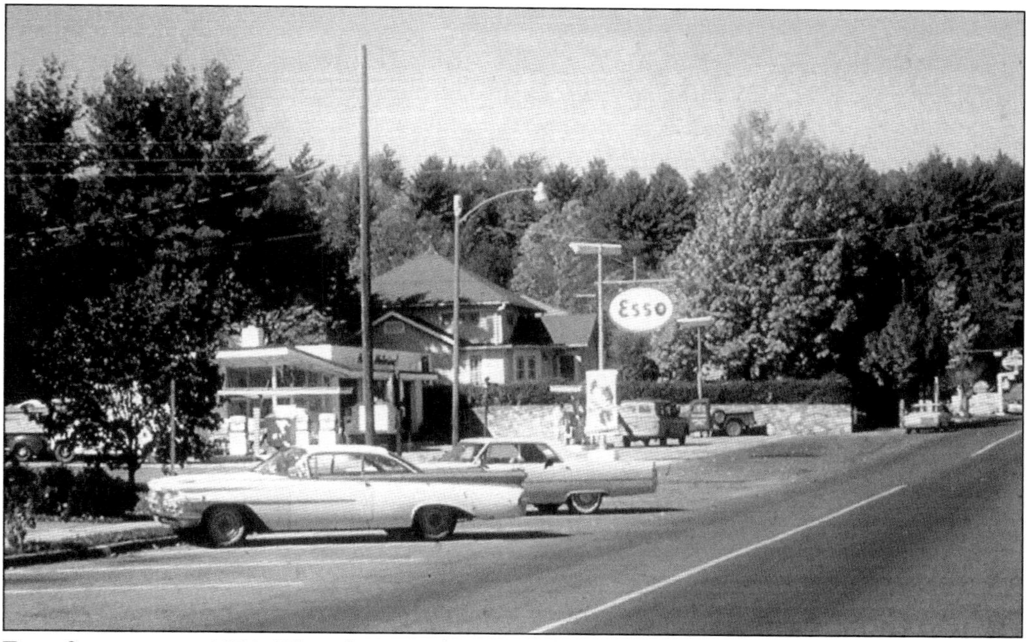

ESSO STATION, C. 1970. This photograph is a northern view of Main Street, showing the Esso Station on the corner. Hayden Pitts was the owner of the store. The site is currently occupied by the Blowing Rock Market and Exxon gas station. (Courtesy of Pug Greene.)

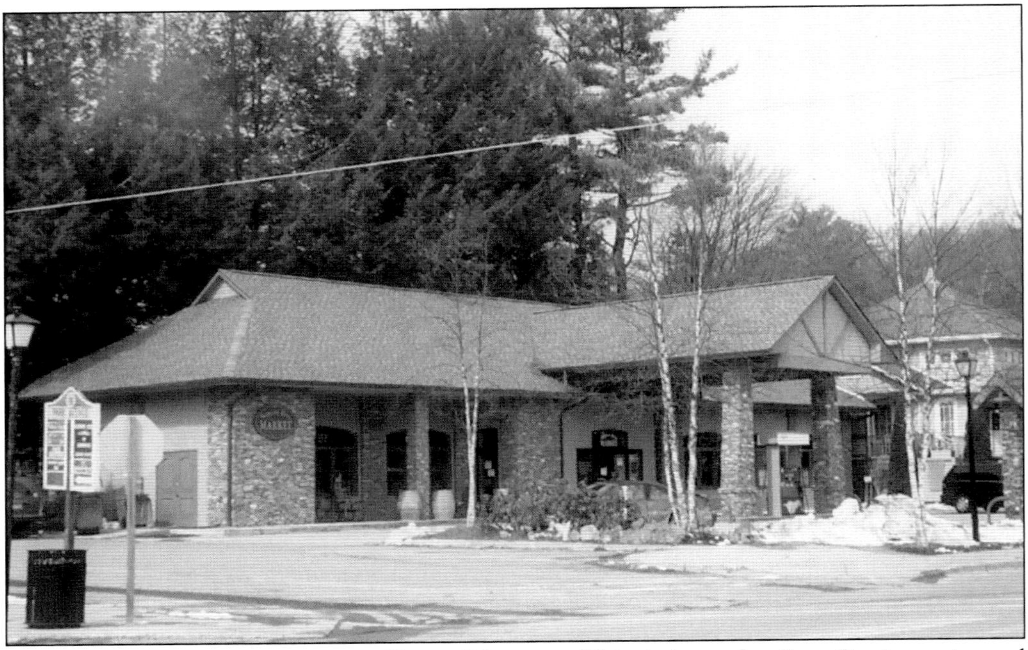

Exxon Station and Blowing Rock Market. This is how the Esso Station, pictured previously, appears today. The new stone building and gas station are one of the more attractive new infill developments in town. (Courtesy of Donna Warmuth.)

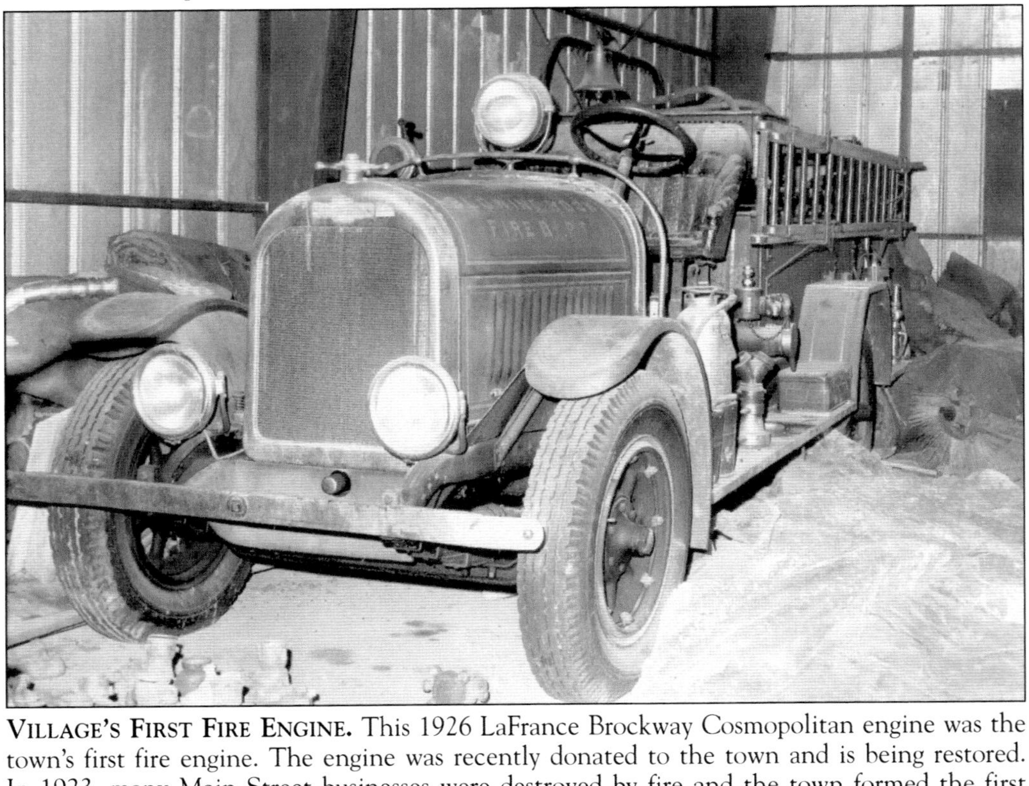

Village's First Fire Engine. This 1926 LaFrance Brockway Cosmopolitan engine was the town's first fire engine. The engine was recently donated to the town and is being restored. In 1923, many Main Street businesses were destroyed by fire and the town formed the first volunteer fire department. (Courtesy of Blowing Rock Fire Department.)

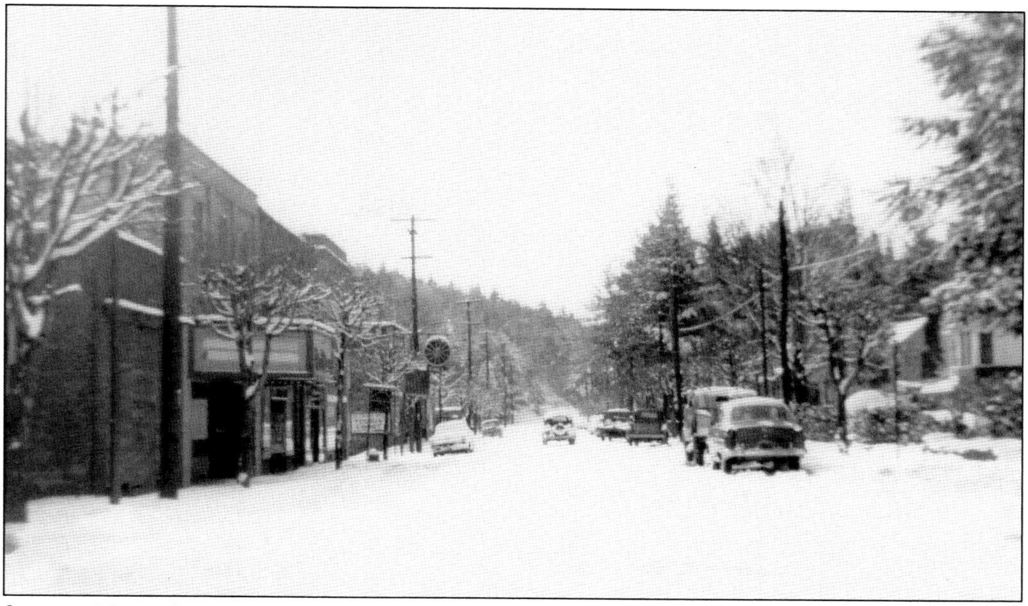

SNOWY MAIN STREET, 1956. This snowy southern view of Main Street shows many of the buildings that are still there today. On the left, the first brick building with the marquee is the Yonahlossee Theatre. The wagon wheel sign for the Wagonwheel Restaurant can also be seen just down the street. (Courtesy of LaVaughn Klutz.)

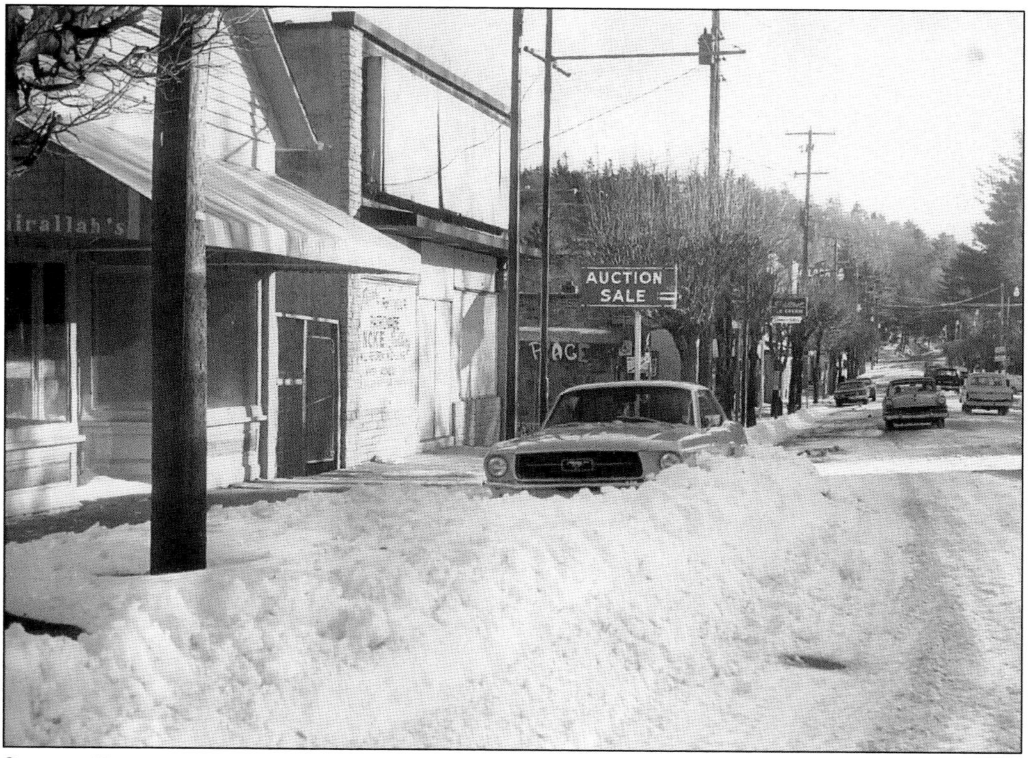

SNOWY DOWNTOWN, C. 1960S. This snow scene of downtown shows the heavy snows so common in the past. Fincke Gallery is shown on the left and various businesses are located along Main Street. (Courtesy of *The Blowing Rocket*.)

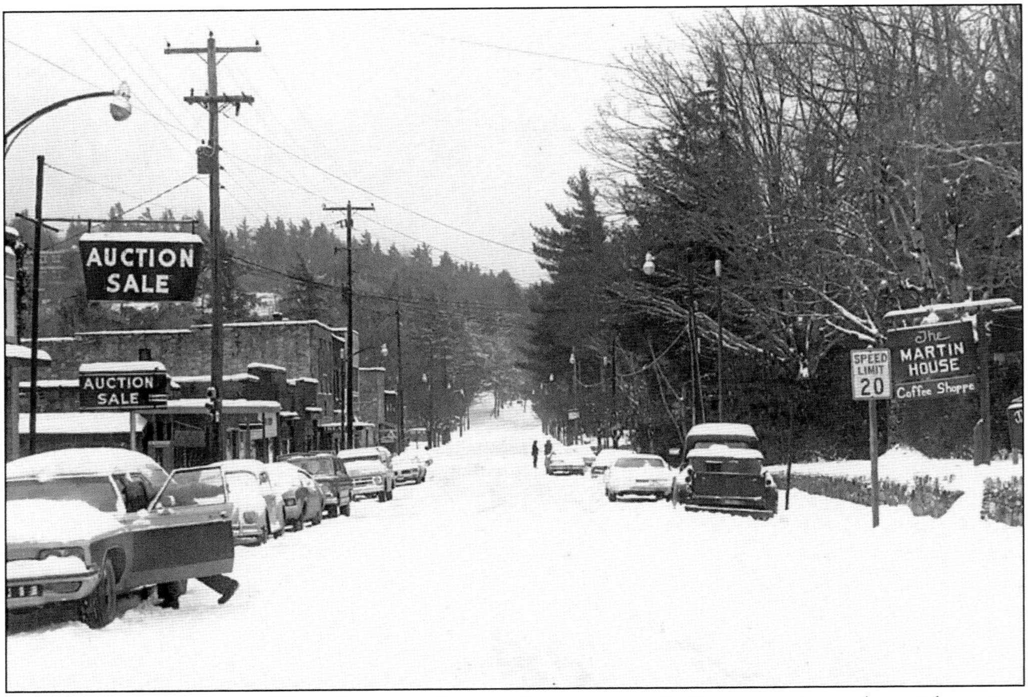

DOWNTOWN, C. 1970S. This photograph was taken on a typical snowy winter day with a view to the south. The auction house is on the left and the Martin House appears on the right. (Courtesy of *The Blowing Rocket*.)

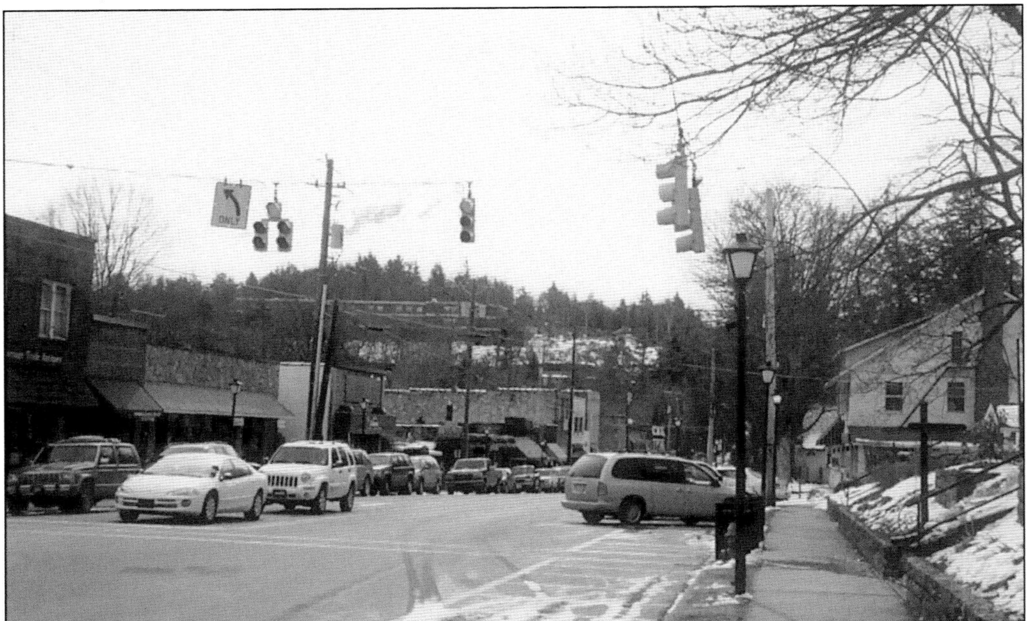

DOWNTOWN TODAY. This same view along Main Street shows the excellent job the village has done in preserving the historic buildings. The Martin House is the first building on the right side of the photograph. Even when thousands of summer visitors throng the street, Blowing Rock retains its quaint, village atmosphere. (Courtesy of Donna Warmuth.)

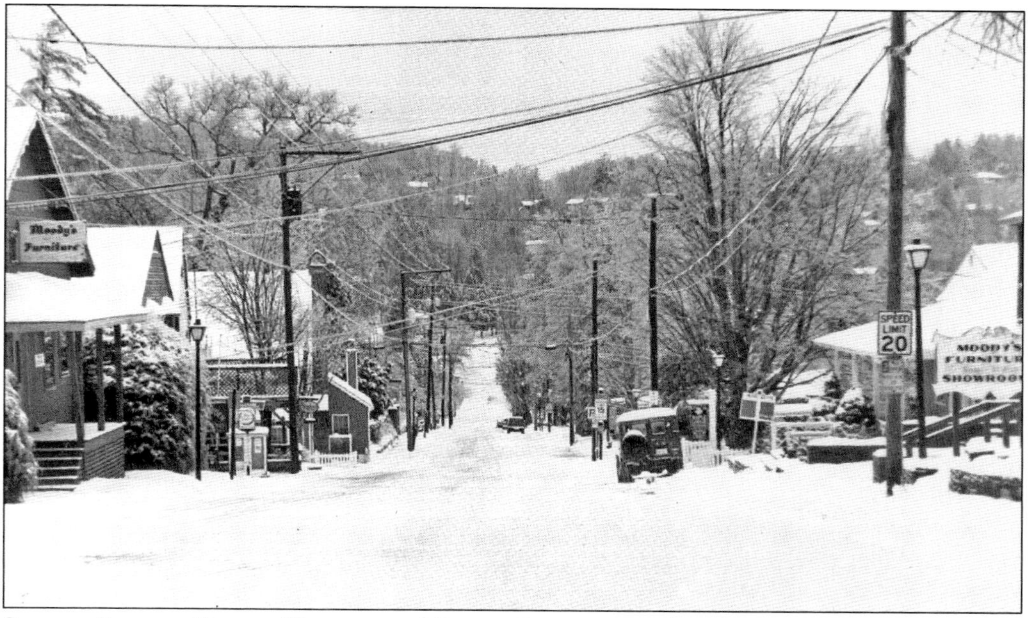

Snowy Sunset Drive. This view of Sunset Drive covered with snow is a true picture of Blowing Rock's winters. The snow has added to the tourist trade, now providing skiing at nearby Appalachian Ski Mountain. Moody's Furniture, on the left and right, is a long-time village business. Ben H. Moody was an early settler and furniture builder. (Courtesy of *The Blowing Rocket*.)

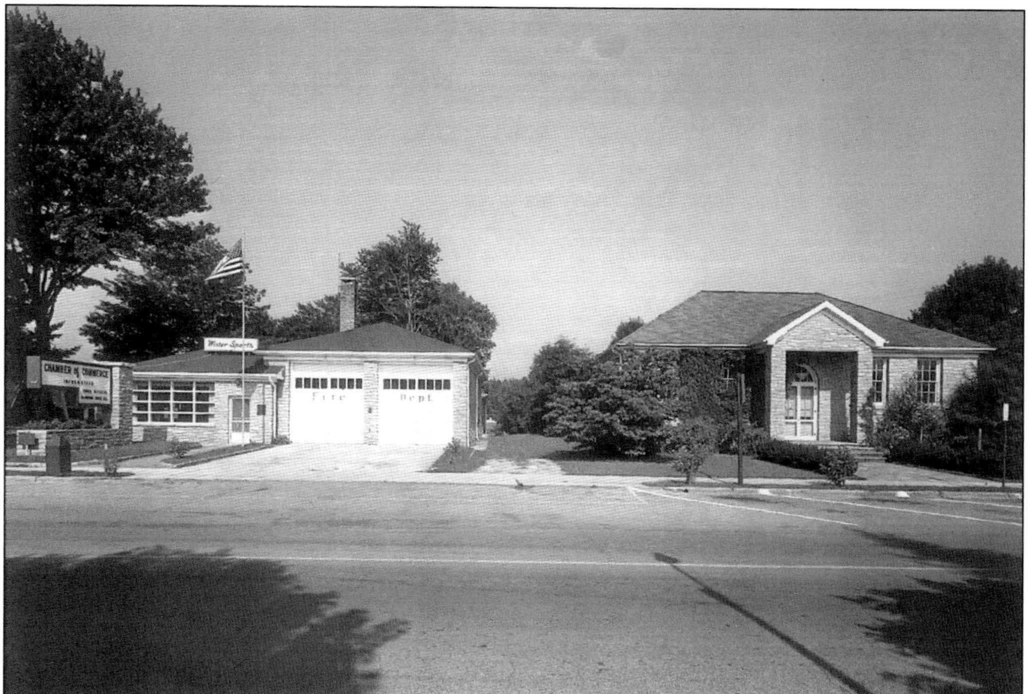

Chamber of Commerce and Library. This view of Main Street shows the combined Chamber of Commerce and fire department and, on the right, the lovely Blowing Rock library. (Courtesy of *The Blowing Rocket*.)

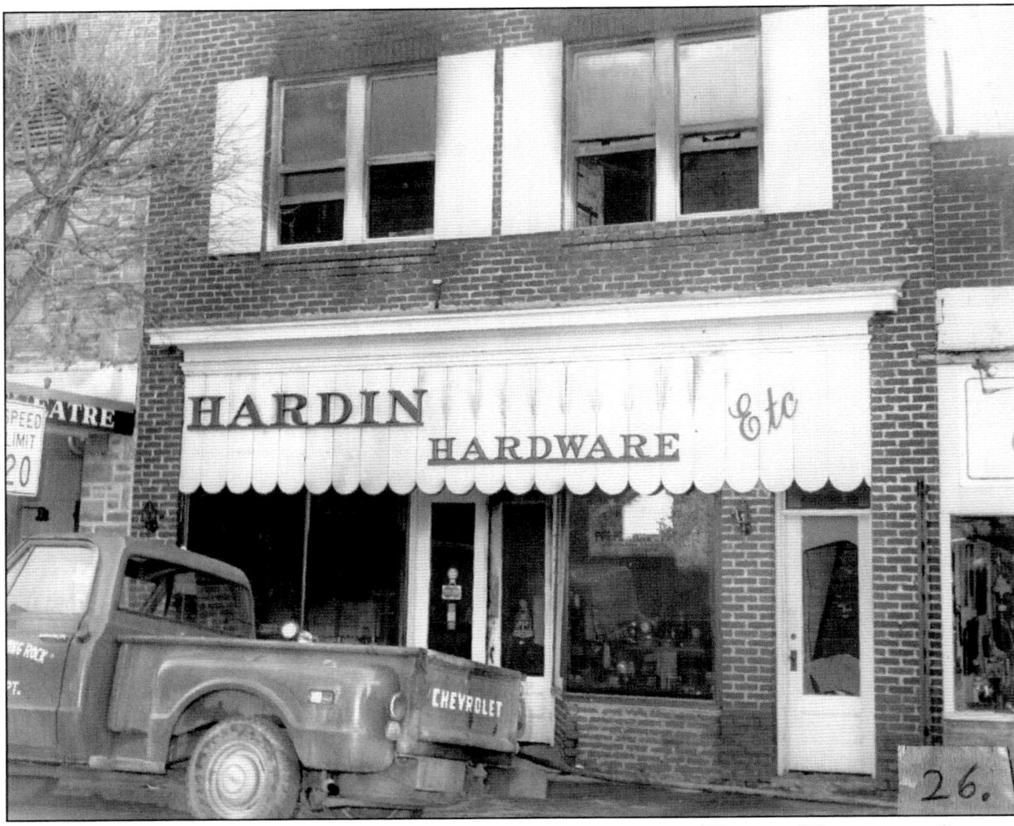

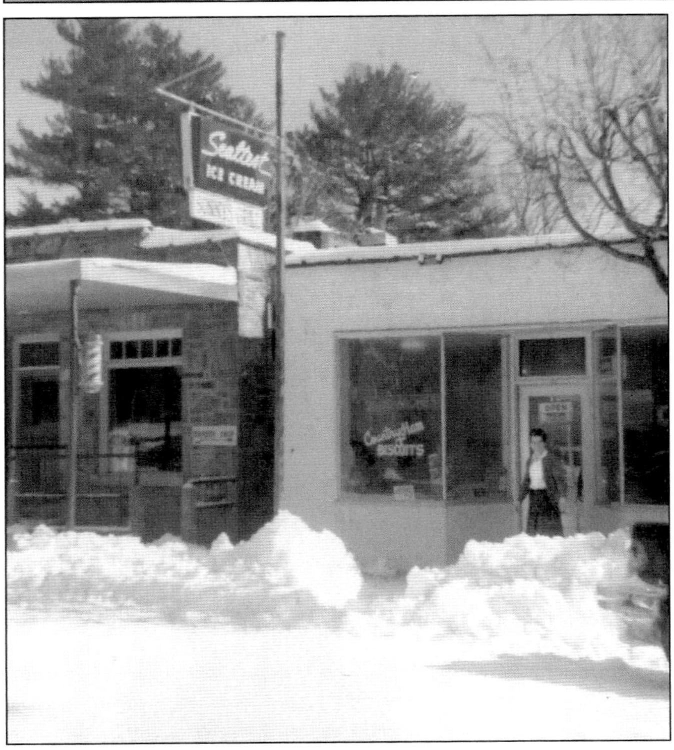

HARDIN HARDWARE STORE. This photograph shows the fire damage to Hardin Hardware store along the east side of Main Street. The Yonahlossee Theatre sign and the theatre building can be seen on the left. (Courtesy of Blowing Rock Fire Department.)

SONNY'S GRILL. Pictured in this 1966 winter photograph are Sonny's Grill on the right and a downtown barber shop on the left. Sonny's Grill was started by Sonny and LaVaughn Klutz in 1946. Jan Karon, a best-selling author who lived in Blowing Rock, used Sonny's Grill as the model for a restaurant in her books on Mitford. (Courtesy of LaVaughn Klutz.)

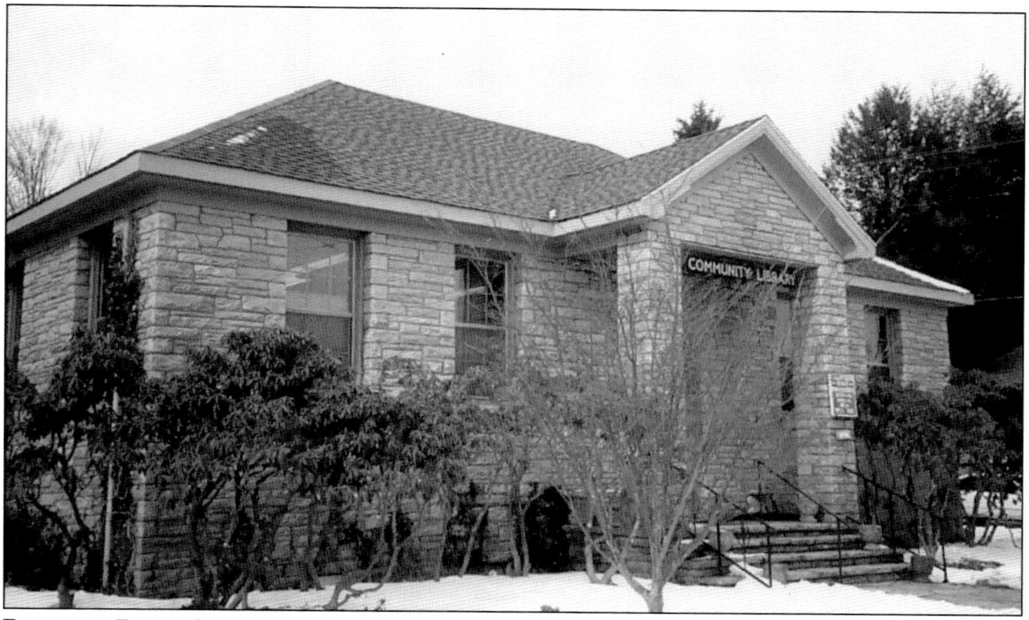

BLOWING ROCK COMMUNITY LIBRARY. The community library, opened in 1928, is located in an attractive native stone building on Main Street and is staffed and funded by the Community Club. The first public library, the "Lend-A-Hand Library" was begun by Mary Nelson Carter and moved from her house to the Mission House Reading Room on Main Street. (Courtesy of Donna Warmuth.)

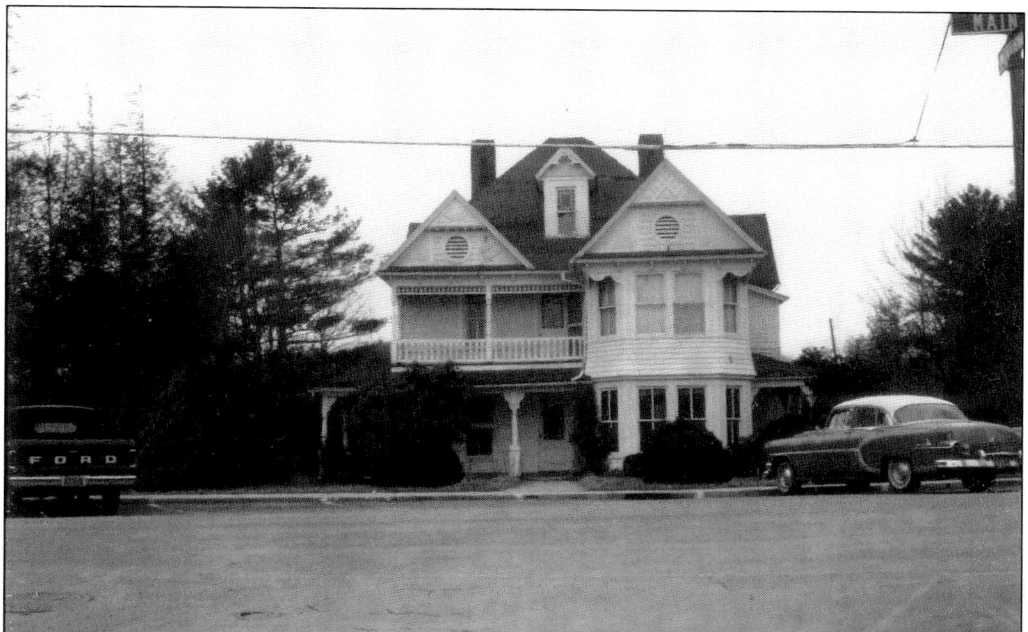

HAYES HOUSE. This house stood along Main Street. When the house was threatened with destruction, the Blowing Rock Historical Society led a community effort to save the historic house and it was moved to a new site along U.S. 221. The house has undergone restoration and is a positive example of historic preservation. (Courtesy of Richard Trexler.)

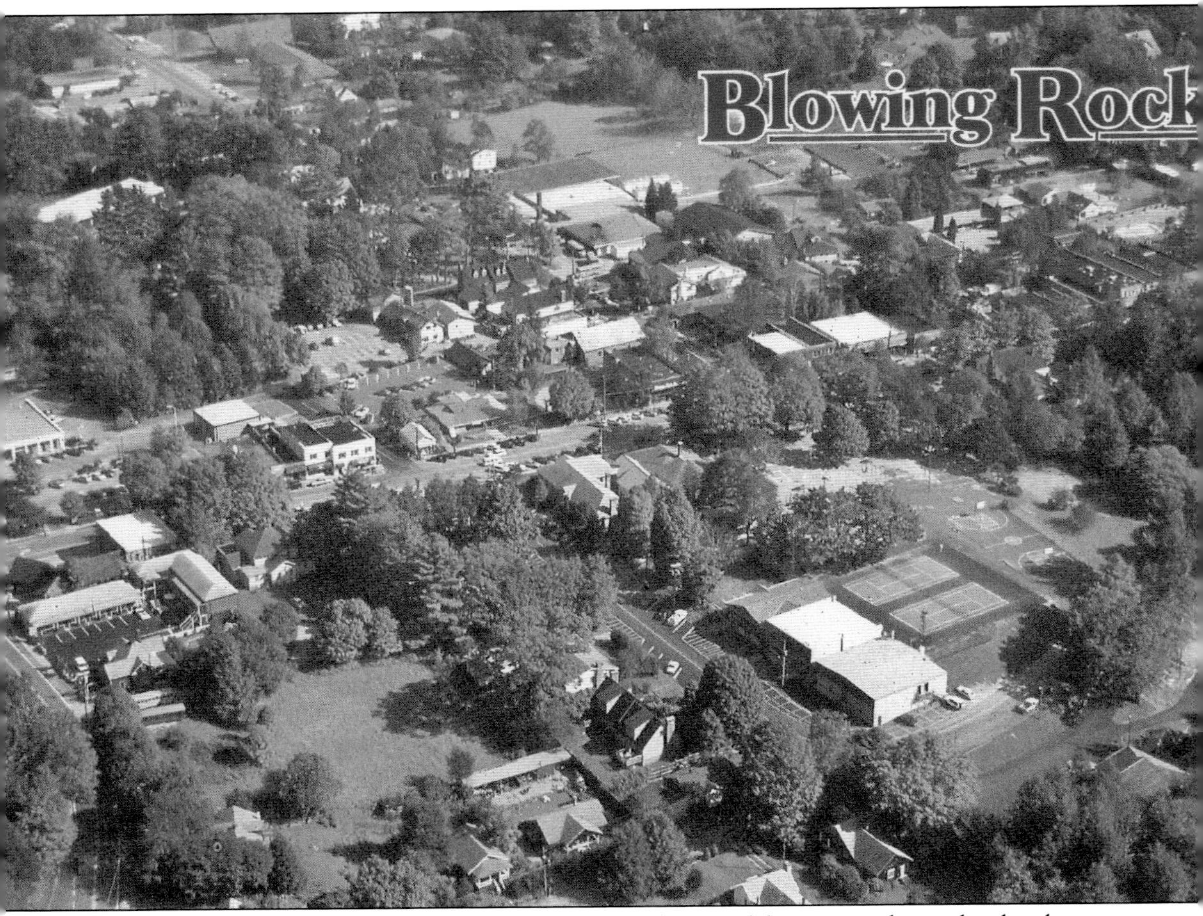

Aerial View, Blowing Rock. This recent aerial view of downtown shows the development that has taken place in Blowing Rock. The tennis courts and recreation offices can be seen in the foreground, U.S. 221 is shown on the far left of the photo, and Main Street runs through the center. The compact size of the town, as well as the sidewalks, makes the town pedestrian friendly to shoppers and tourists. The trees and Memorial Park add green space to the town and enhance its old-fashioned appeal. From a town of summer houses and small shops, the village has transformed itself into a sophisticated blend of old and new. Many historic buildings have been preserved, although they may have changed their function. The Chamber of Commerce has actively promoted events and activities in the town to enhance its reputation as a tourist attraction. (Courtesy of Richard Trexler.)

Two

SCHOOLS AND CHURCHES

Religion has always been important to the people here. Circuit riding preachers provided the first religious guidance for the early settlers and often folks would meet in each others' houses to worship. Most of the settlers were Protestant and originally Presbyterian in faith. However, other religious groups later flourished in the area, and the village has an assortment of Protestant and Catholic churches to offer. The first church in the area was the Mount Bethel Reformed Church, dating to 1882. The town's earliest grave and marker, dating from 1794, is located in the adjacent graveyard. The earliest church in the town limits was the Episcopal Church built in 1890. Schools were also a necessary institution for the settlers. One-room schoolhouses were the earliest schools, but few remain. In Blowing Rock, Sandy Flat School was the first public school. Silver Lake School was an early school, located just past the Parkway overpass on U.S. 321. Skyland Institute, established by Emily C. Prudden in 1887, provided lodging and education for local children. Globe Academy, located in adjacent Caldwell County, was a training school for locals to continue their education. Other early schools were located on Possum Hollow Road and the Old Spring School off Laurel Lane in town. A school was built at the current Blowing Rock school location after 1918, but it was demolished in 1927 to build the brick school. Sandy Flat, Silver Lake, and Blowing Rock Village school districts were combined into the new facility. Most of this brick school was torn down in 1966 and the Blowing Rock Elementary School was built in 1957.

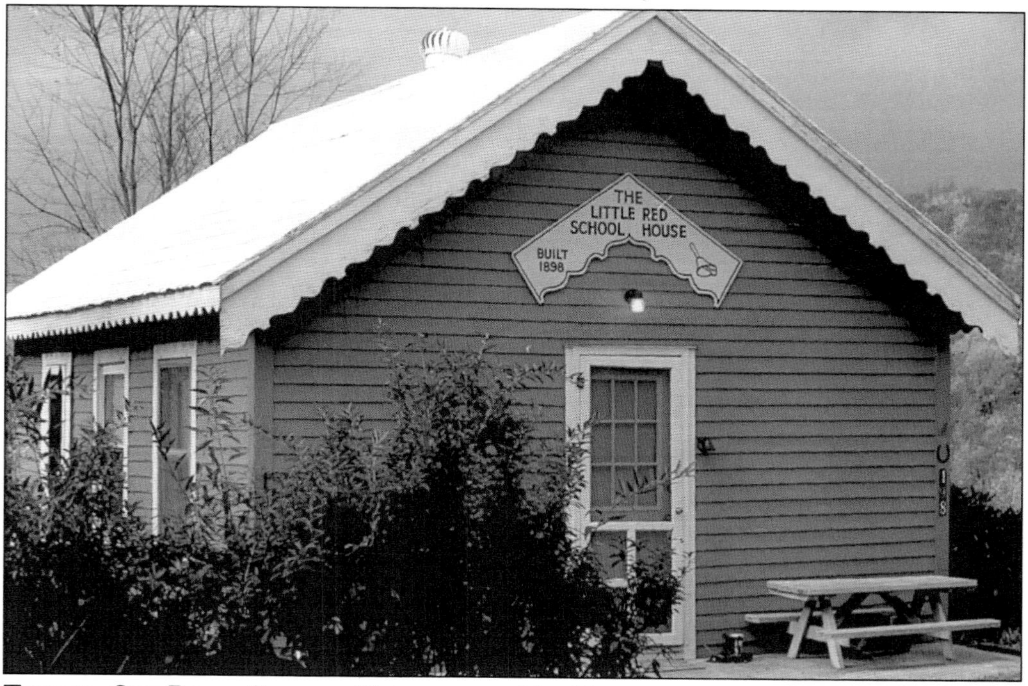

TYPICAL ONE-ROOM SCHOOL. This renovated building was once a one-room schoolhouse on the Cone Estate. The building was saved and moved to Sandy Flats. These reminders of early educational history are important to preserve in the community. (Courtesy of *The Blowing Rocket*.)

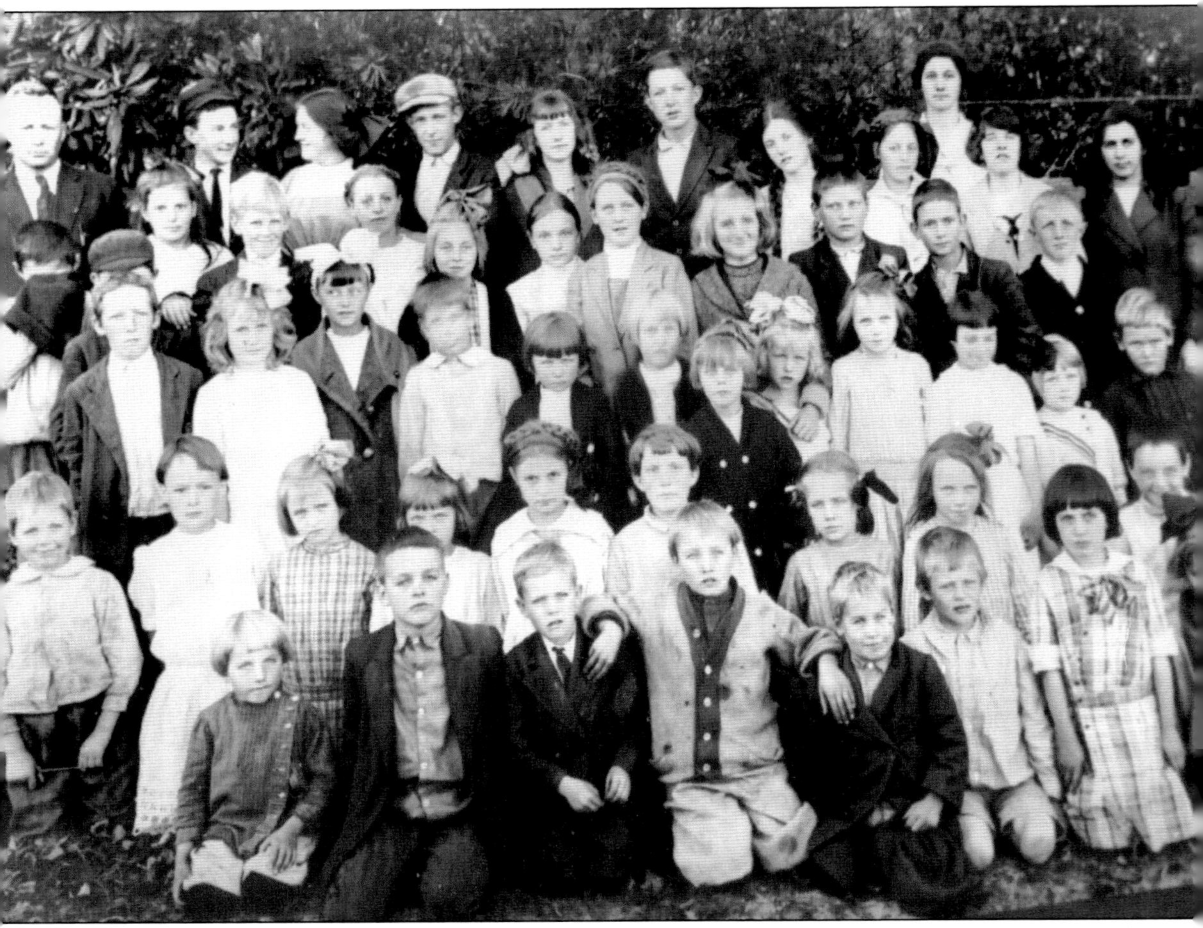

BLOWING ROCK PUBLIC SCHOOL, CLASS OF 1912. Pictured from left to right are (first row) Hal Teague, Randall Foster, Herman Hartley, Ralph Teague, Rhonda Foster, Spencer Greene, Mary Suddreth, and Dorothy Hayes; (second row) Hal Benfield, Helen Critcher, Pauline Hartley, Mary Holshouser, Lena Robbins, Rae Critcher, Mary Raby, Grace Bollinger, and Ben Greene; (third row) Eubert (Peck) Holshouser, Lula Ward, Anna Lee Crisp, Howard Benfield, Ella Crisp, Ann Greene, Ruth Robbins, Bess Ward, Gertie Bollinger, Carrie Miller, Ethel Holshouser, and George Robbins; (fourth row) James Suddreth, Hal Ward, Eloise Greene, Fred Benfield, Nellie Brown, Pearl Winkler, Doris Brown, Ella Winkler, Elley Coffey, George Crisp, Lloyd Robbins, and Thomas Coffey; (fifth row) Hardin Brown (principal), Caskie Hodge, Blanch Miller, Eugene Holshouser, Mary Ward, Cecil Critcher, Bess Peoples, Katy Holshouser, Lena Miller, Dorothy Suddreth, and Myrtle Suddreth (teacher). (Courtesy of Emma Jean Bowman Wynn.)

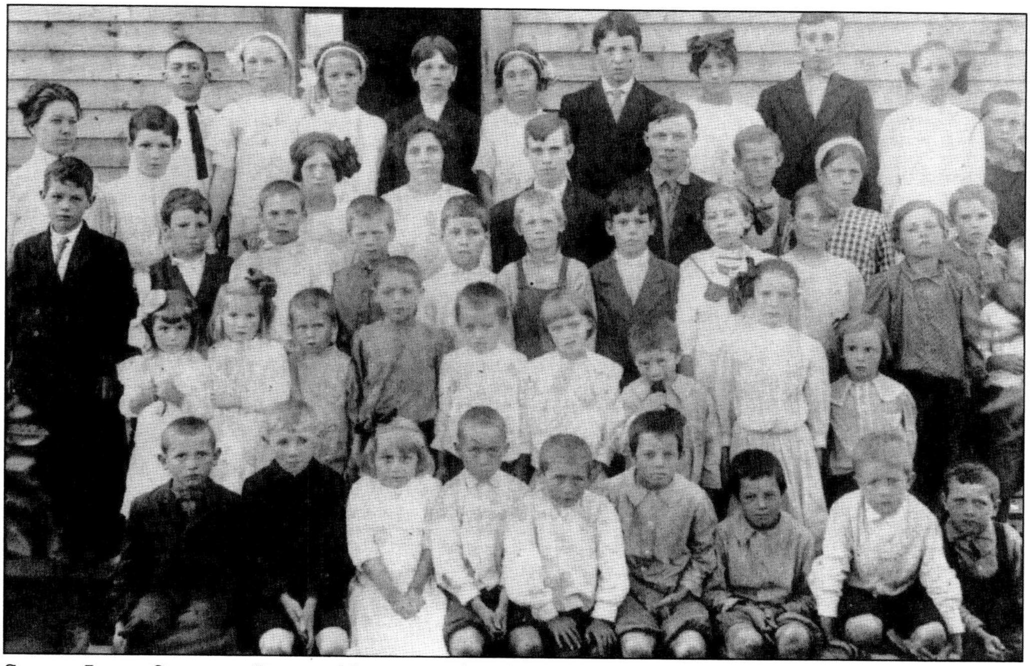

Silver Lake School. Pictured here is a class from Silver Lake School in the early 1900s. The school building was located just south of the overpass of the Blue Ridge Parkway on U.S. 321. (Courtesy of Ralph E. Lentz II.)

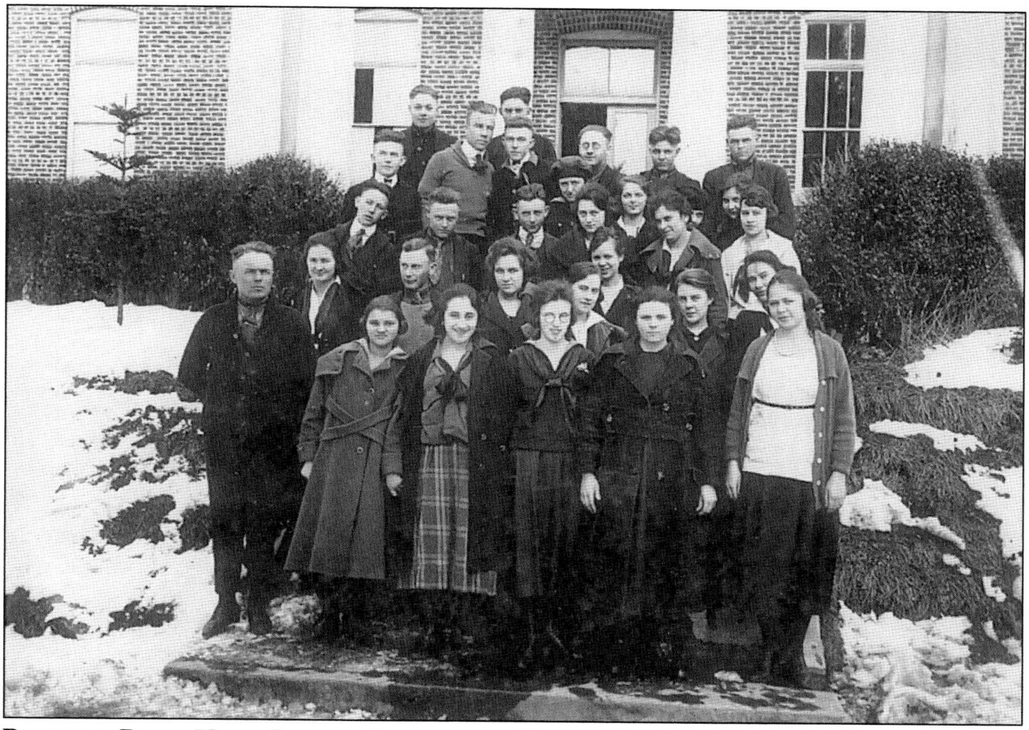

Blowing Rock High School Sophomore Class. This photograph is of Blowing Rock's sophomore class in 1920–1921. Local students attended high school here in the town until the construction of the consolidated high school in 1965. (Courtesy of *The Blowing Rocket*.)

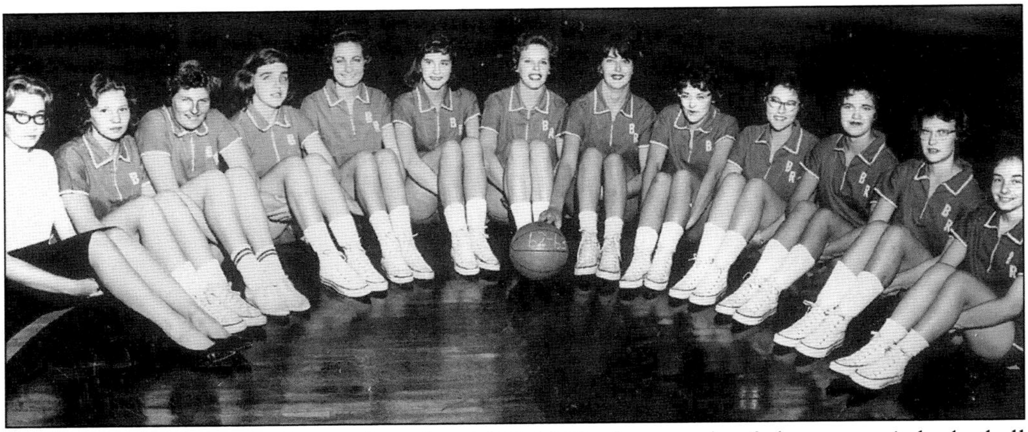

Women's Basketball. Pictured in this 1962–1963 photograph of the women's basketball team at the high school are, from left to right, Linda Rainey Campbell, Emma Coffey, Mary Francis Tipton, Patricia Pitts Greene, Linda Luttrell Davis, Shirley Holoway, Marie Greene Ponn, Brenda Holoway, Shannon Ashley, JoAnn Lentz, Janice Cook, Janice Dotson Kelly, and Betty Hartley Green. (Courtesy of *The Blowing Rocket*.)

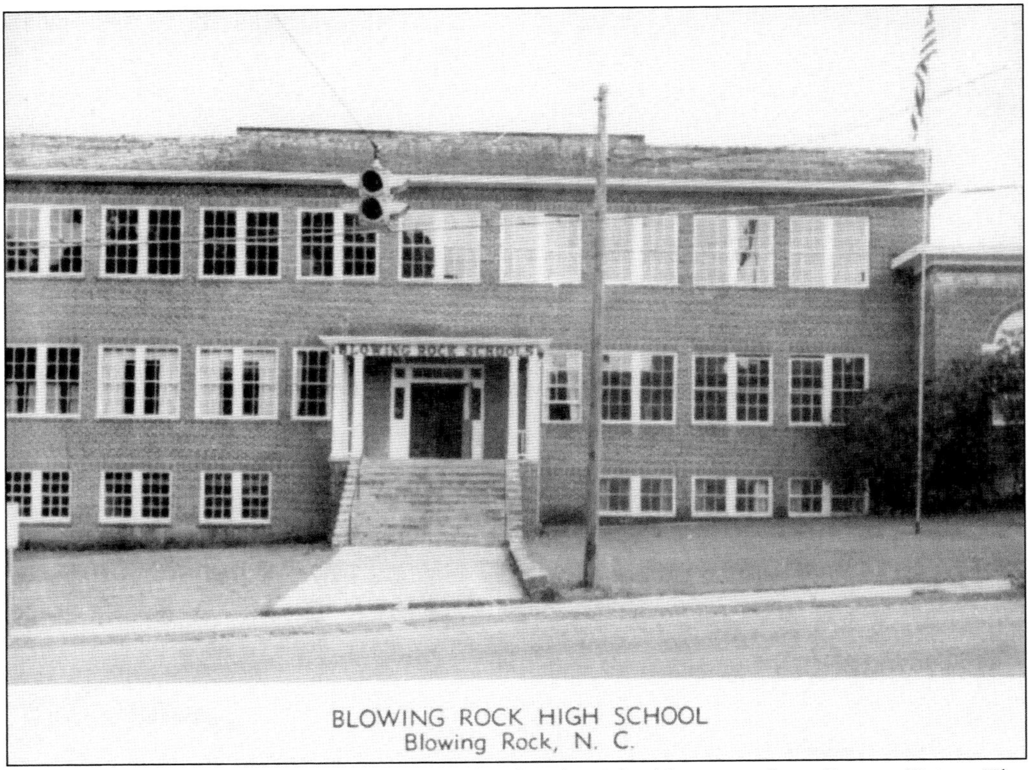

Blowing Rock School. This attractive brick school building stood on Sunset Drive. The gymnasium was added as part of the Works Project Administration (WPA). Smaller community schools such as Boone Fork, Aho, Whiting, Middle Fork, and Cool Springs were consolidated with Blowing Rock School. In 1957, a new Blowing Rock Elementary School was built. (Courtesy of Richard Trexler.)

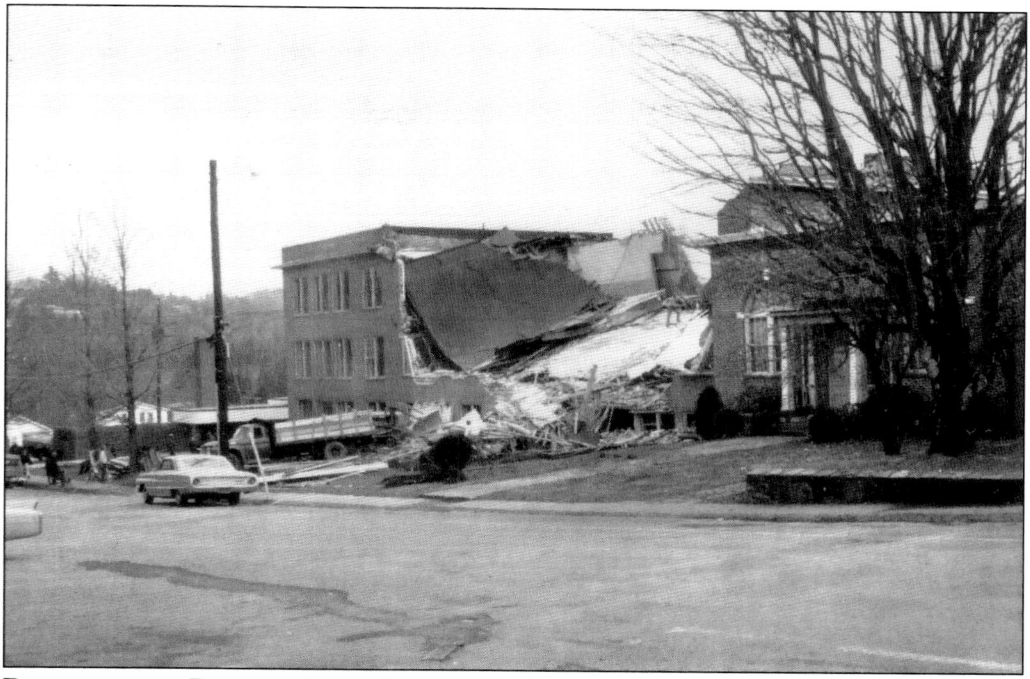

DEMOLITION OF BLOWING ROCK SCHOOL. In this view along Sunset Drive, one can see the demolition of Blowing Rock School taking place in 1966. A consolidated high school was begun in Boone in 1965. The building section on the right side of the photo was preserved and later became the Blowing Rock Stage Company. (Courtesy of Richard Trexler.)

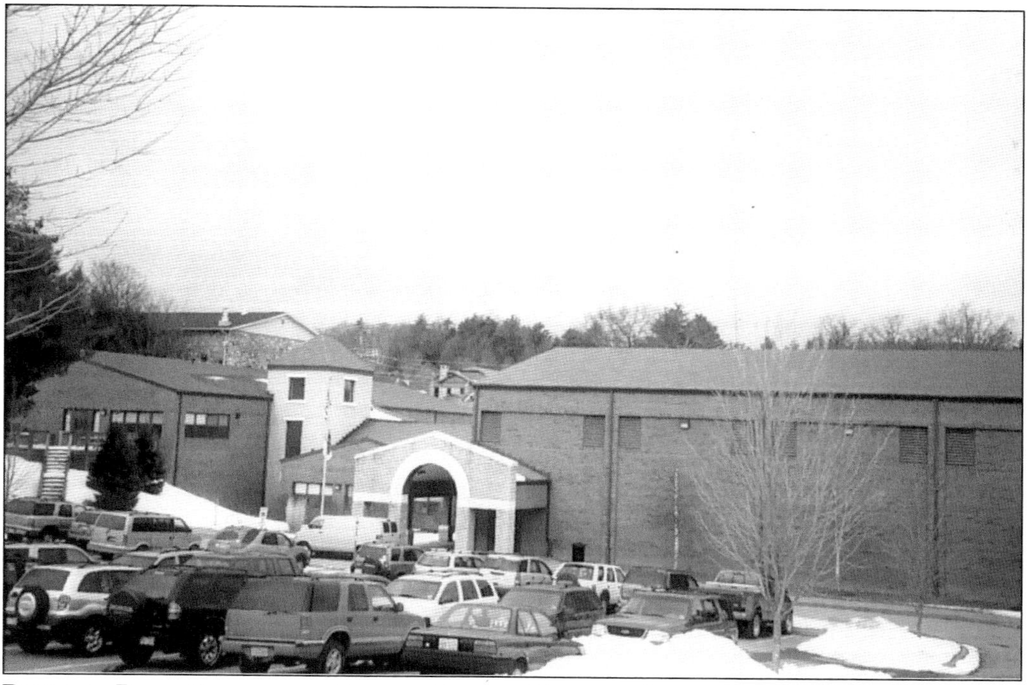

BLOWING ROCK ELEMENTARY SCHOOL TODAY. The new elementary school was built in 1957 and additions have been constructed as needed. The school regularly receives the highest state ratings for its quality education. (Courtesy of Donna Warmuth.)

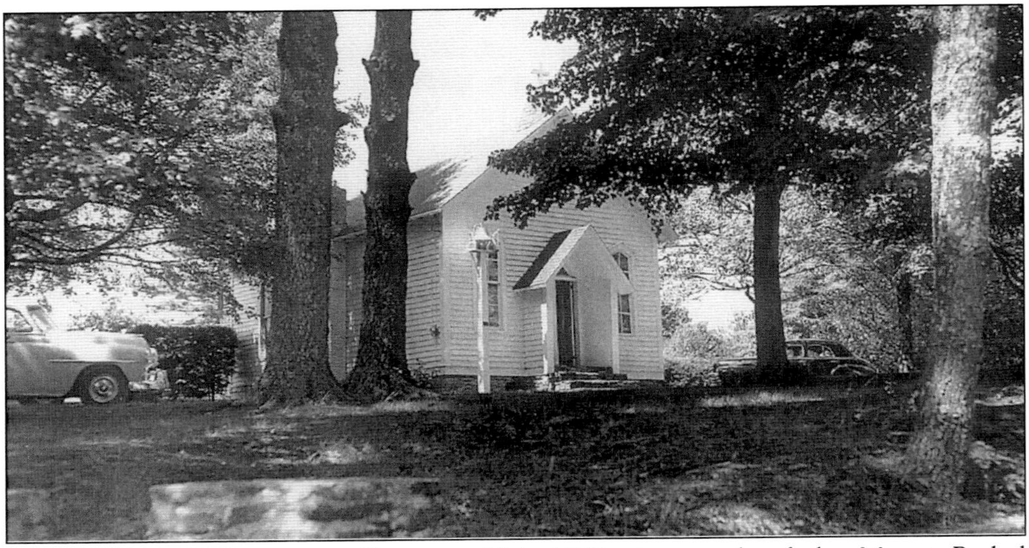

Mount Bethel Reformed Church. This 1943 photograph of the Mount Bethel Reformed Church shows its simple beauty. The church was built in 1882 and has several old gravestones surrounding it. It is part of the Blowing Rock Assembly Grounds. (Courtesy of *The Blowing Rocket.*)

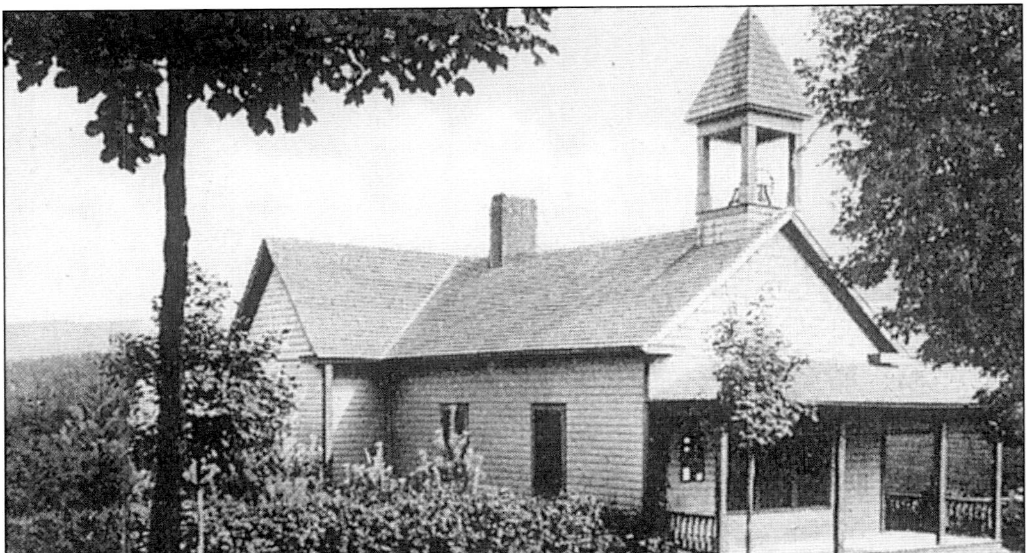

Episcopal Church and Reading Room. This church and early library were built in 1890 at the current location of Sonny's Grill. This was the only public library from 1902 until the Blowing Rock library was formed in 1918. It was destroyed by a downtown fire. (Courtesy of *The Blowing Rocket.*)

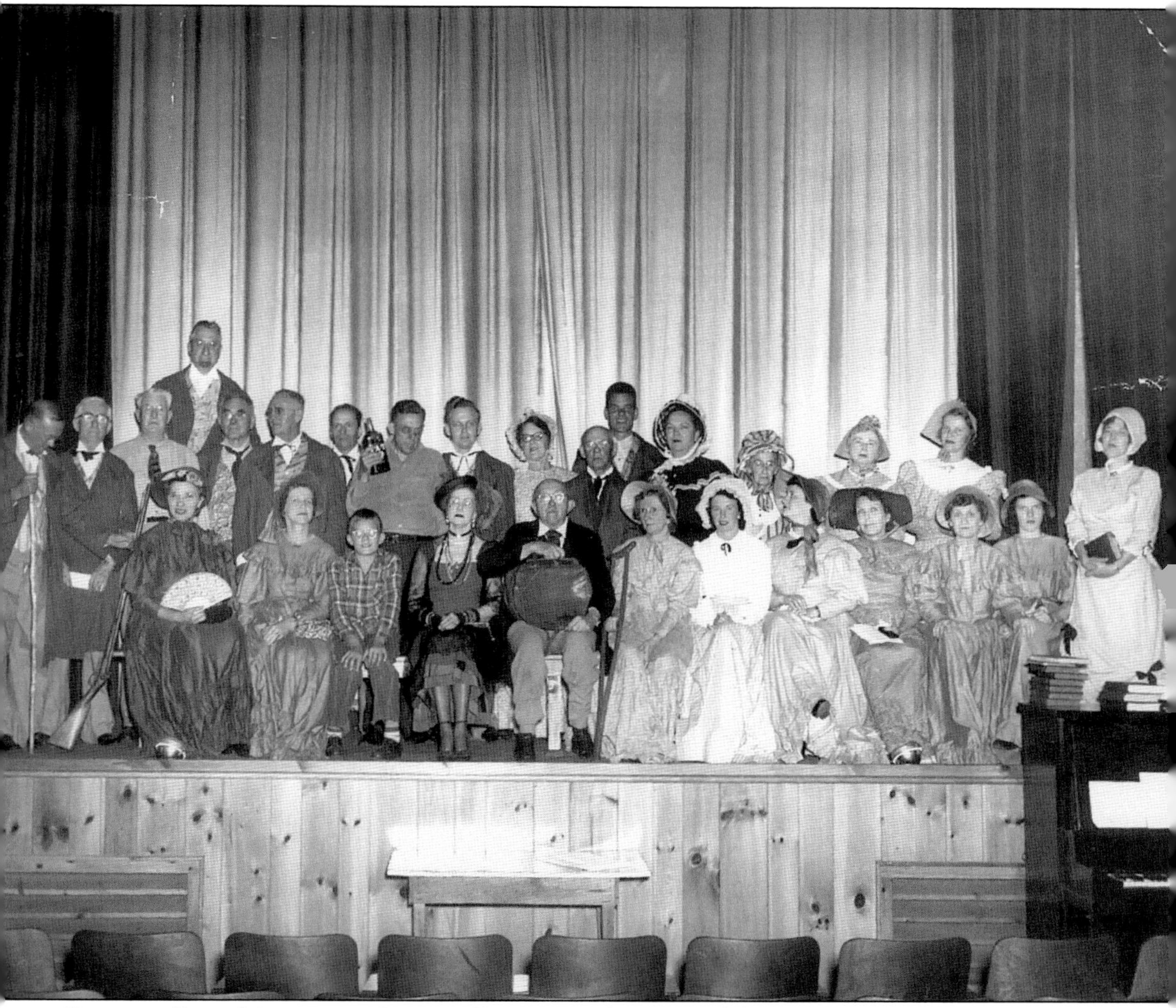

Blowing Rock Methodist Church Pageant. This 1950 celebration of the 50th anniversary of the Blowing Rock Methodist Church was a popular community event and was held at the Yonahlossee Theatre downtown. The Methodist church on Main Street is a beautiful church built after 1900 from native stone and chestnut siding. The church is open seasonally. Pictured from left to right are (front row) Grady Ransom, Grover Robbins, Mrs. Charles Brown, Mrs. H.P. Holshouser, Dennis Rash, Mrs. J.F. Schenck Sr., Dr. H.E. Spence, Mrs. L.H. Smith Sr., Miss B. Pardue, Mrs. Irene Coffey, Mrs. Hal Hartley, Mrs. Ernest Banner, Miss Lett, and Mrs. Margaret Reineking; (back row) Clarence Grider, Dr. Schmeisser, George Sudderth, Lawrence Rankin, Fuller Sams, L.H. Smith Sr., ? Jones, Mrs. H.E. Spence, W.E. Boger, Marvin Culberth, Mrs. Alice Gayton, Mrs. Clarence Grider, Mrs. Ella Bess Schmeisser, and Mrs. Fuller Sams. (Courtesy of *The Blowing Rocket*.)

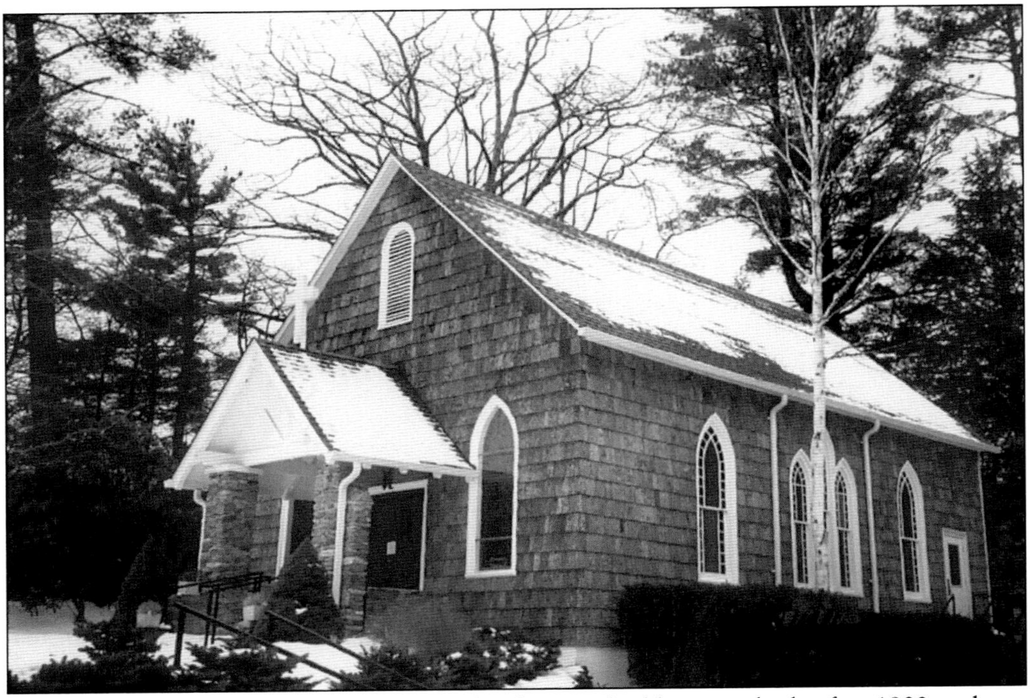

Blowing Rock Methodist Church. This historic building was built after 1900 and was originally constructed of chestnut bark siding and native stone. Poplar bark siding replaced the chestnut bark, but the building retains its original appearance. The church is open seasonally for summer residents and local residents. (Courtesy of Donna Warmuth.)

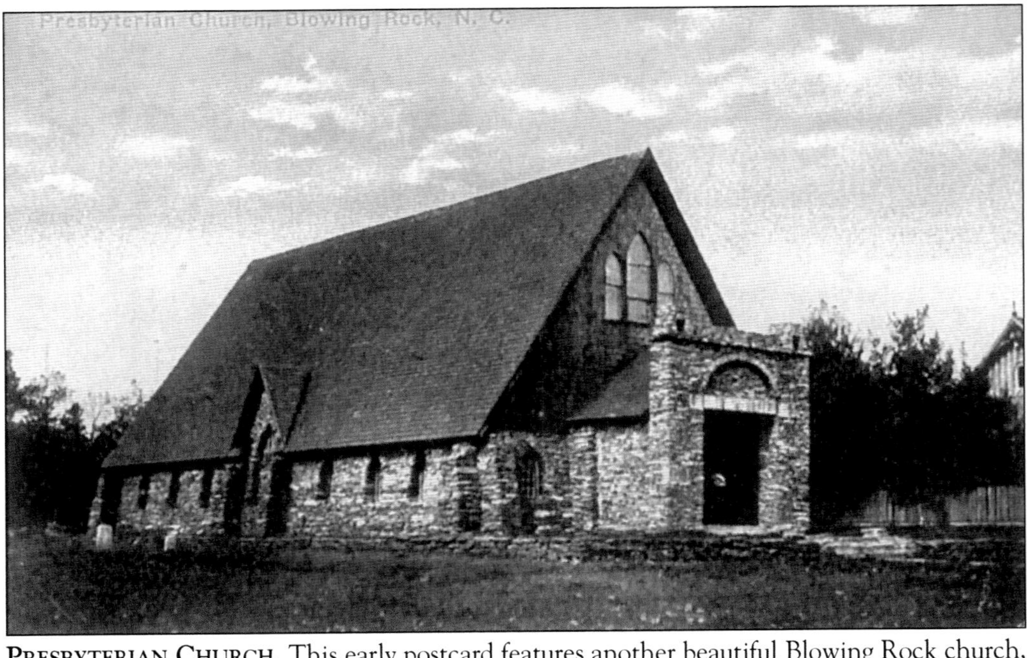

Presbyterian Church. This early postcard features another beautiful Blowing Rock church, the Rumple Memorial Presbyterian Church. The original church was dedicated in 1886. This stone church was finished in 1912 and still stands today. The gravestones in the side yard dated from the early days. (Courtesy of Ginny Stevens.)

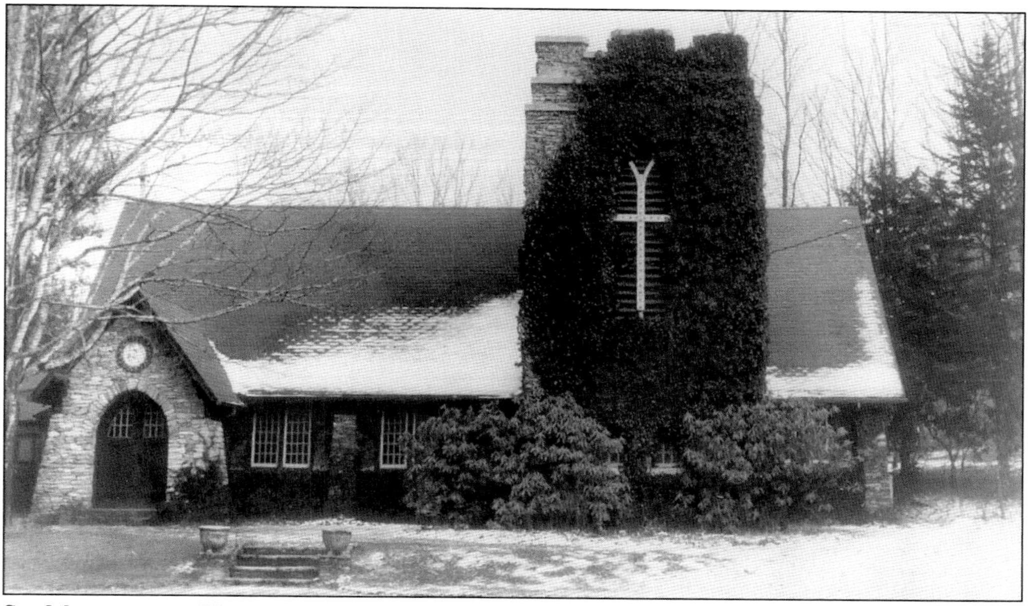

ST. MARY OF THE HILLS EPISCOPAL CHURCH. Completed in 1921, this church was first known as the Stringfellow Memorial Church, after W.W. Stringfellow, then owner of Chetola Estate. After famous artist Elliott Daingerfield donated his painting, *Madonna of the Hills*, the building was renamed St. Mary of the Hills. The design is said to be patterned on an English country church. (Courtesy of *The Blowing Rocket*.)

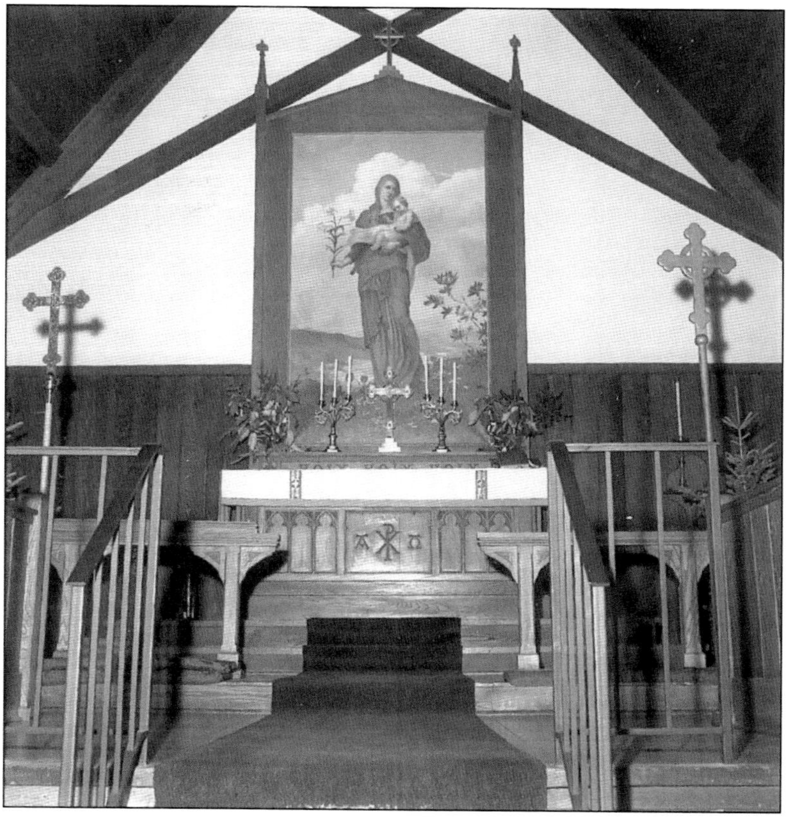

MADONNA OF THE HILLS. Painted by famous artist Elliott Daingerfield, this masterpiece graces the St. Mary of the Hills Episcopal Church. The painting is based on the legend of a lady who walks the hills every year on the first day of summer. Daingerfield painted *Madonna of the Hills* in 1918 and donated it to the church. (Courtesy of *The Blowing Rocket*.)

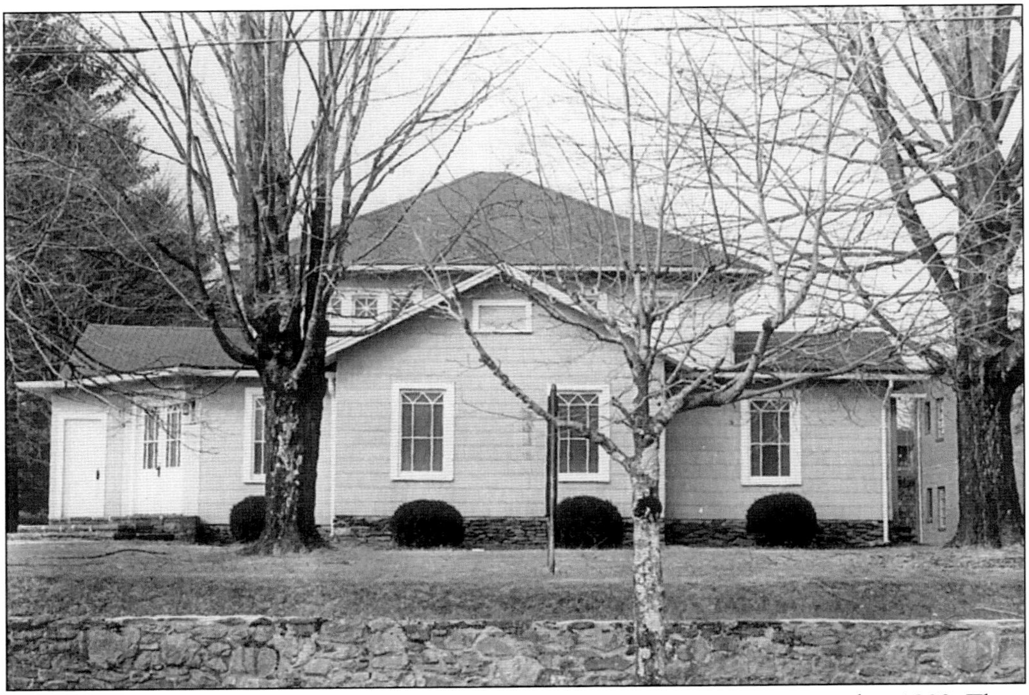

FIRST BAPTIST CHURCH. The First Baptist Church congregation was organized in 1903. Their first church building, shown in this photograph, was built on Main Street in 1905. It now is used as a restaurant. In 1968, a larger building was built on Sunset Drive, which is the home of the church today. (Courtesy of *The Blowing Rocket*.)

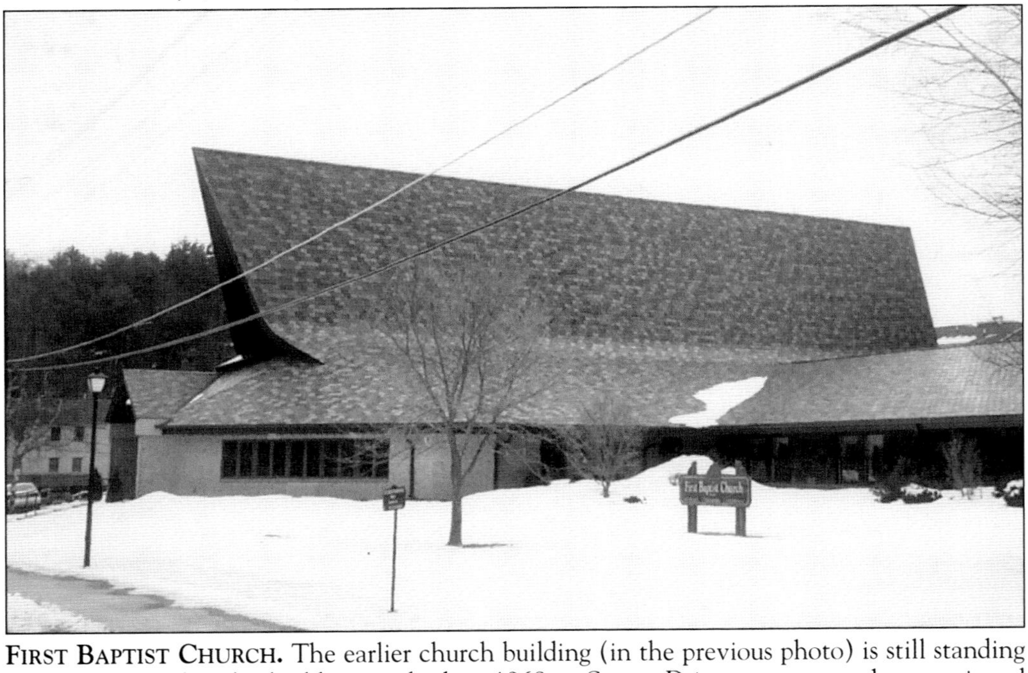

FIRST BAPTIST CHURCH. The earlier church building (in the previous photo) is still standing on Main Street, but this building was built in 1968 on Sunset Drive to accommodate continued growth. The Baptist Church has always been active in the Blowing Rock community and was one of the first to remain open year-round in town. (Courtesy of Donna Warmuth.)

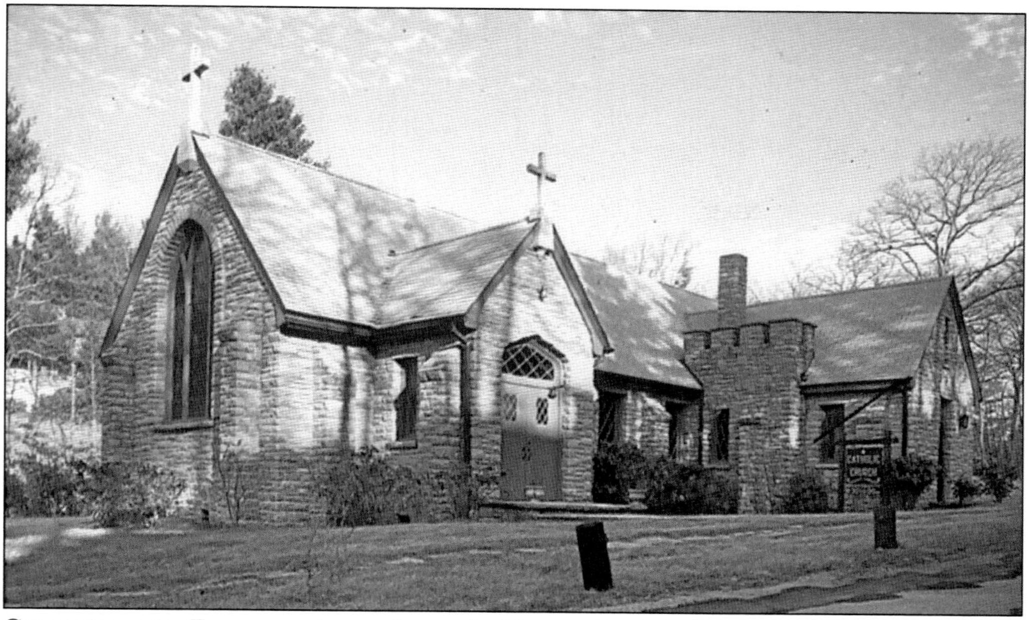

CHURCH OF THE EPIPHANY. Located near the Blowing Rock Golf Course, this Catholic church was built in 1948. Earlier Catholic congregations met at Mayview Manor and the Yonahlossee Theatre. The Gothic architecture and native stone add to its aesthetic appeal. (Courtesy of Ginny Stevens.)

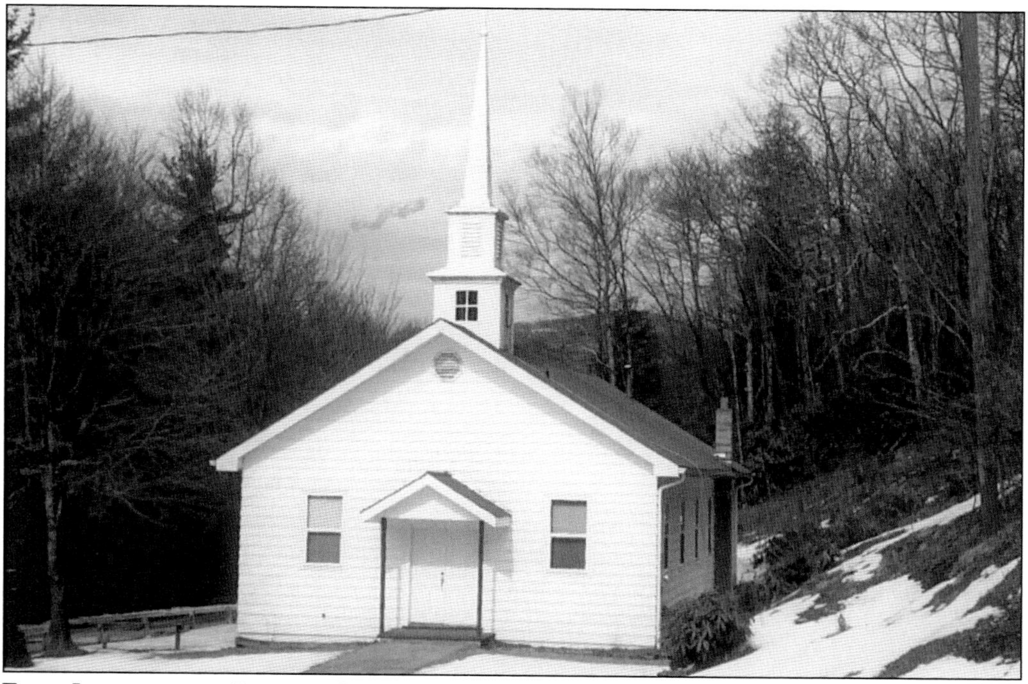

FIRST INDEPENDENT BAPTIST CHURCH. Located on Possum Hollow Road, this church was first incorporated and built in 1949 as the Blowing Rock Negro Community Church. The African-American population in Blowing Rock has historically been small and was later reduced by out-migration. In 1982, the church became the First Independent Baptist Church. (Courtesy of Donna Warmuth.)

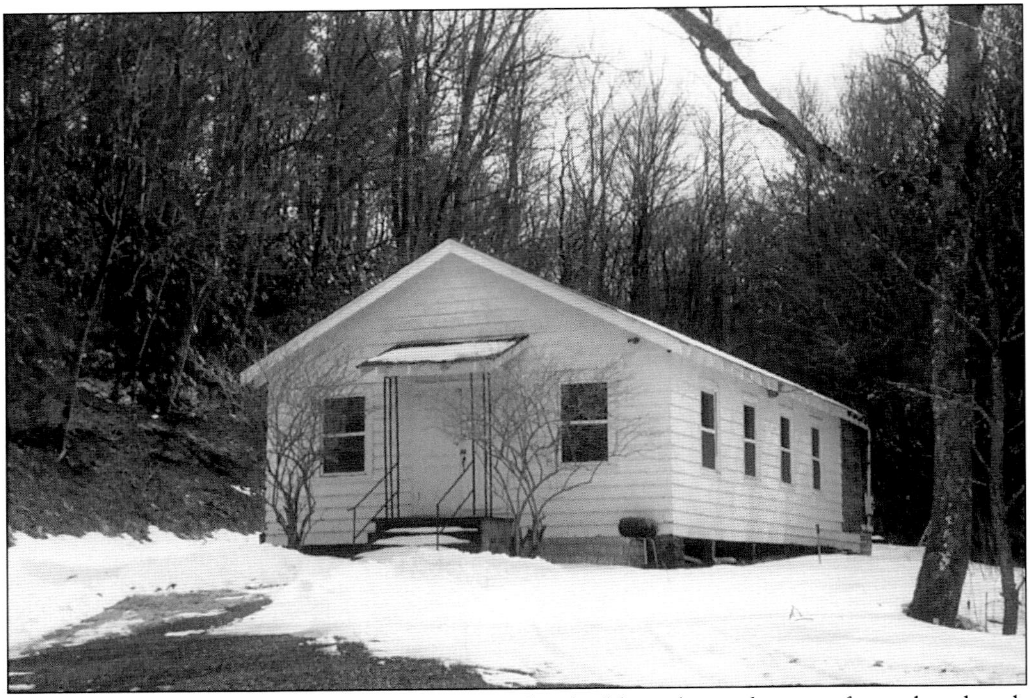

AFRICAN-AMERICAN COMMUNITY CENTER. This building, located across from the church in the previous photo, was the community center for the African-American population. The building provided a key location for families to meet and visit. (Courtesy of Donna Warmuth.)

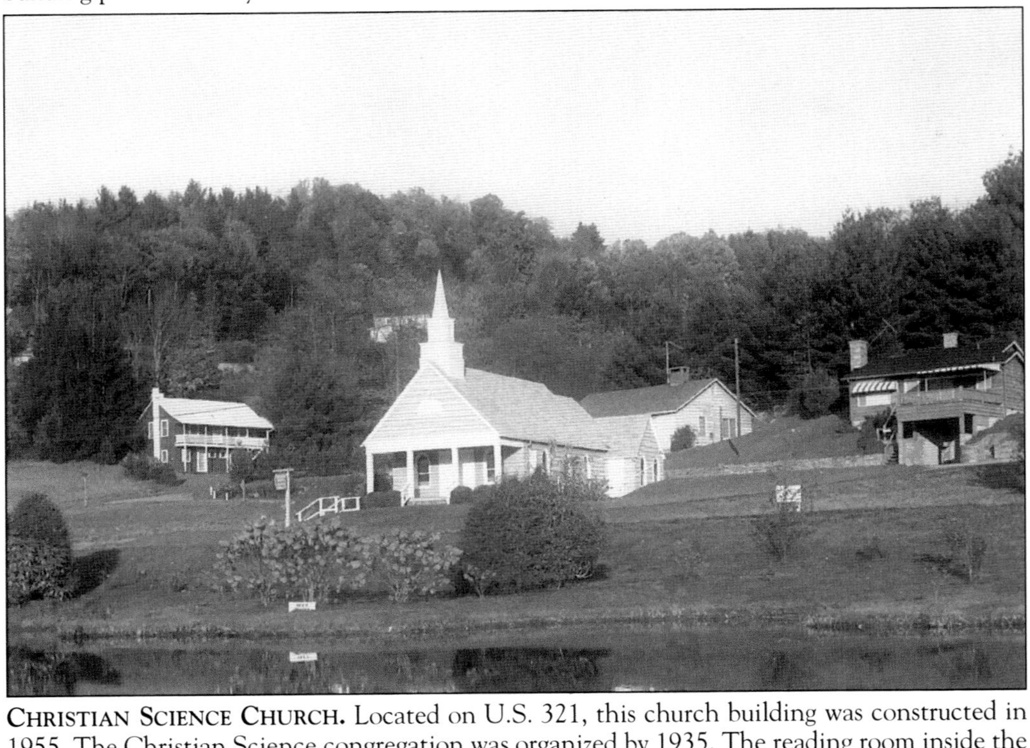

CHRISTIAN SCIENCE CHURCH. Located on U.S. 321, this church building was constructed in 1955. The Christian Science congregation was organized by 1935. The reading room inside the church provides religious materials to the public. (Courtesy of *The Blowing Rocket*.)

Three

ESTATES, HOTELS, HOUSES, AND BUSINESSES

Blowing Rock has been fortunate to have such a diverse mixture of businesses and residences. The more affluent and prominent left their marks on the town's history through philanthropic projects and construction of landmark estates and houses. Estates such as the Cone Mansion, Westglow, and Chetola live on as reminders of these influential families. The simple houses of the local population have their own charm, and a few older examples, such as the Martin House on Main Street, still remain. Several of these houses became inns, boarding houses, and restaurants to serve the increasing number of tourists. Elegant hotels began to be built after the Civil War to draw discriminating tourists to "America's Switzerland." Of the many grand hotels, only one grand dame, the Green Park Hotel, is still standing and hosting summer visitors. Local residents operated boarding houses and inns from their houses to meet the demands for lodging. Later, motor courts or the new "motor hotels" were built in the town and surrounding area to provide lodging to the new tourists traveling by automobile. Businesses always have responded to consumer demand and that is evident in Blowing Rock, too. Livery stables, blacksmith shops, and general stores have given way to craft stores, antique shops, gift shops, and art studios. Downtown Blowing Rock has an eclectic mixture of shops and restaurants, from home-town diners, such as Sonny's Café, to imported European linen stores. The range of stores and shops along Main Street are sure to provide a day's worth of shopping to even the most discriminating consumer.

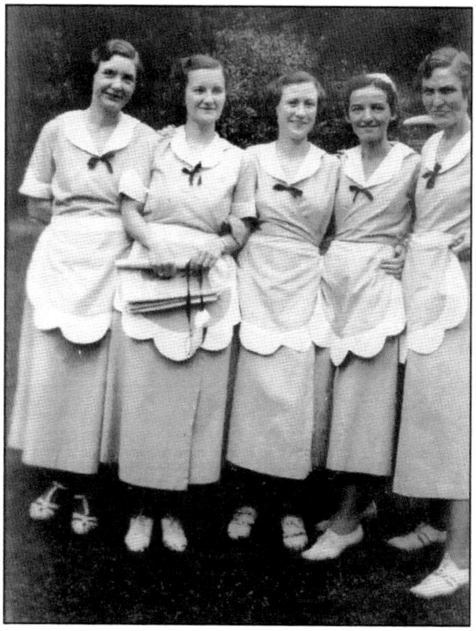

WAITRESSES OF THE GREEN PARK HOTEL. Several waitresses of the Green Park Hotel pose in this September 1934 photograph. From left to right are Mary, Sue, Pauline, Kat, and Marion. (Courtesy of Blowing Rock Historical Society.)

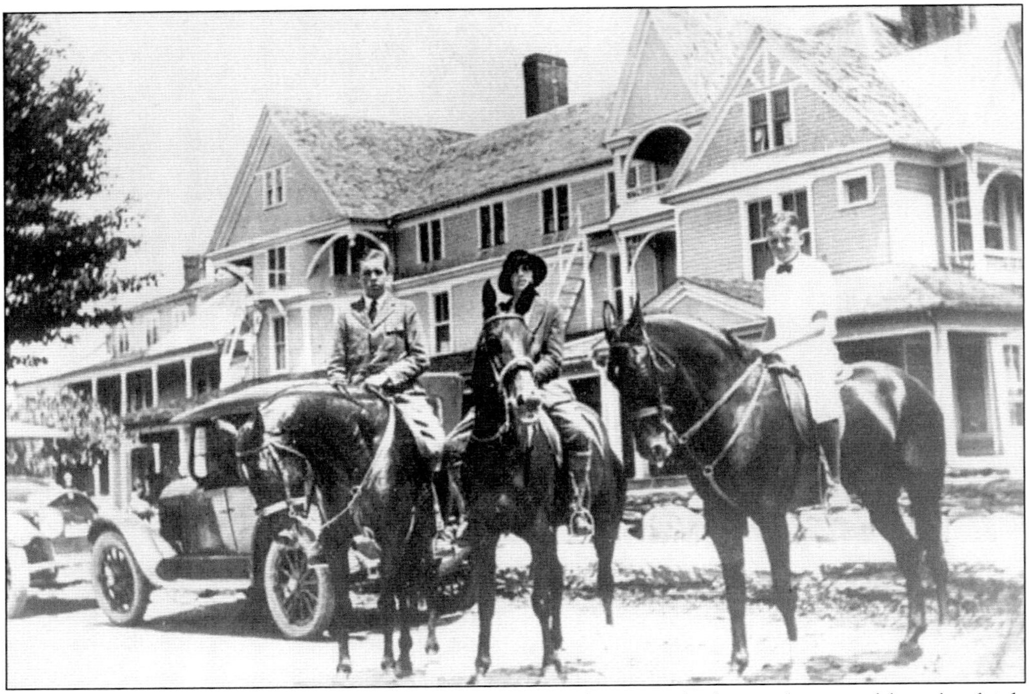

RIDERS AT THE GREEN PARK HOTEL. This *c.* 1920 photograph shows the grand hotel, which opened in 1891 and was a community gathering place as well as a hotel. The old hotel had its own post office and casino and it sponsored dances for the community. This hotel continues to be a popular place to stay in the mountains and is proud to be one of the remaining grand hotels in town. (Courtesy of *The Blowing Rocket*.)

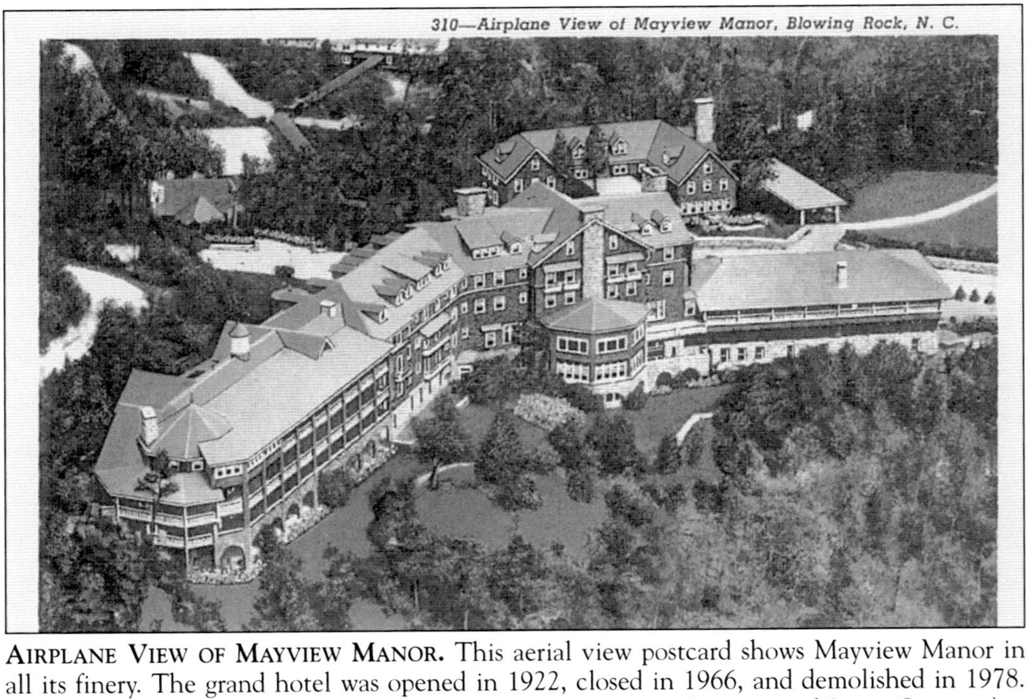

AIRPLANE VIEW OF MAYVIEW MANOR. This aerial view postcard shows Mayview Manor in all its finery. The grand hotel was opened in 1922, closed in 1966, and demolished in 1978. Currently, condominiums occupy the manor's former location. (Courtesy of Ginny Stevens.)

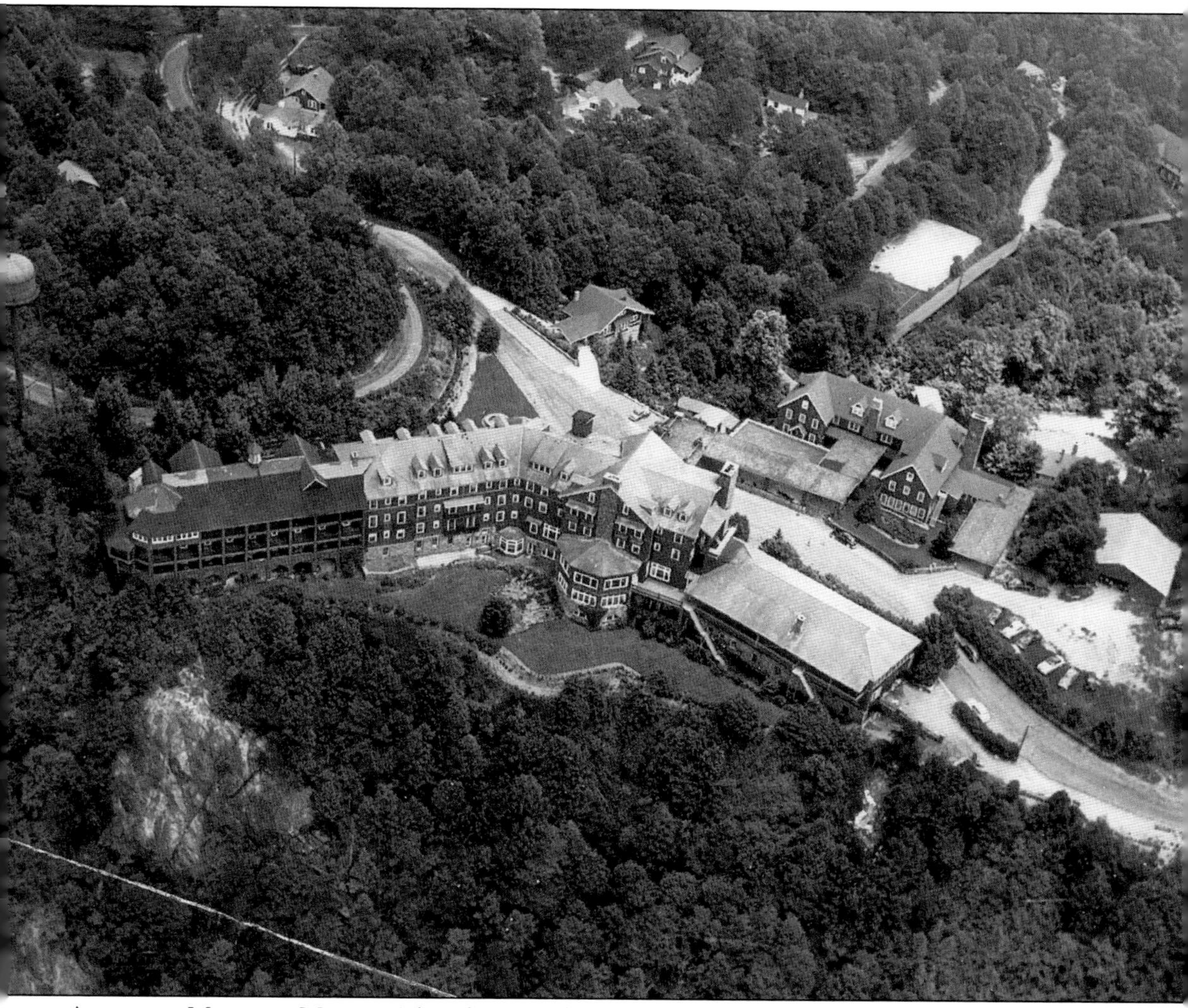

AERIAL OF MAYVIEW MANOR. This photograph, taken by Palmer Blair, a Boone photographer, shows the grandeur of the Mayview development. Walter L. Alexander developed Mayview Park in 1917 and was primed to develop the town into "America's Switzerland." The grand hotel was opened in 1922 and built precariously on the edge of John's River Gorge. The "mountain" architecture featured chestnut bark and native stone fireplaces. The hotel had a total of 138 rooms and a rustic, not fancy, mountain charm. Many famous people, such as Annie Oakley and other celebrities, were guests at the manor. Social events, fine entertainment, and wonderful food drew visitors and locals. The manor was the symbol of a grand era, with its horse show breakfasts, fashion shows, and afternoon teas. The hotel closed in 1966 and, sadly, in 1978 the manor was demolished. Many residents regret that the hotel could not have been saved. Currently, condominiums occupy the manor's former location. (Courtesy of *The Blowing Rocket*.)

CHETOLA ESTATE. This postcard shows the Chetola Manor House. The estate has been owned by the Estes, Stringfellow, and Snyder families and is now a highly rated year-round resort and restaurant. Chetola means "haven of rest" in Cherokee. (Courtesy of David Harwood.)

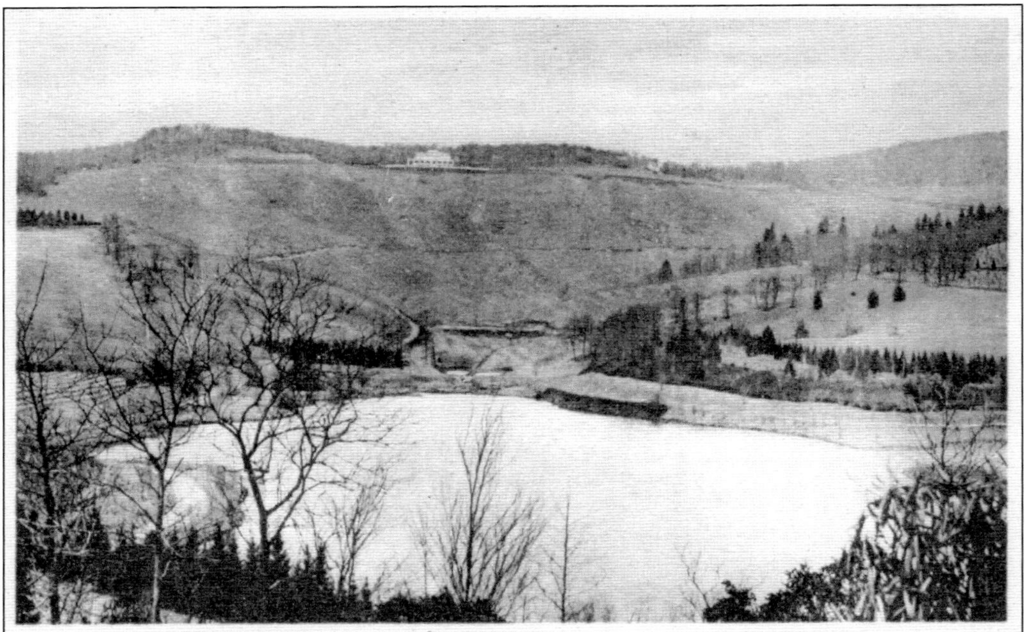

CONE ESTATE. This early postcard shows the Cone Estate, which is now part of the National Park Service. The original estate, owned by Moses Cone, included 3,600 acres with walking trails, riding paths, orchards, and elaborate landscaping. Flat Top Manor was built in 1900 and now houses the Southern Highland Handicraft Guild. (Courtesy of David Harwood.)

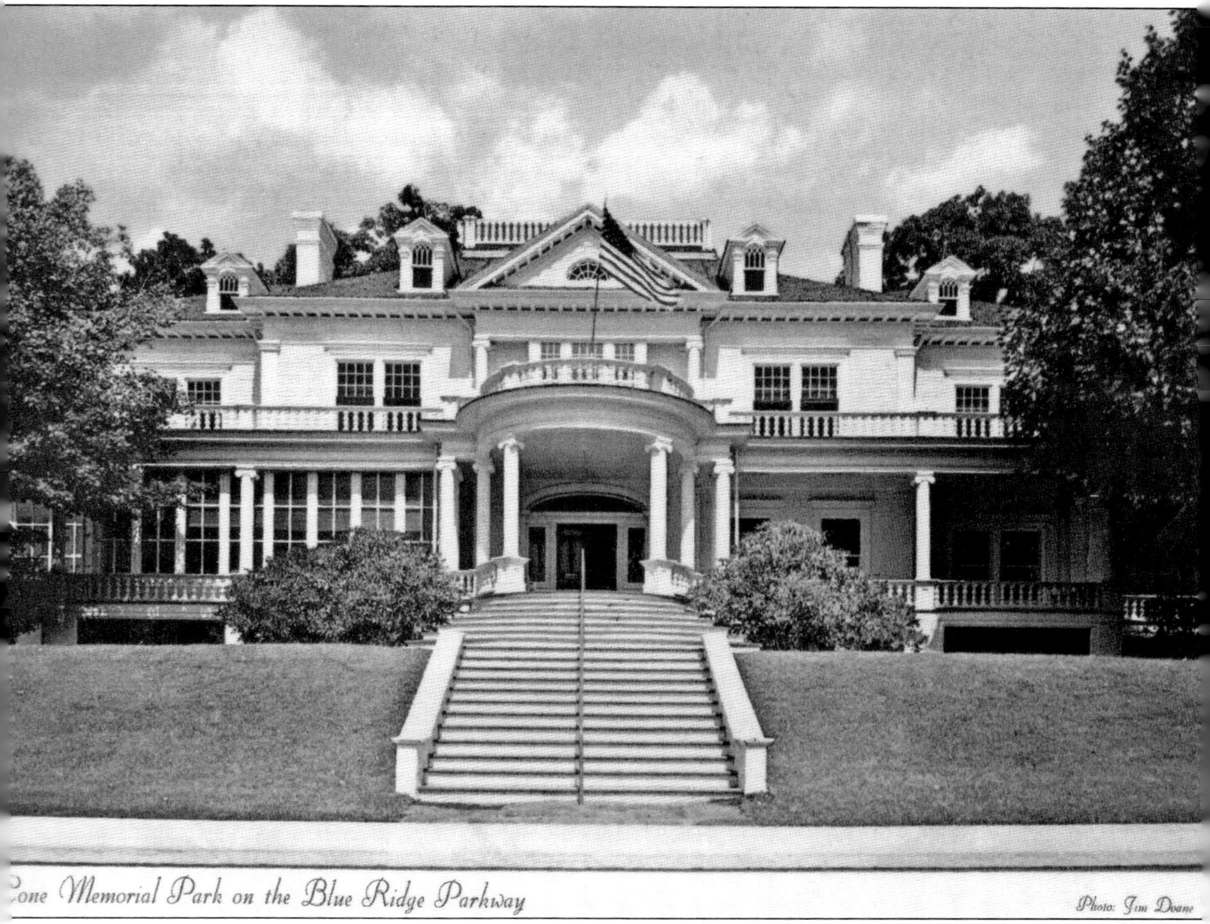

THE CONE MANSION. Located on the Blue Ridge Parkway, the Cone Mansion or Flat Top Manor, is part of the Cone Estate and is operated by the National Park Service. The Southern Highland Handicraft Guild is located within the house and the first floor is open for tours. Moses Cone, otherwise known as "The Denim King," acquired the land in the 1890s and in 1900 built Flat Top Manor, a 23-room colonial revival house. The mansion was innovative for its time and included a gaslight plant, wood burning central heating, and ornate woodwork. Cone planned his house and estate as a self-sufficient farm. His 3,600-acre gentleman's farm included lakes, walking and riding trails, gardens, apple orchards, grazing lands, a Grade A dairy, and extensive landscaped grounds. An important economic force in the area, the Cone estate employed or supported 30 local families in the area. The Cones entertained various well-known guests at the manor including the Secretary of the Navy under President Wilson and the governor of North Carolina. The Cones also frequently invited local children to the estate and served them homemade ice cream. We are fortunate the estate was donated to the National Park Service and is preserved for public use. (Courtesy of Richard Trexler.)

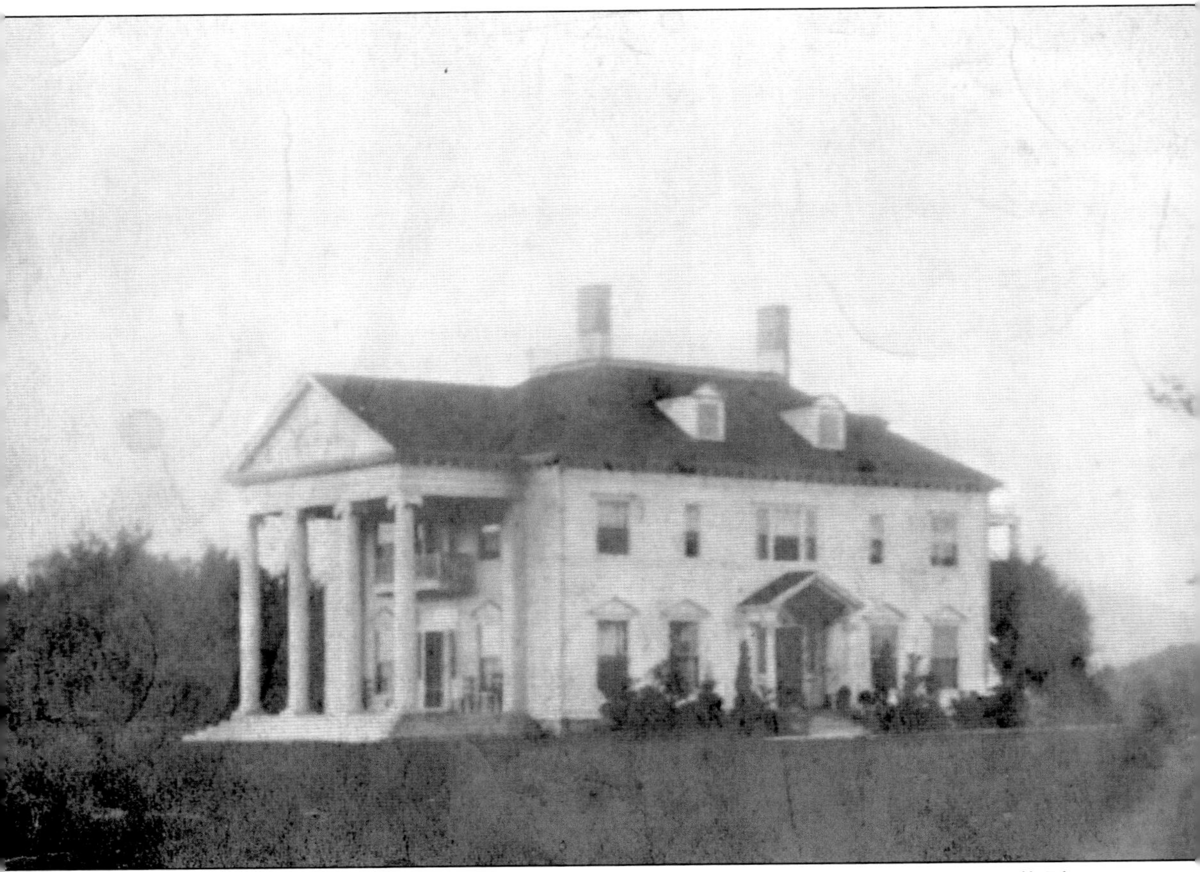

Daingerfield House. Elliott Daingerfield was the most well-known artist to call Blowing Rock home. Westglow was built in 1917 at a cost of $20,000 on a hill overlooking the Blue Ridge vistas. The house had its own 32-volt light plant. Visitors from all over the world and art students were housed at the mansion when the Daingerfields were there. Westglow was a popular social gathering place for their friends and neighbors. When the Daingerfields lived there, the house was filled with valuable artwork and antiques. The Grecian columns along the front of the house were imported from Italy and had to be hauled by oxen up the mountain. Elliott Daingerfield's works are part of the collections of the most notable museums, including the National Gallery and the Metropolitan Museum. Mr. Daingerfield donated *Madonna of the Hills* to the Stringfellow Memorial Church in Blowing Rock, which was then named St. Mary's of the Hills Episcopal Church. Many visitors stop by the church each year to admire the painting. Westglow is listed on the National Register of Historic Places. The house is now the Westglow Spa, a luxury resort and spa. (Courtesy of Joe Dulaney.)

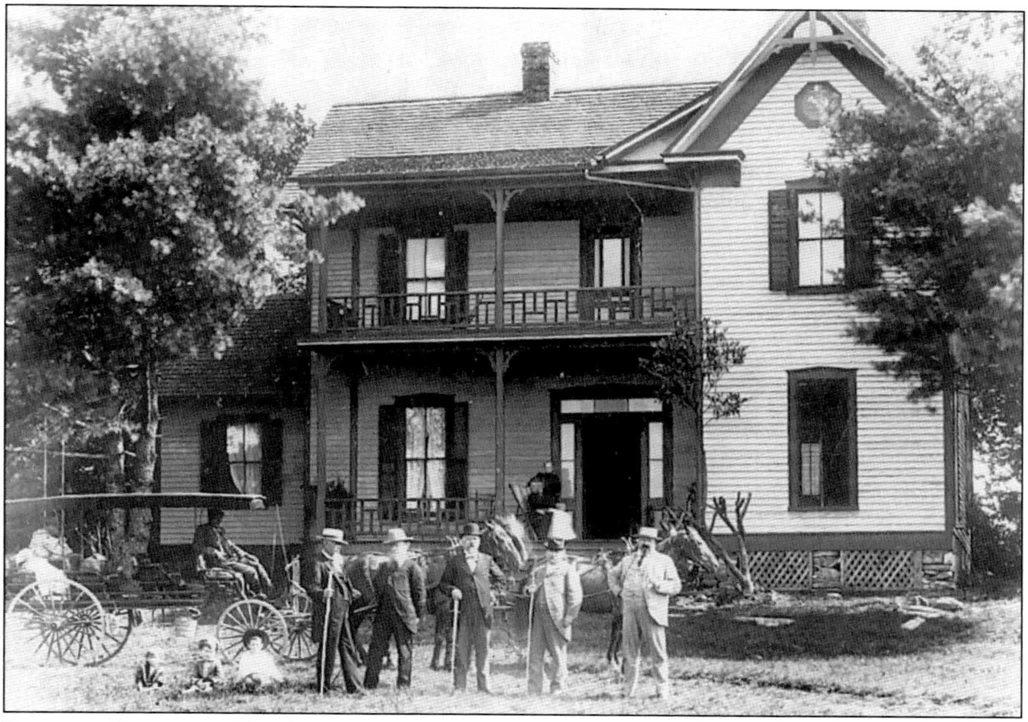

BOYDEN COTTAGE. This house was built in 1860 and is still located on U.S. 321 between the town and Green Park Inn. Known as "Norwood," the house has recently been renovated. Reportedly, Mr. Patterson, the owner, offered the house for use as a Yankee hospital so that it would be spared burning during the Civil War. (Courtesy of *The Blowing Rocket.*)

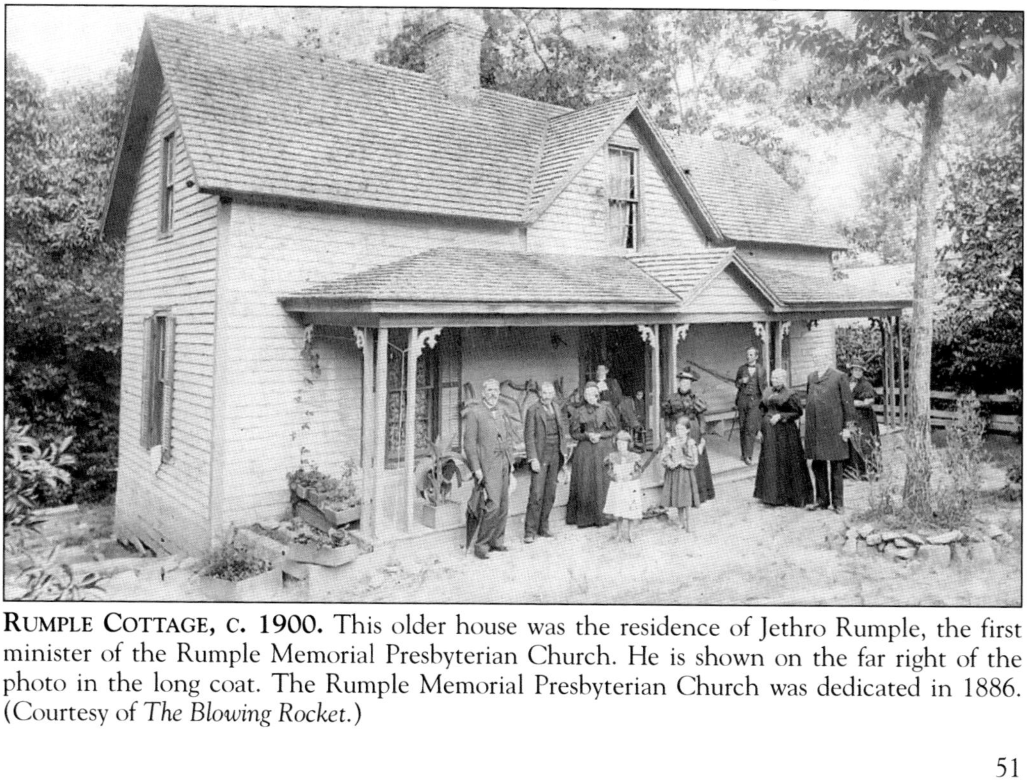

RUMPLE COTTAGE, C. 1900. This older house was the residence of Jethro Rumple, the first minister of the Rumple Memorial Presbyterian Church. He is shown on the far right of the photo in the long coat. The Rumple Memorial Presbyterian Church was dedicated in 1886. (Courtesy of *The Blowing Rocket.*)

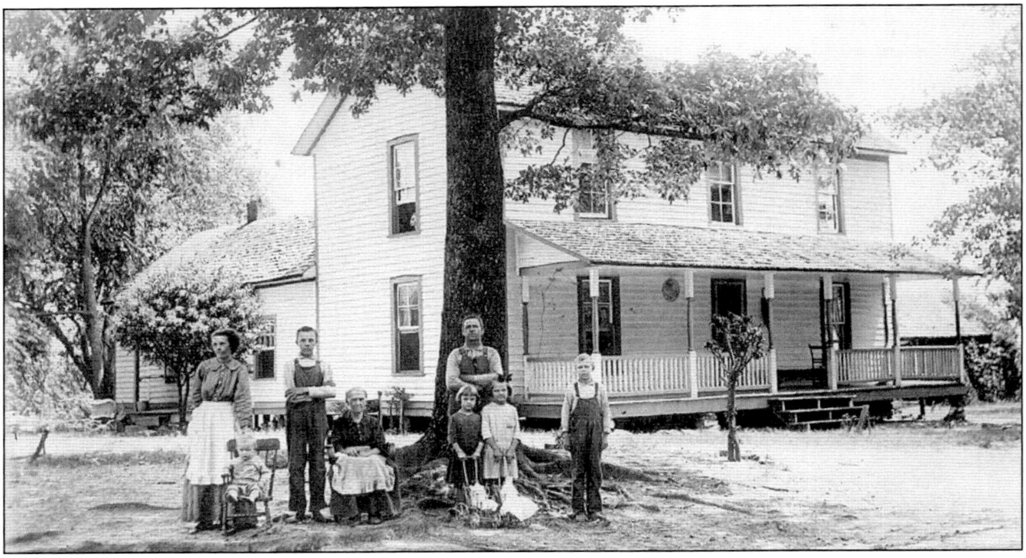

HOLSHOUSER HOME. This photograph was taken of the old Holshouser family house, which was located on Main Street beside the present-day Wachovia Bank. The I-house floor plan is typical of vernacular architecture in rural towns in the south. Note the baby carriages held by the two girls. (Courtesy of *The Blowing Rocket.*)

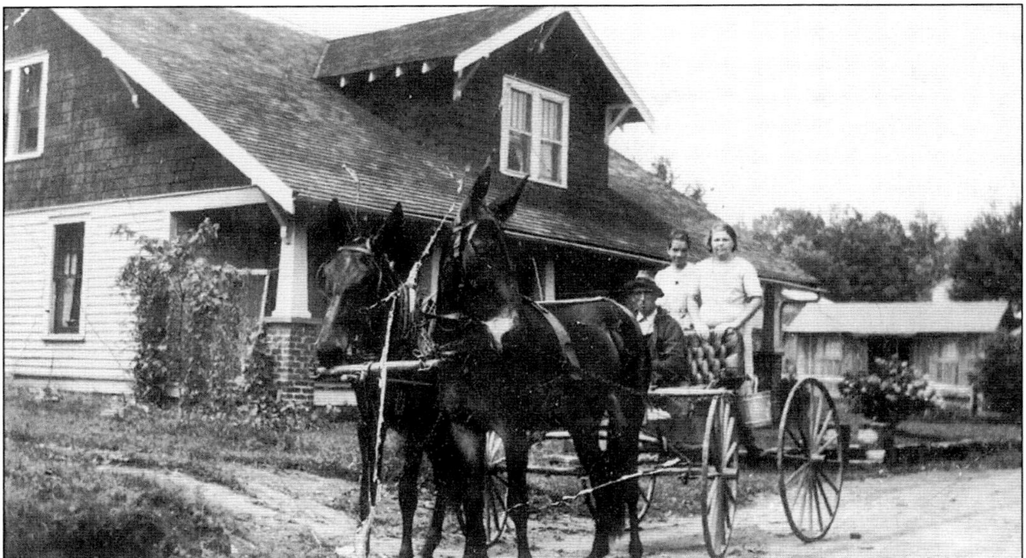

GUY COON RESIDENCE. This house stood on Morris Street at the current location of the Hemlock Motel. One of Dr. H.R. Reid's summer rental cabins can be seen on the right. Driving the wagon is Eddie McLean, and the passengers are Belle McLean and Lovell Estes. The McLeans peddled produce in town during summers, a good way to earn extra cash for the local families. (Courtesy of *The Blowing Rocket.*)

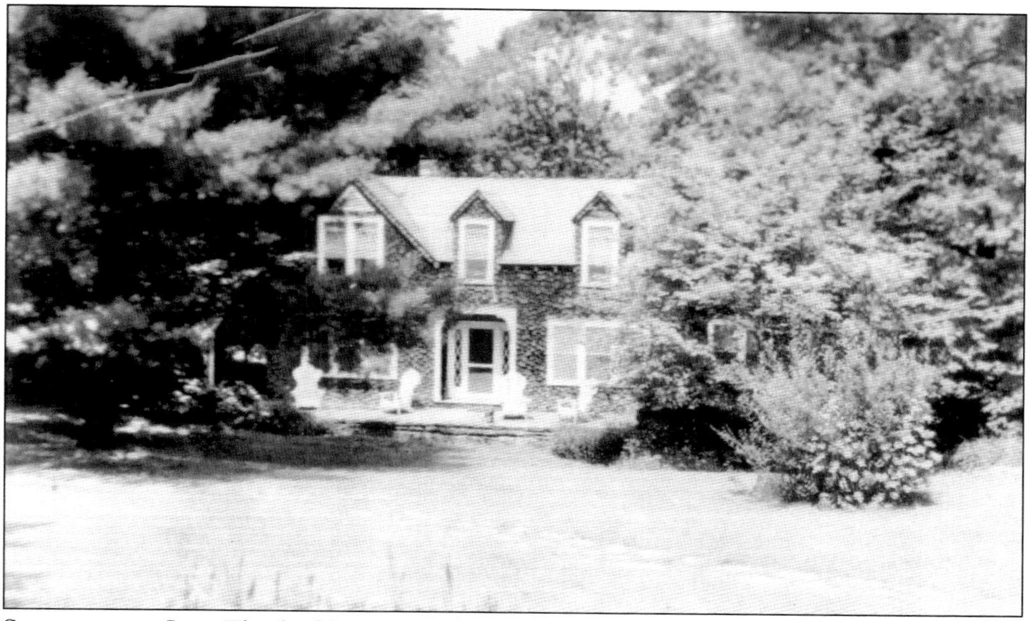

SPRINGHAVEN INN. This building is now located at the intersection of South Main Street and Globe Road. The inn began at a different location as the old toll house inn for the Yonahlossee Turnpike, the road running up the mountain from Lenoir. The stagecoaches dropped the passengers at the inn while fresh horses were exchanged. The building was moved to its present location in the early 1900s. (Courtesy of Richard Trexler.)

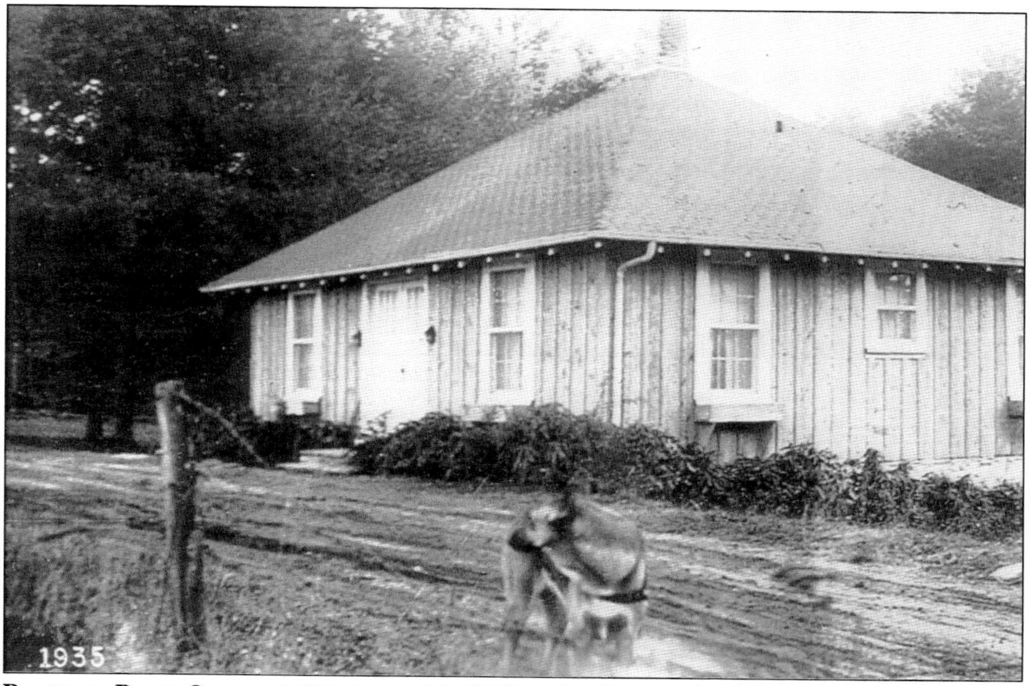

BLOWING ROCK CLINIC, 1935. Mary Cabell Warfield, Blowing Rock's first female physician, is credited with setting up the Warfield Clinic, which developed into the Blowing Rock Hospital. Dr. Warfield had a German shepherd who accompanied her on house calls and sat in the front seat of the car. The dog in this photograph is likely her dear pet. (Courtesy of Heidi Ellis.)

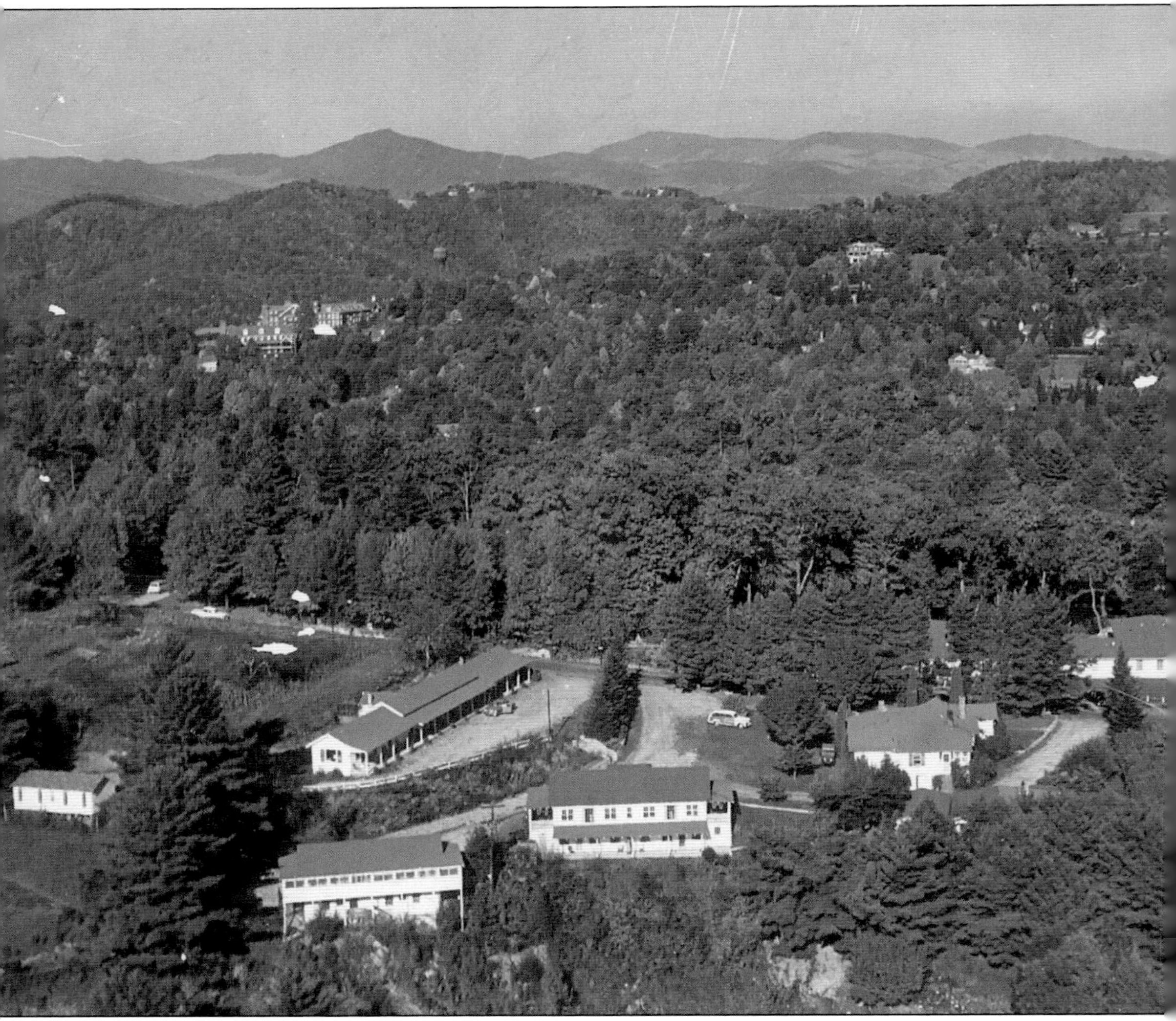

AERIAL VIEW, C. 1940S. This photograph shows the Hart Motor Court and Cottages along Ransom Street. Several of the Hart Cottages were moved to the Farm House Inn and Restaurant property and then demolished when the Farm House was torn down. The clinic, which preceded the Blowing Rock Hospital, is located on the right of the photo. Mayview Manor is the large building shown in the upper left of the view. The increasing development of the town can be seen in the photograph, although the development is not as dense and compact as it is today. (Courtesy of *The Blowing Rocket*.)

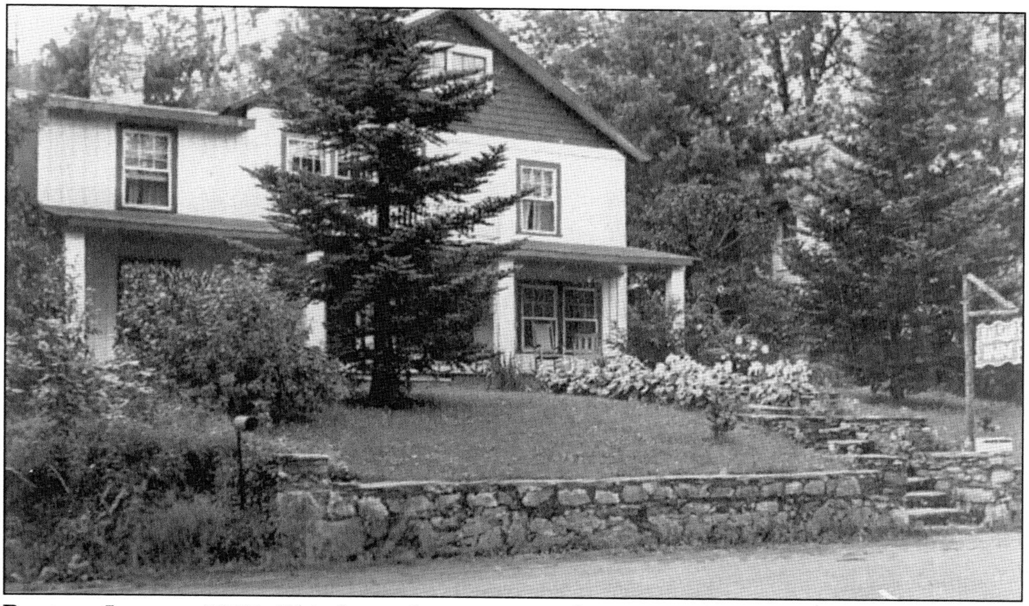

Balsam Inn, c. 1915. This house became an early inn in Blowing Rock. It is no longer standing and may have been located along U.S. 221 near town. Many larger houses were turned into boarding houses and then inns as the tourism industry increased. (Courtesy of *The Blowing Rocket*.)

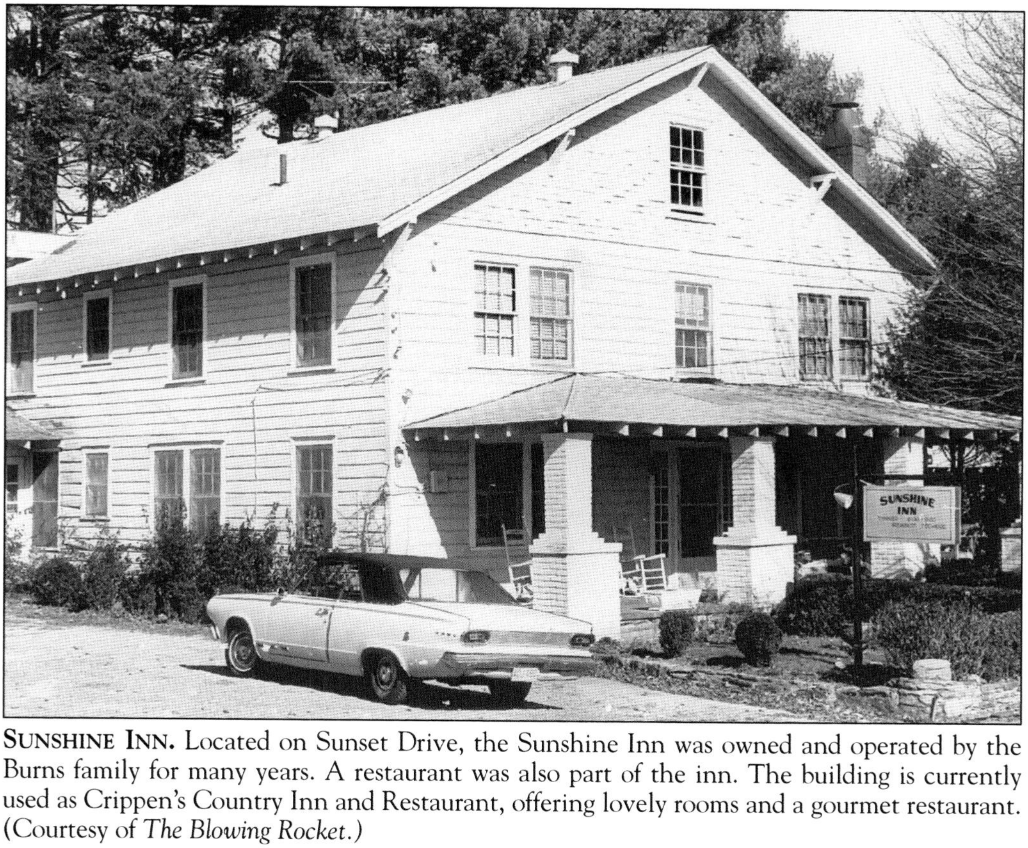

Sunshine Inn. Located on Sunset Drive, the Sunshine Inn was owned and operated by the Burns family for many years. A restaurant was also part of the inn. The building is currently used as Crippen's Country Inn and Restaurant, offering lovely rooms and a gourmet restaurant. (Courtesy of *The Blowing Rocket*.)

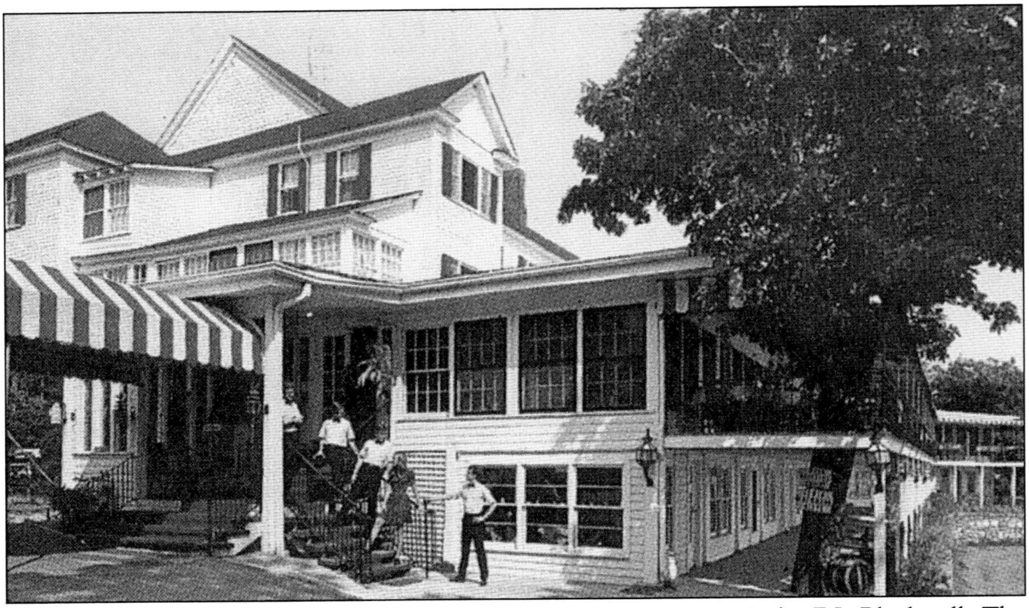

FARM HOUSE INN. This Blowing Rock tradition was begun in 1951 by E.J. Blackwell. The building dates back to 1891, when it was the Skyland Inn and later the Stuart Hotel. The Farm House Inn's unique draw was singing waiters and waitresses. E.J. Blackwell Jr. and Shirley Blackwell operated the restaurant from 1954 until a few years ago, when it was closed and the building was demolished. (Courtesy of *The Blowing Rocket*.)

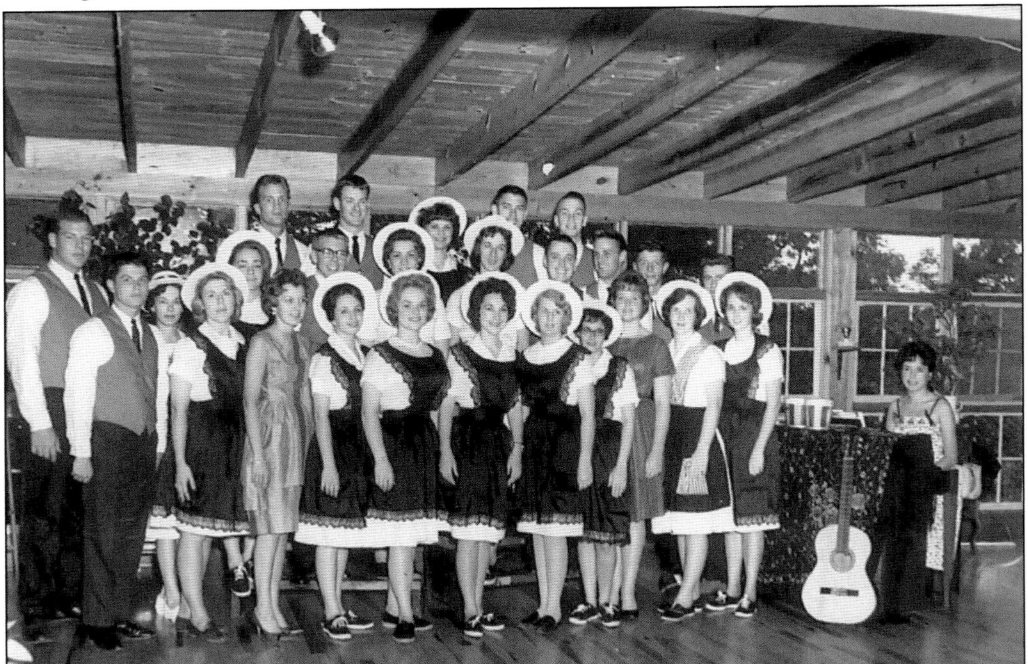

FARM HOUSE INN ENTERTAINERS. The Farm House Restaurant drew crowds and became a tradition with good food and lively entertainment. The ability to carry a tune was a requirement for employment at this restaurant that was a Blowing Rock tradition. (Courtesy of *The Blowing Rocket*.)

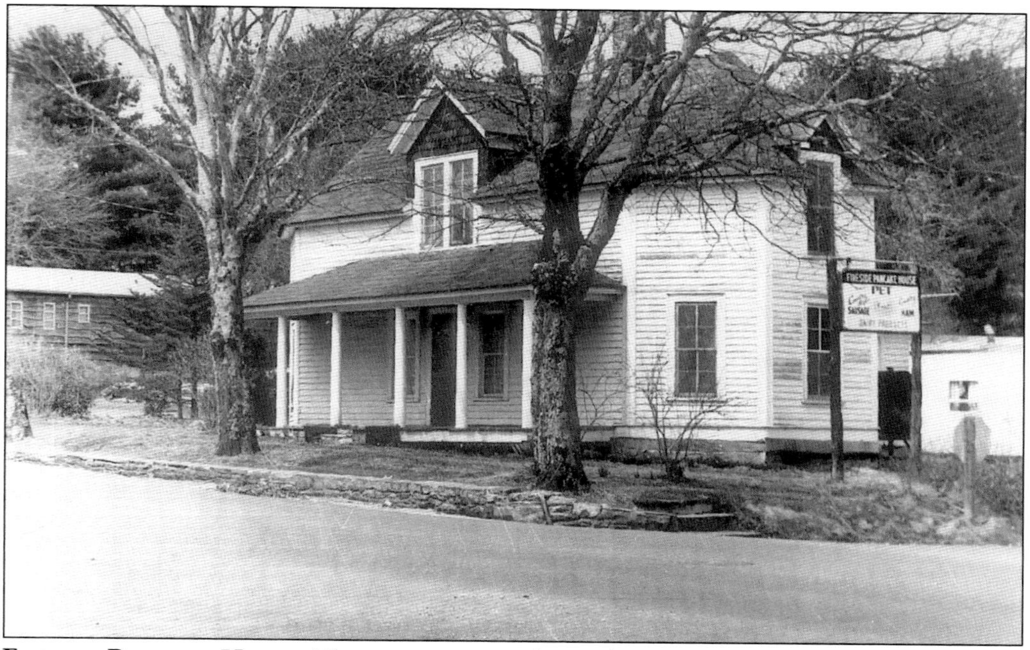

FIRESIDE PANCAKE HOUSE. This restaurant was located on Sunset Drive and Ransom Street. Locals and tourists remember good breakfast food available there. The Hillwinds Inn is now located on the lot. (Courtesy of *The Blowing Rocket*.)

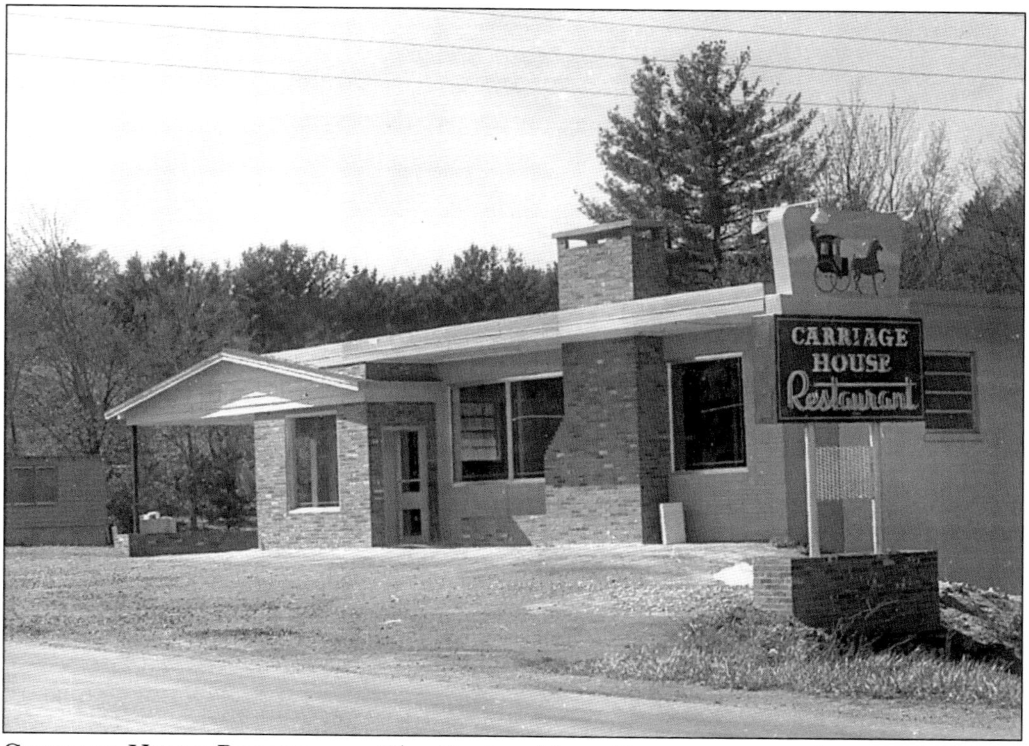

CARRIAGE HOUSE RESTAURANT. The Carriage House Restaurant was a location for home-cooked food when it operated in the early 1960s. The building now houses the Village Pharmacy, Blowing Rock's only drug store. (Courtesy of *The Blowing Rocket*.)

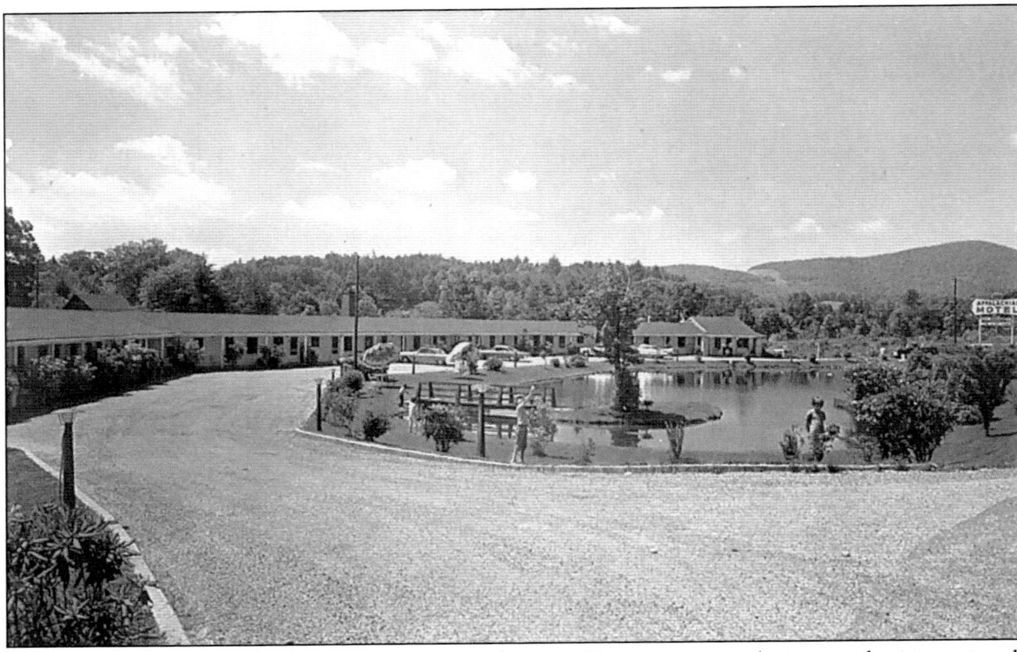

APPALACHIAN MOTEL. This postcard touts the excellent accommodations, televisions in all rooms, and a beautiful lake. The motel is still located on U.S. 321 and is now known as the Brookside Inn. These vehicle oriented hotels bring back the nostalgia for the 1950s family vacations. (Courtesy of Ginny Stevens.)

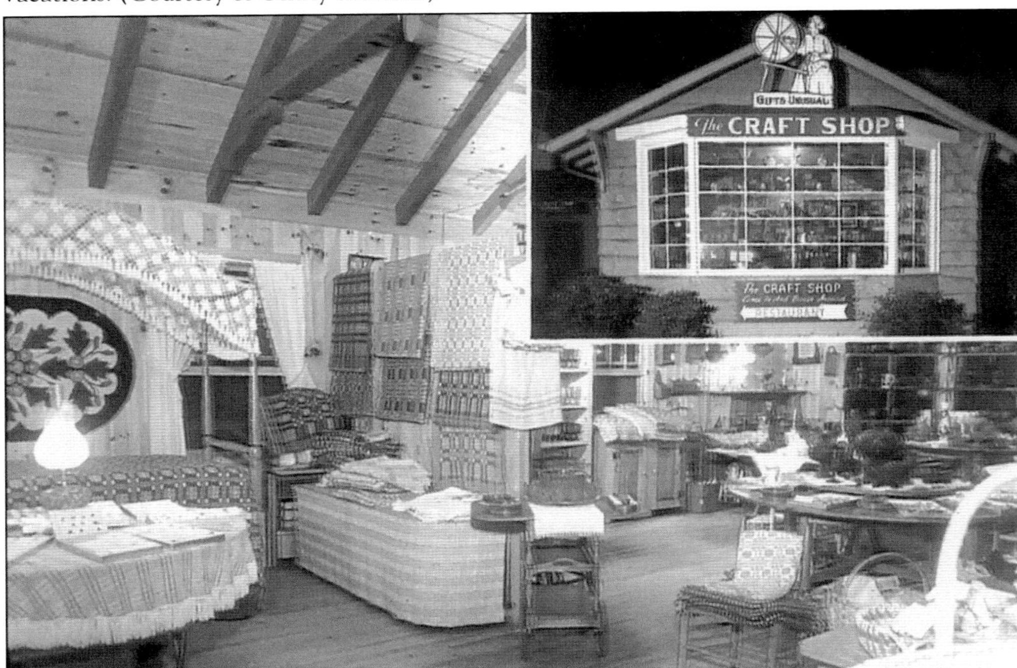

GOODWIN WEAVERS. This weaving business has long been a part of the town's history. Located on U.S. 321, the business provided a showroom of mountain crafts and is home to the Goodwin Guild. The colonial patterns of woven bedspreads and throws have been prized collectibles for locals and visitors alike. (Courtesy of Ginny Stevens.)

Four

Agriculture and Transportation

Agriculture was about the only way of life for the earliest settlers in Blowing Rock after the Revolutionary War. The subsistence farmer hoped to produce enough extra to transport cabbage, potatoes, beans, corn, or livestock down the mountain to Lenoir to trade. Transportation became essential to getting goods off the mountain and onto the mountain. Constructed after 1845, the Lenoir–Blowing Rock Turnpike improved the route between the two towns and allowed tourism to develop after the Civil War. When the East Tennessee & Western North Carolina Railroad came through Boone, long distance markets were opened. The lumber industry grew in the area in the late 1800s and early 1900s and provided jobs for local workers and another function for the railroad line. People in the mountains traveled by horse or oxen and wagon, on horseback, or by foot. Transportation improvements, such as the automobile, allowed trade to increase and were critical in bringing tourists to the area. Agriculture has become less important in the economy, while the service industry has expanded. However, it is still possible to drive in the country here and see hayfields, cattle, tobacco fields, and rows of corn.

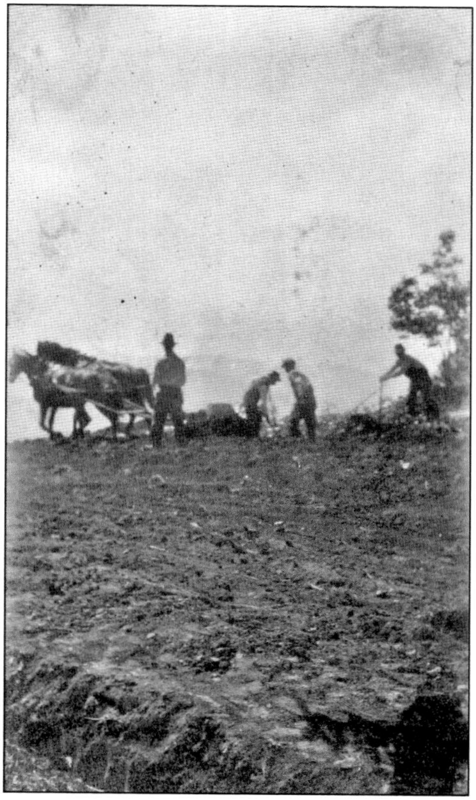

Plowing by Horse. This photograph reflects the toil required to till the soil in days gone by. The steep terrain required great fortitude from the farmer. This photo was likely taken on the Westglow Estate. (Courtesy of Joe Dulaney.)

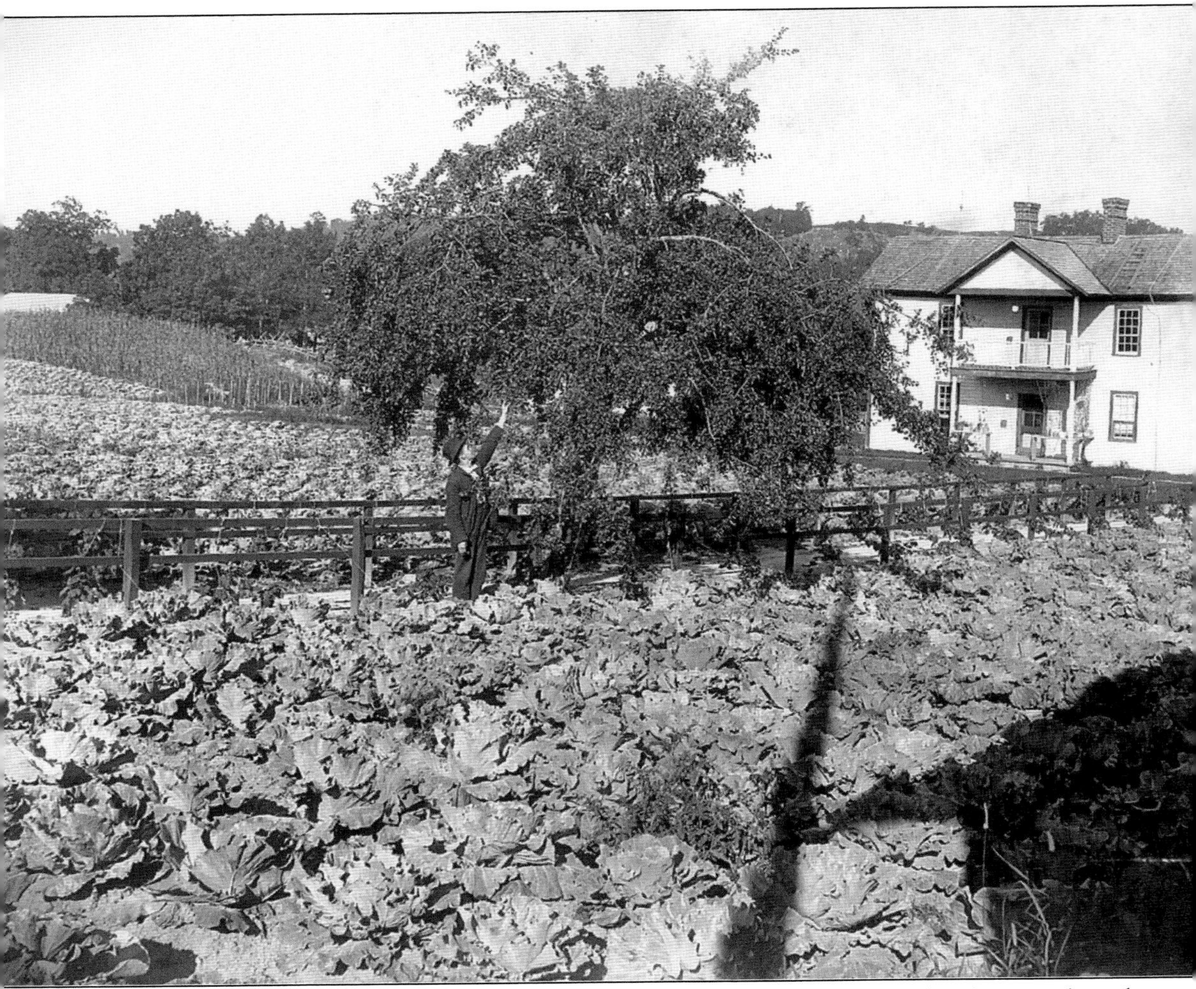

Typical Mountain Farm. Pictured in this early photograph is an example of a typical rural mountain farm. Crops such as corn, cabbage, and apple trees provided sustenance for the farmer and often enough to barter for other necessities. Agricultural products were transported by oxen and wagon to Lenoir, a very long day's journey or a two-day journey camping overnight along the way. Construction projects, such as the Yonahlossee Trail and the Cone Estate provided extra cash to help local families. The advent of the logging industry in the late 1800s and early 1900s also provided jobs to supplement incomes. In 1900, most of the Blowing Rock households reported themselves as farmers. Today, the small percentage of the population involved in farming does it on a part-time basis and usually holds down a regular job. (Courtesy of *The Blowing Rocket*.)

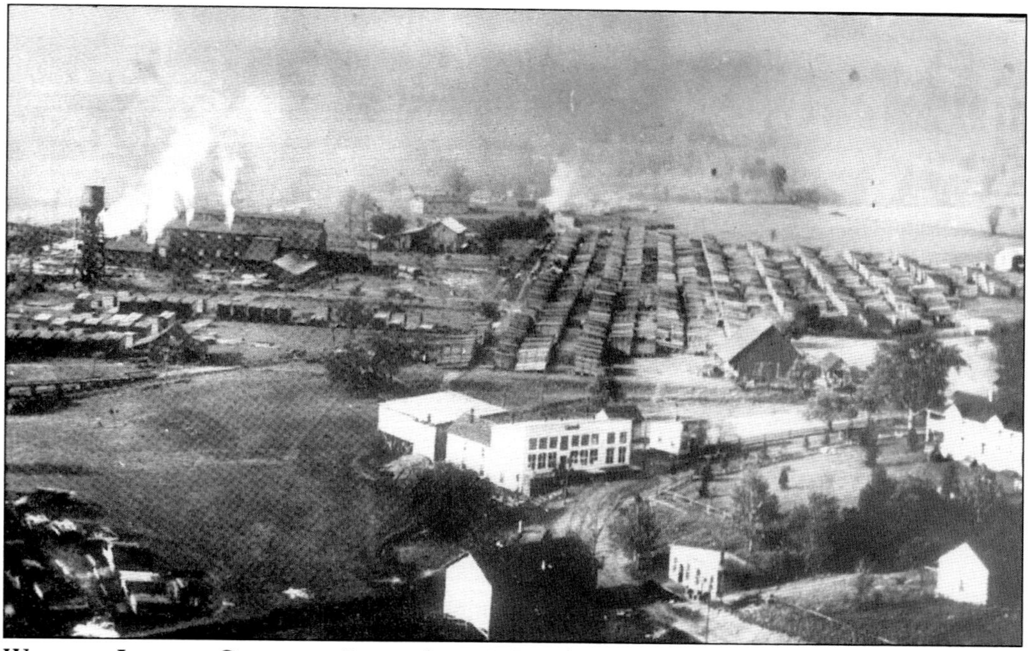

WHITING LUMBER COMPANY. Pictured in 1917 is the Whiting Lumber Company, which was once located in the Shull's Mill community. It included sawmills and a timber plant and provided employment for many folks in the area. However, the wholesale lumbering caused erosion, road maintenance problems, and forest fires. The lumber was transported by a rail line through Shull's Mill to Tennessee and distant markets. The large building on the right of the photo is the Shull's Mill Hotel. The lumber company built a nearly self-sustaining community, which included a drug store and movie theatre. In the photograph below is a view of the sawmills and the timber plant located in the Shull's Mill area. (Courtesy of *The Blowing Rocket*.)

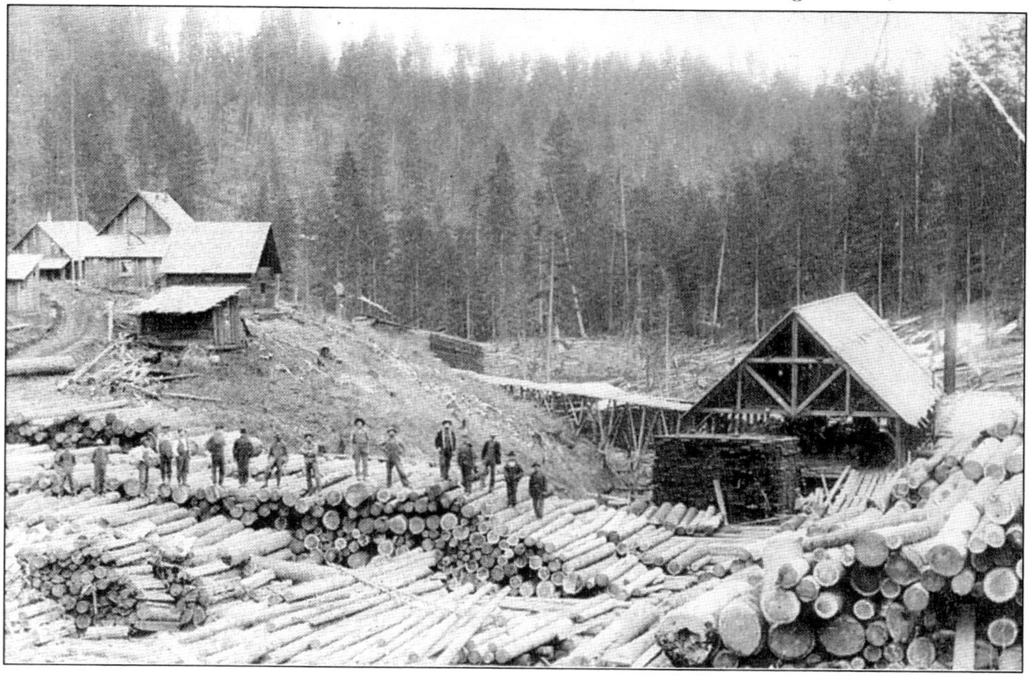

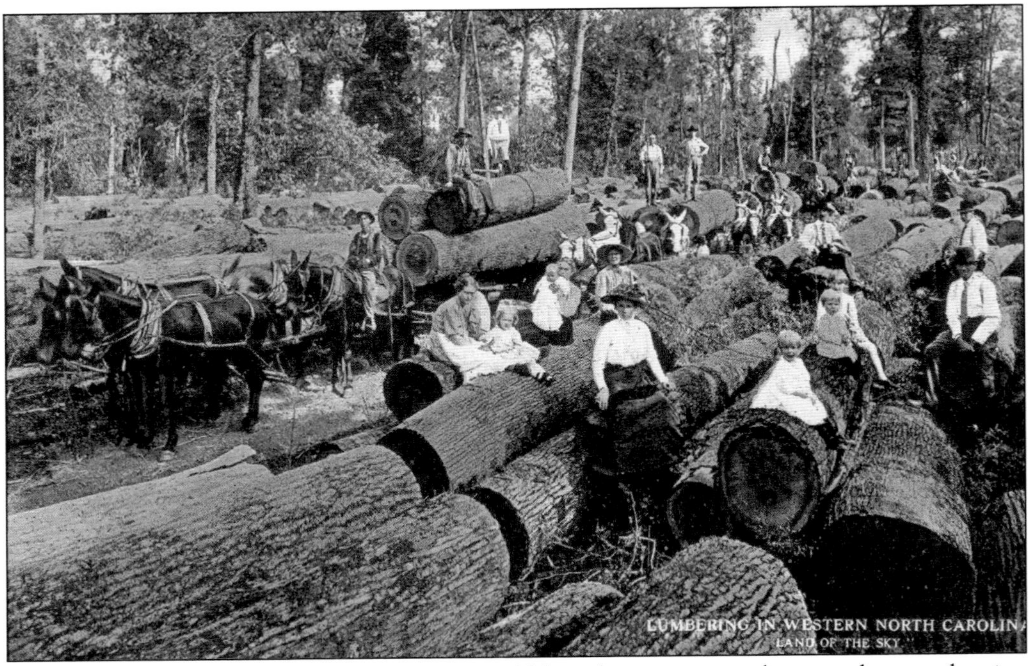

LUMBERING IN WESTERN NORTH CAROLINA. Although an economic boon to the area, logging led to erosion and slope damage in many areas. The logs were transported for milling and then sent by the Eastern Tennessee & Western North Carolina train to be sent all over the nation. (Courtesy of David Harwood.)

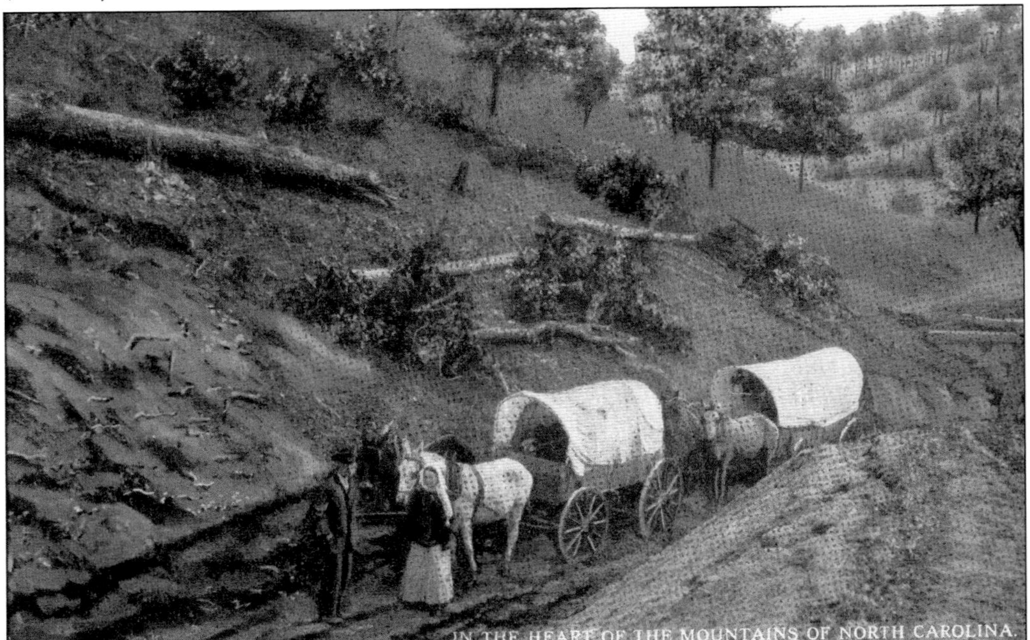

WAGONS UP THE MOUNTAIN. These two flatbed wagons are drawn by a team of two mules. The lumbering is evident on the slopes and did not improve road conditions. However, the stalwart mountain pioneer traveled through all these poor conditions to transport agricultural goods down the mountain for trade. (Courtesy of David Harwood.)

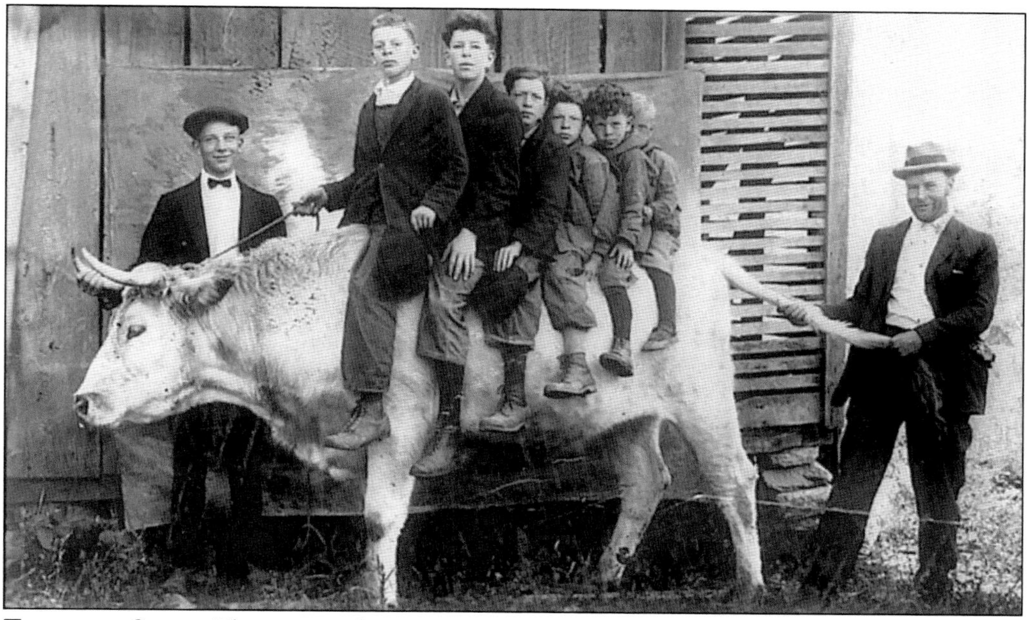

Travel by Steer. These young boys are getting to ride in style aboard a steer. The gentleman at the back of the steer may be trying to "steer" it by its tail. If a family did not have a horse, it was not unheard of to ride cattle or oxen. (Courtesy of *The Blowing Rocket*.)

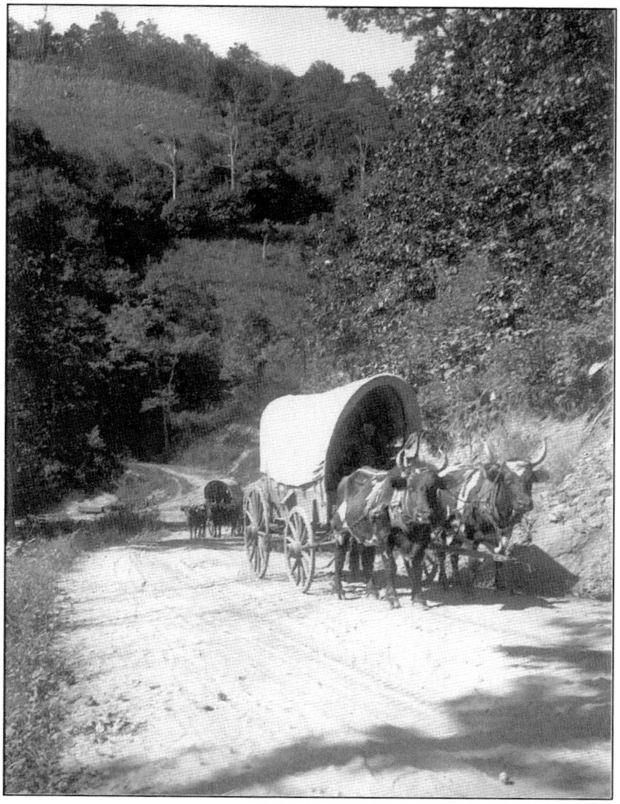

Lenoir–Blowing Rock Turnpike. The oxen are pulling schooner or crooked bed type wagons up the Lenoir–Blowing Rock Turnpike. Farmers in the area would transport wagonloads of potatoes, cabbage, apples, dried fruit, chestnuts, dried beef, and hams "down the mountain" to supplement their income. Back then, the trip took one long hard day or two days with camping overnight. (Courtesy of *The Blowing Rocket*.)

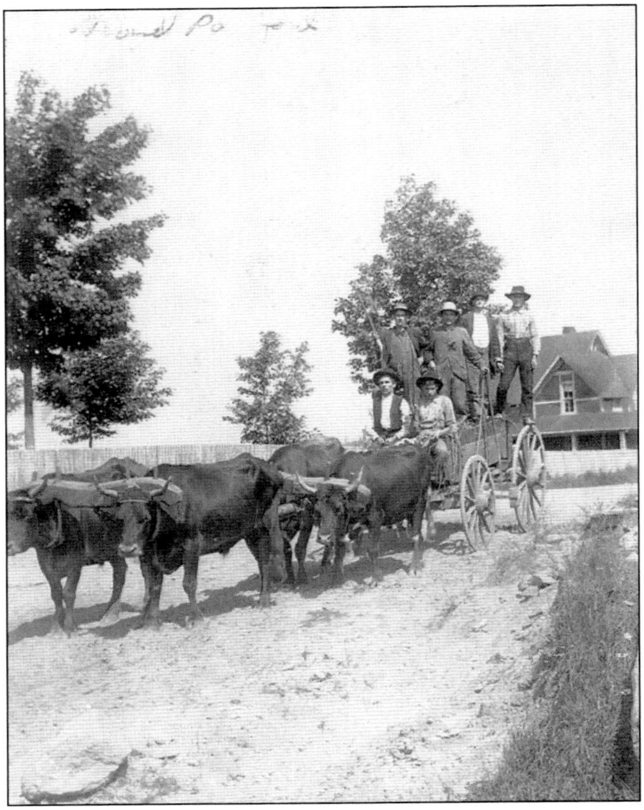

Oxen Pulling Wagon, c. 1900. This photograph illustrates the old-fashioned mode of transportation used in the mountains—wagons pulled by oxen. Note the poor condition of the local roads. (Courtesy of Heidi Ellis.)

Ladies Out for a Wagon Ride. Oxen pull an old wagon in this Blowing Rock area photo. Oxen were used for quite a long time in the mountains due to poor road conditions and steep slopes. (Courtesy of *The Blowing Rocket*.)

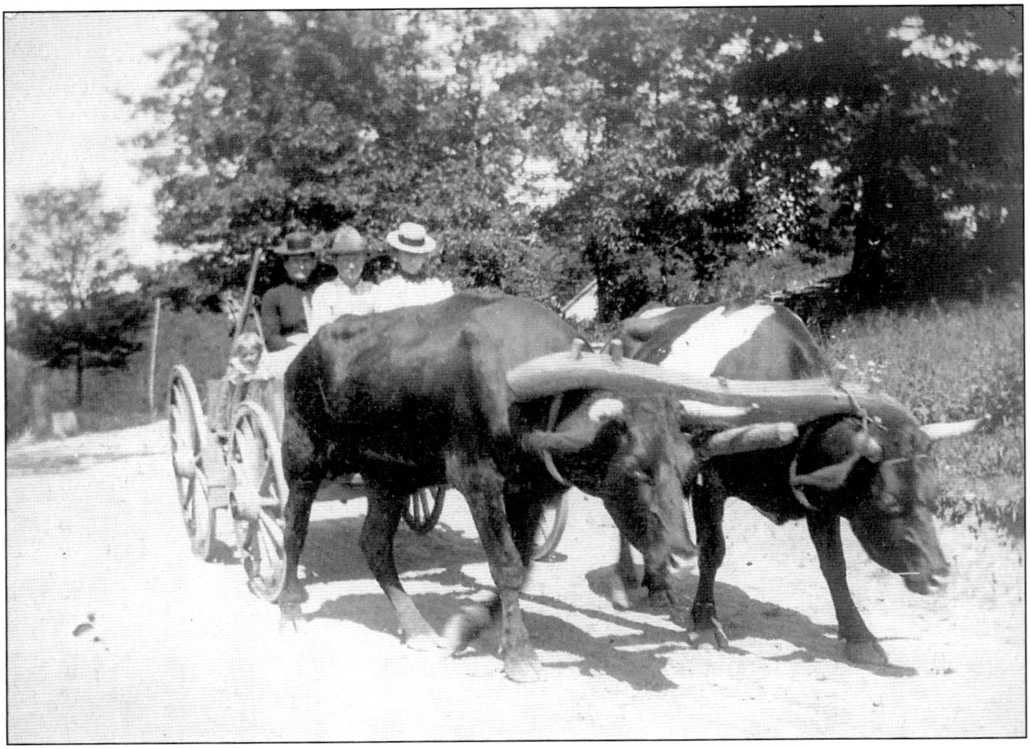

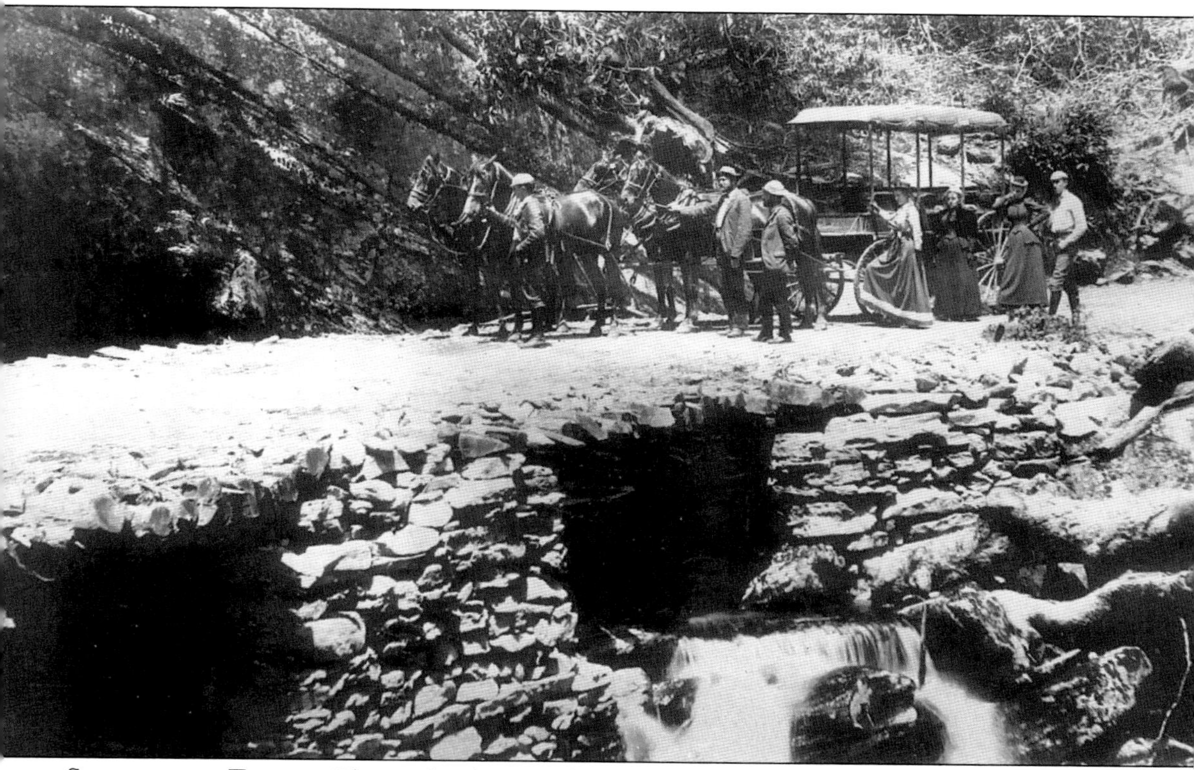

Stagecoach Travel. This early photograph reflects the perils of mountain travel. This stagecoach is traveling along the Yonahlossee Trail (Black Bear Trail, now U.S. 221). Note the rock pillars holding up the road and the waterfall cascading down the slope. Stagecoach lines were operated from Lenoir up to Blowing Rock. Locals also set up several livery stables in Blowing Rock to provide transportation by buggy and coach through the area. Taking these sometimes dangerous rides on the rough mountain roads was a popular pastime for summer tourists. (Courtesy of *The Blowing Rocket*.)

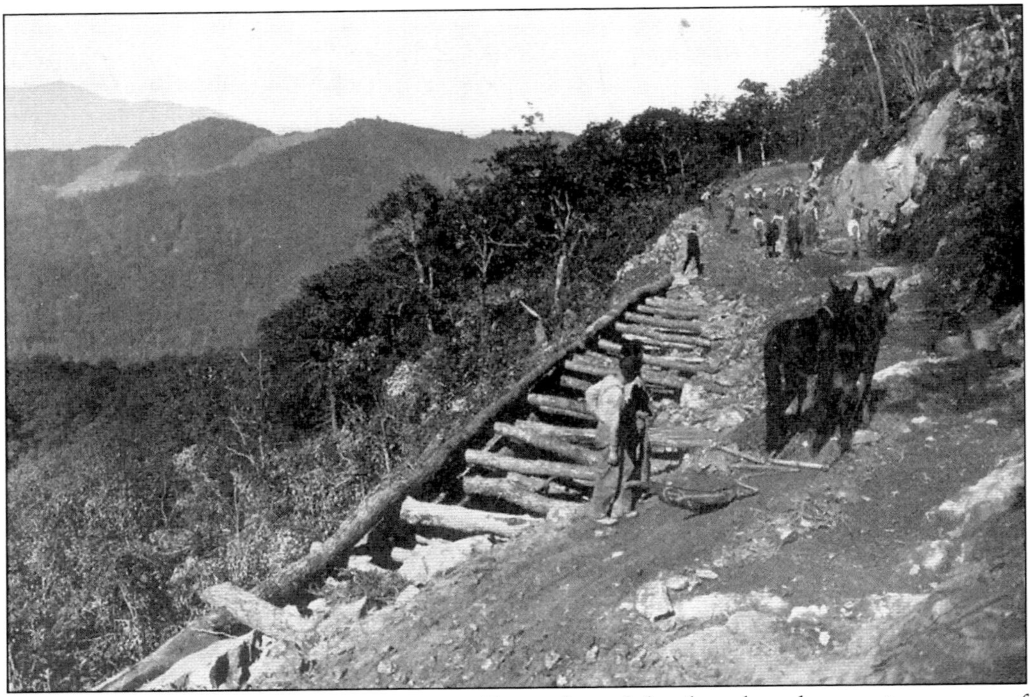

ROAD CONSTRUCTION ON WONDERLAND TRAIL. It took hard work and a certain amount of bravery to forge out roads in these days. This photograph shows the construction of Wonderland Trail above the John's River Gorge in the early 1900s. (Courtesy of *The Blowing Rocket*.)

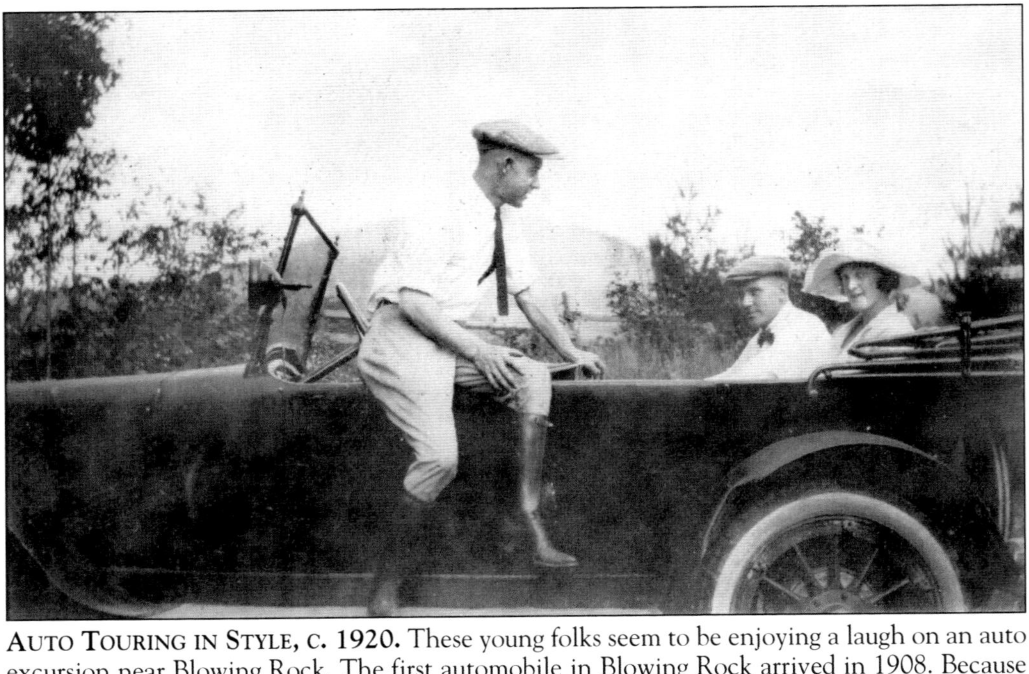

AUTO TOURING IN STYLE, C. 1920. These young folks seem to be enjoying a laugh on an auto excursion near Blowing Rock. The first automobile in Blowing Rock arrived in 1908. Because of the unpaved and often muddy roads, travel by automobile was sometimes risky. (Courtesy of Joe Dulaney.)

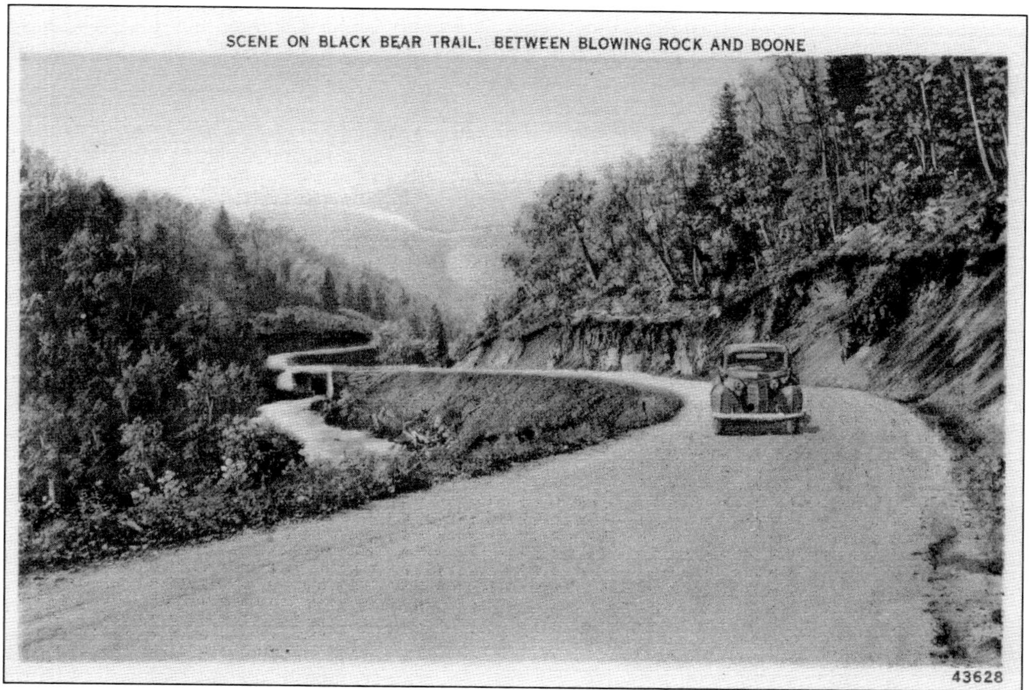

SCENE ON BLACK BEAR TRAIL. This scene from the past along Black Bear Trail (now U.S. 221) shows the rough roads, but the beautiful scenery made road trips worthwhile. (Courtesy of Brian Lambeth.)

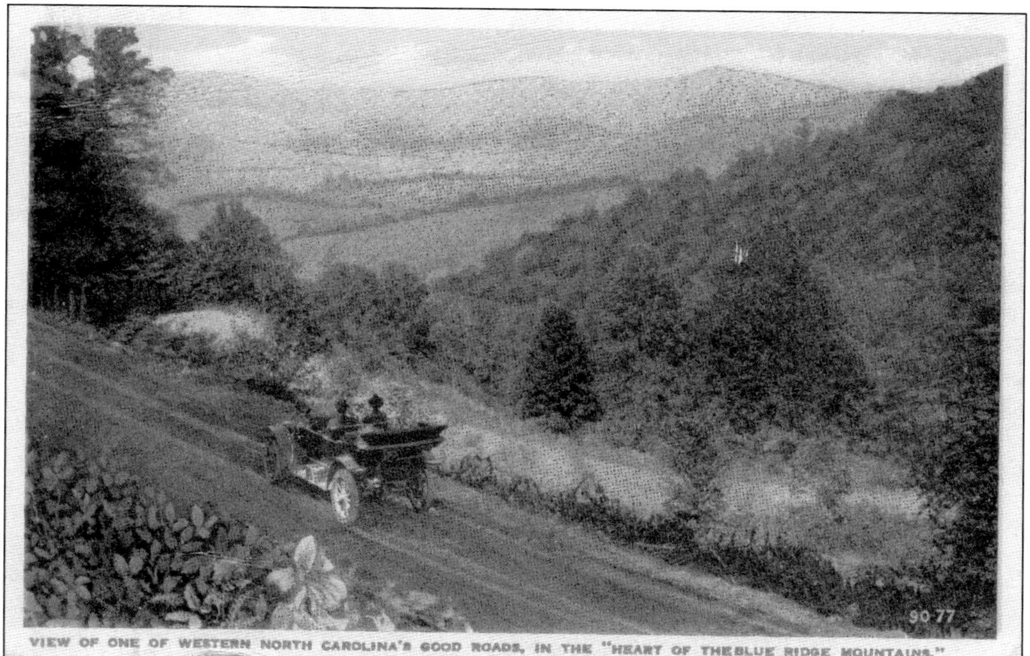

VIEW OF WESTERN NORTH CAROLINA MOUNTAINS. These early tourists admire the long-range views and vistas from the rough roads. The road conditions did not deter tourists in the 1800s and 1900s, but improvements have definitely made the trip up to the mountains more comfortable, safer, and quicker. (Courtesy of David Harwood.)

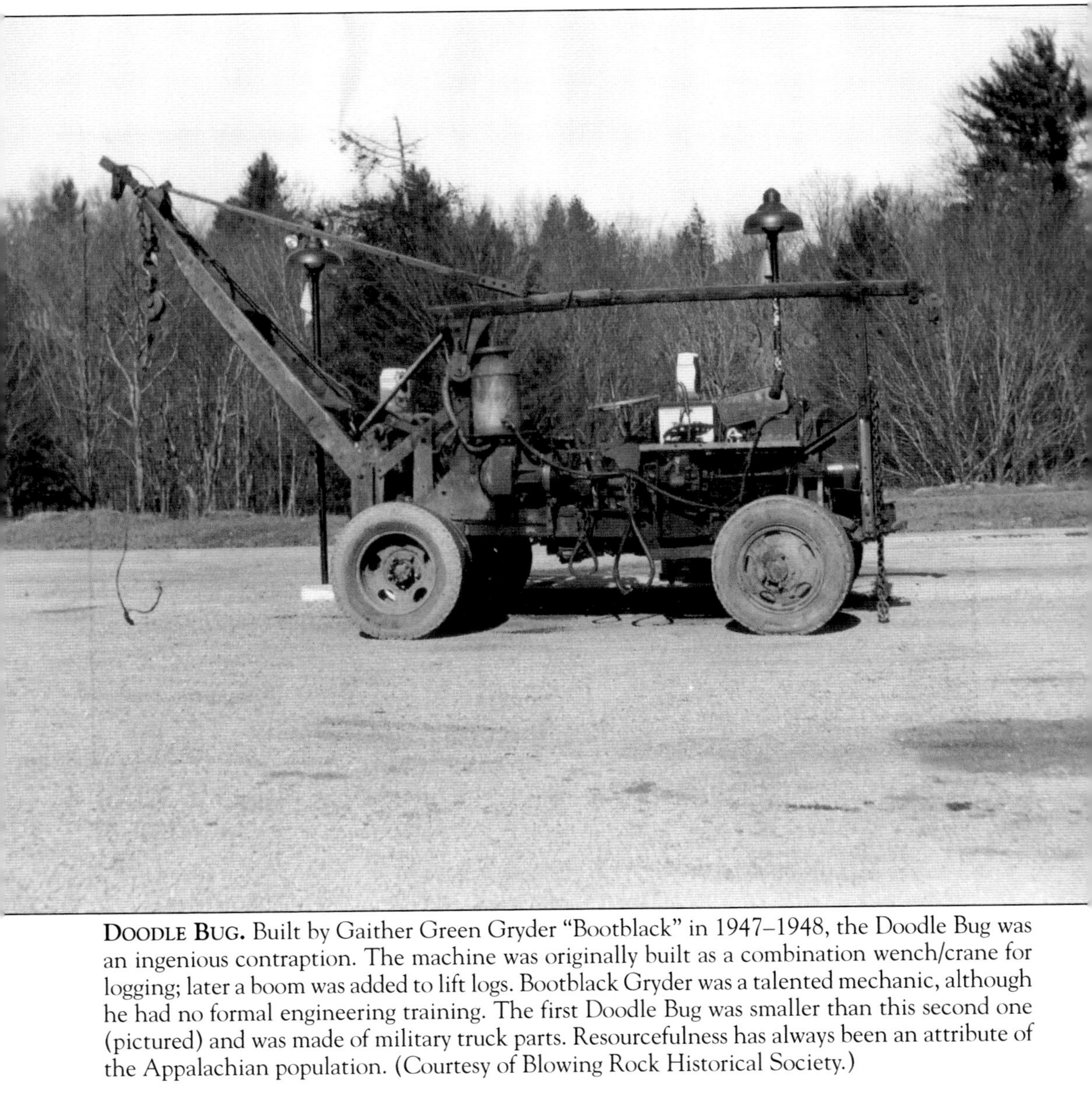

DOODLE BUG. Built by Gaither Green Gryder "Bootblack" in 1947–1948, the Doodle Bug was an ingenious contraption. The machine was originally built as a combination wench/crane for logging; later a boom was added to lift logs. Bootblack Gryder was a talented mechanic, although he had no formal engineering training. The first Doodle Bug was smaller than this second one (pictured) and was made of military truck parts. Resourcefulness has always been an attribute of the Appalachian population. (Courtesy of Blowing Rock Historical Society.)

Five

FRIENDS AND NEIGHBORS

Today, we marvel at the hardships the early settlers endured in this region, such as harsh winters, isolation, the short growing season, and the steep terrain. These settlers came in search of freedom and inexpensive land on which to prosper. The ancestry of most settlers in this region is Ulster-Irish, Scottish, Irish, German, English, Welch, and Swiss. Early family names in the Blowing Rock area, many of which are still represented today, included Greene, Hayes, Storie, Estes, Bolick, and Coffey. The early town was built by these stalwart and brave pioneers. Prominent and wealthy tourists began to summer here and provided another economic means of survival to many local families. Certain social events, such as church socials, were one method by which "locals" and tourists could intermingle. Often, though, the seasonal residents organized and created their own social events. The contributions of the tourists and summer dwellers to the town, its economy, educational system, and arts community are readily acknowledged. It took hard work and commitment on everyone's part to make this town the success that it is today.

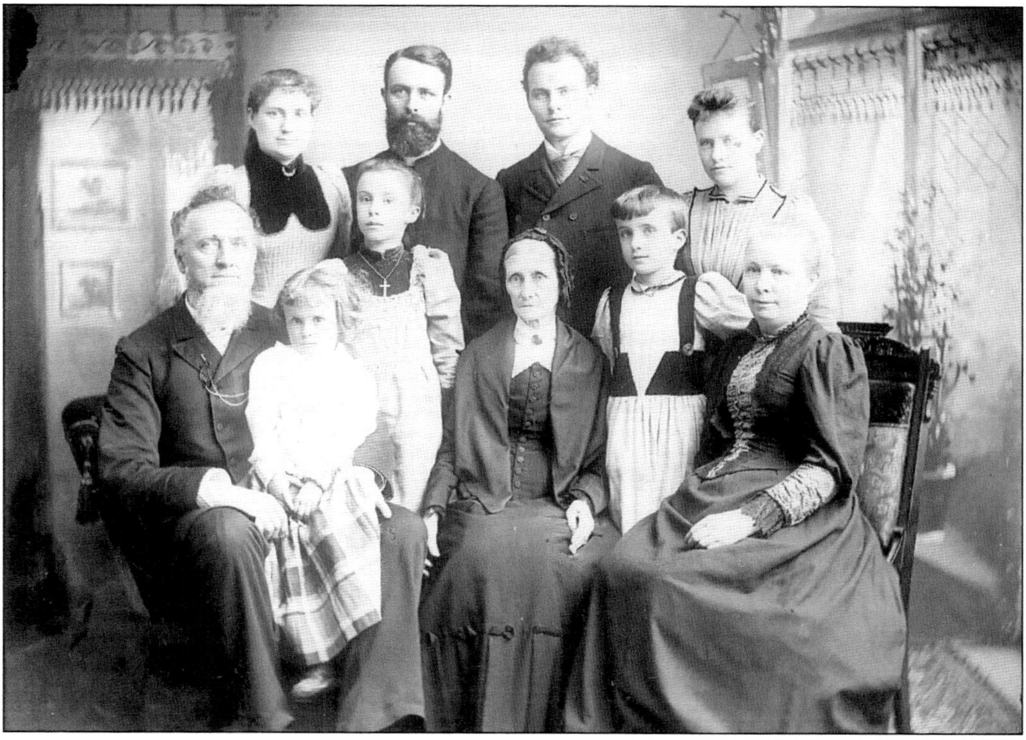

EDMISTEN AND HOLSHOUSER FAMILIES. This c. 1865 photograph shows members of the Edmisten and Holshouser families, two early Blowing Rock families. The Holshouser family ran a store in the town. Descendents from these two pioneering families still live in the area. (Courtesy of *The Blowing Rocket*.)

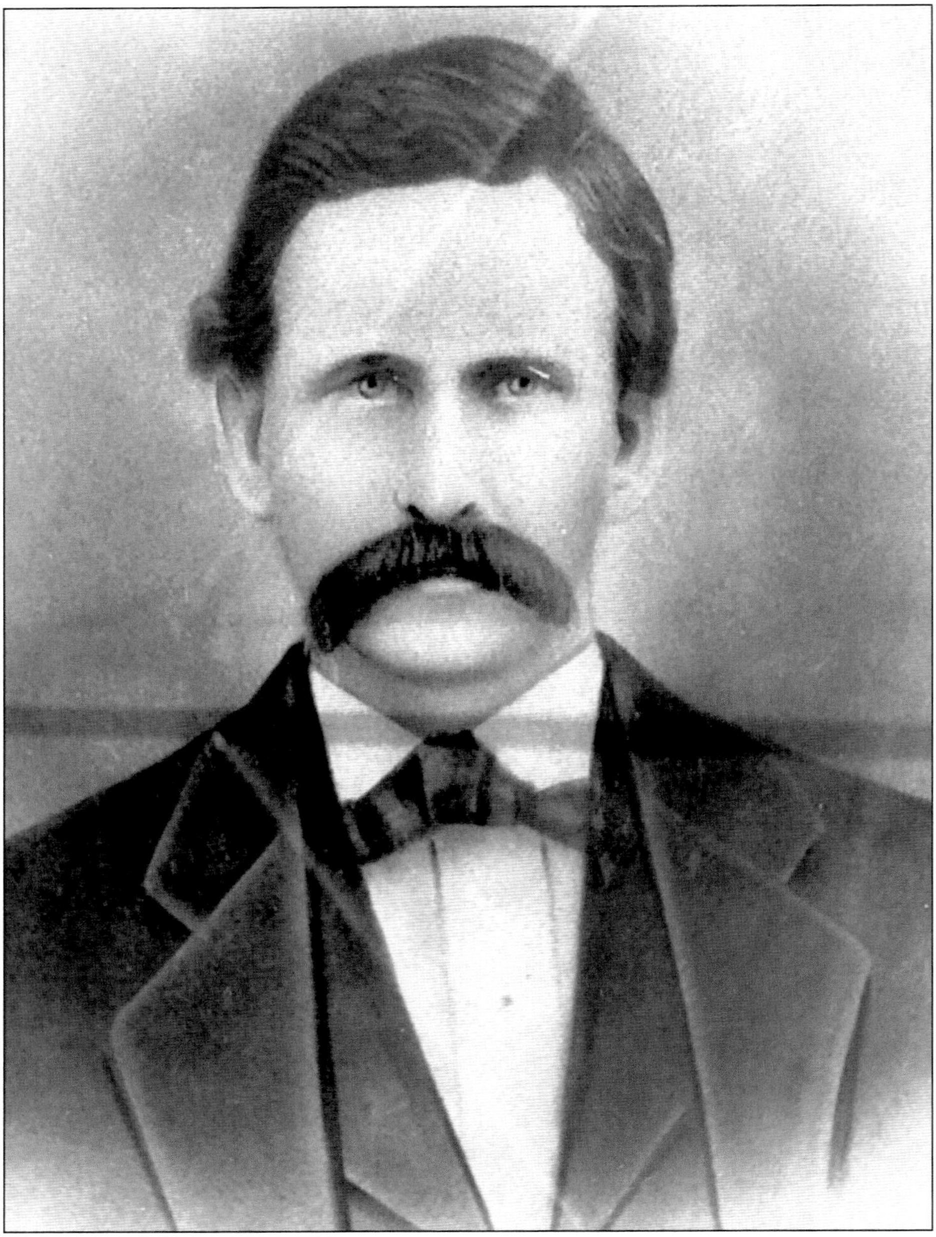

MAYOR JOE CLARK. Joseph Bogle Clark, a Civil War lieutenant, became the first mayor of Blowing Rock. Newspaper accounts show he served in the office in 1889, 1890, 1892, 1894, 1900, 1903, and 1910, and he likely was the mayor in some of these years in between. He was an officer of the Caldwell & Watauga Turnpike company. Clark owned a general merchandise store along with the Martins. He was a colorful character, dressing in formal black coat while the tourists were up in the summer, but then going about in casual short sleeves while they were absent in the winter. He administered the first census in 1886 for the new town. After having too much to drink one night, Mayor Clark is reported to have stampeded a herd of cattle down Main Street. In court the following day, he convicted himself of drunk and disorderly conduct and fined himself. Mayor Clark guided the town through its early development and growth. (Courtesy of *The Blowing Rocket*.)

Gen. Matt W. Ransom (1826–1904). Matt Ransom served as attorney general of North Carolina, a brigadier general in the Confederate Army, a U.S. senator from 1872 to 1889, and an ambassador to Mexico. General Ransom was a summer resident in Blowing Rock beginning in 1902. The housed he lived in is located on Main Street, diagonally across from the former location of the Blowing Rock Hotel. (Courtesy of Cullie Tarleton.)

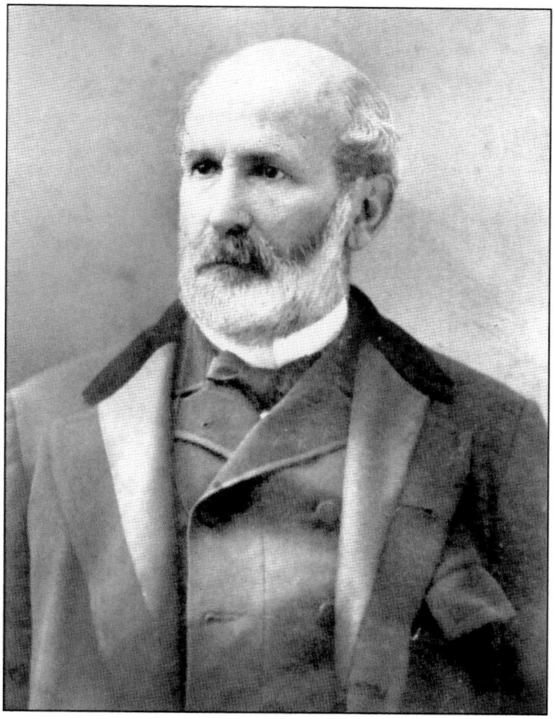

Local Families. This 1903 photograph shows representatives from several of the pioneering families of Blowing Rock. Pictured from left to right are Cora Blair, George Sudderth Sr., Dasy (sic) Gragg, Roby Greer, and Maud Harris. (Courtesy of *The Blowing Rocket*.)

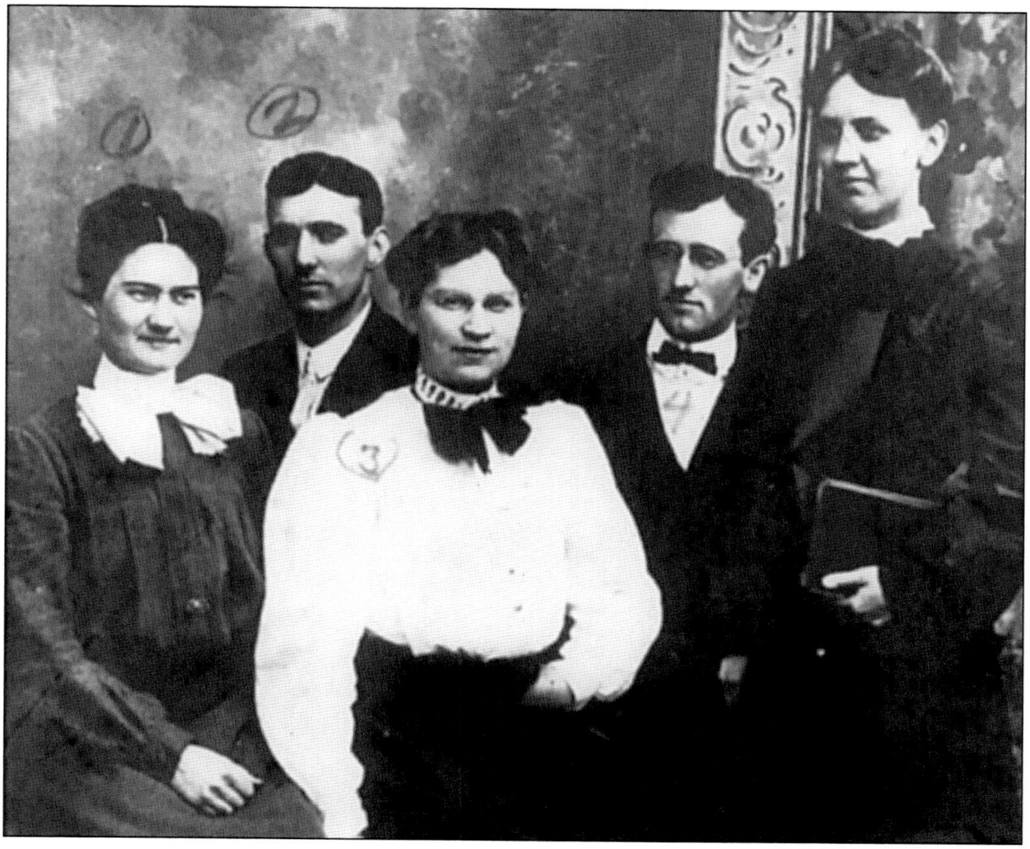

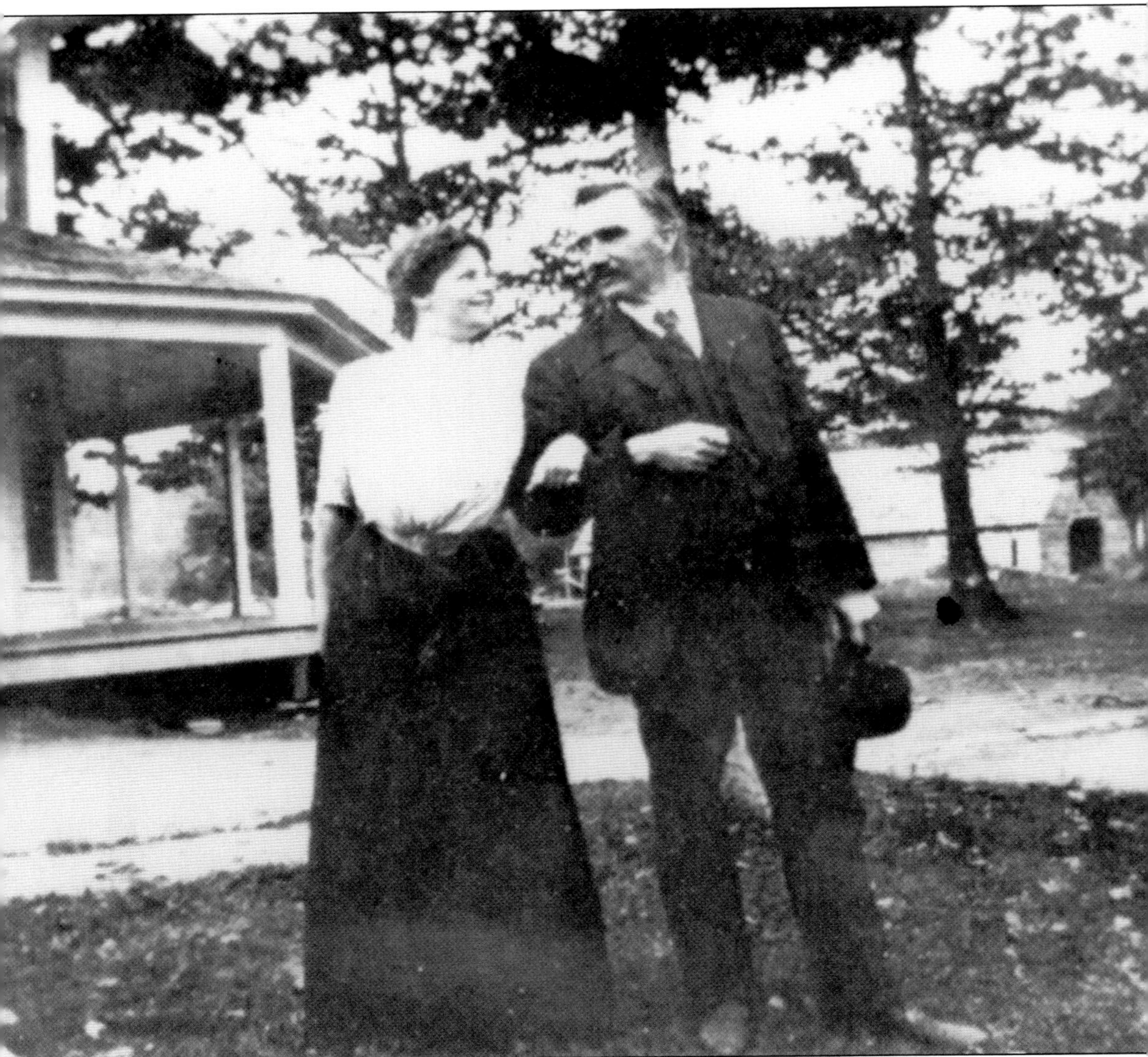

Dr. Parlier and Skyland Institute Teacher. This photo shows Dr. Calvin J. Parlier and an unidentified teacher from Skyland Institute. Dr. Parlier was mayor in 1901, served on the board of the Caldwell and Watauga Turnpike, and helped establish the Bank of Blowing Rock in 1907. Skyland Institute was founded in 1887 by Miss Emily Prudden. This private school was located at the intersection of Main Street and U.S. 321 bypass at the present site of Chateau Cloud Condominiums. Miss Prudden provided a basic Christian education to many mountain children. The school was later administered by the American Missionary Movement as a boarding school mainly for girls, although a few boys were enrolled. The campus included classrooms, a chapel, and dormitories. The school was closed in 1912 and was reopened as the Wonderland Hotel. The building is no longer standing. (Courtesy of *The Blowing Rocket.*)

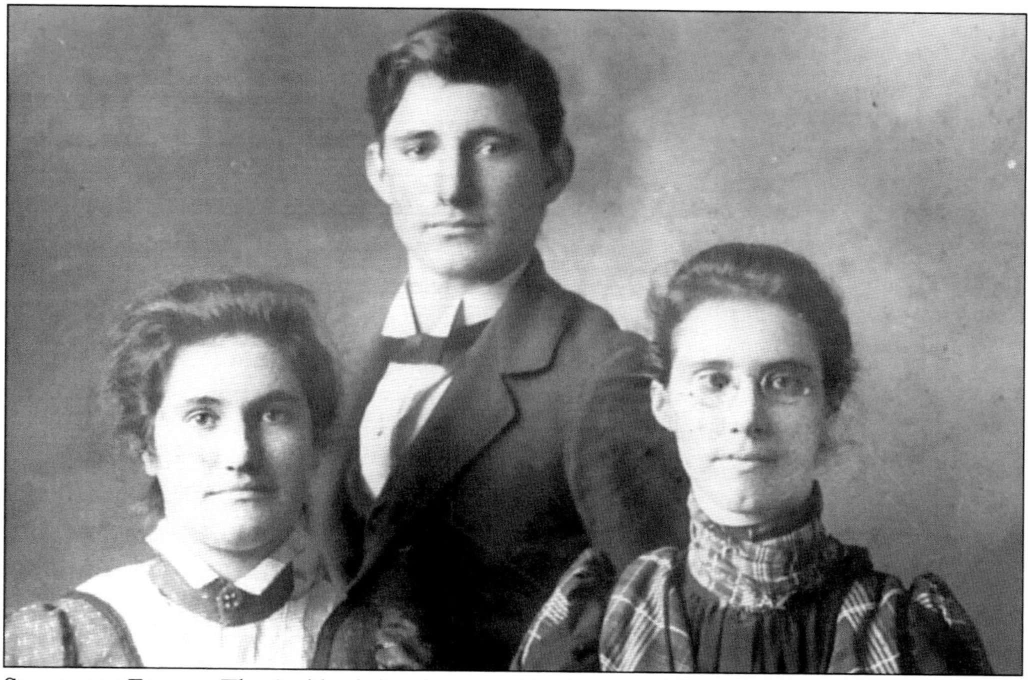

SUDDERTH FAMILY. The Sudderth family is an older family in Blowing Rock and members have been active in town politics and local businesses. Pictured from left to right are Sallie Sudderth, George M. Sudderth, and Bettie Sudderth. George Sudderth was one of the founders of the Blowing Rock Bank. (Courtesy of *The Blowing Rocket.*)

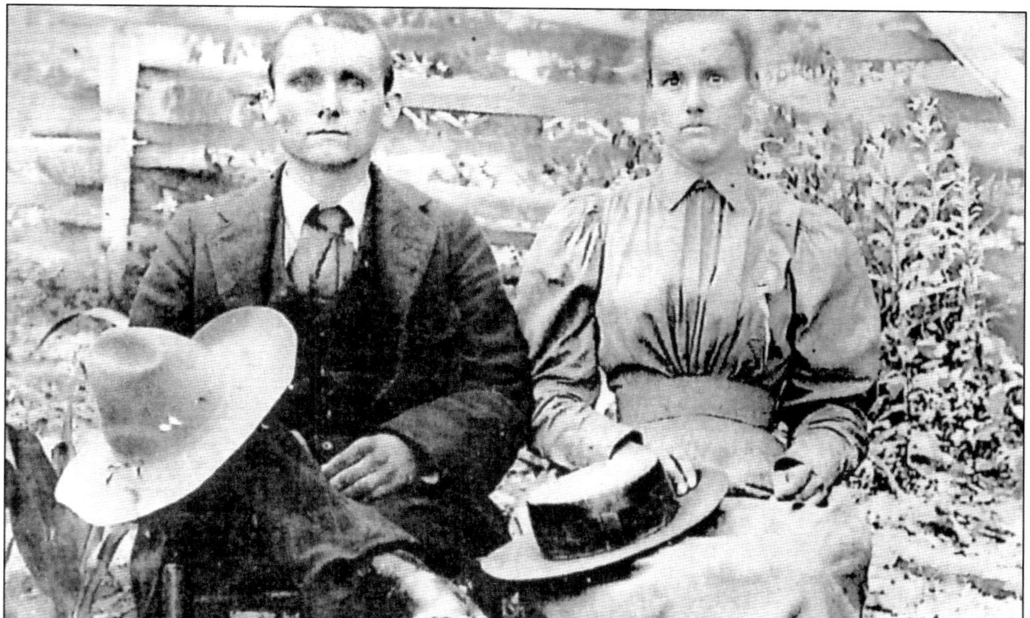

JOHN CLINTON FORD (1878–1945) AND BARBARA BOLICK FORD (1878–1953). John Ford was a sawmill operator, surveyor, and business owner in the Blowing Rock area. He owned one of the first automobiles in town. Ford owned the Blowing Rock, the nearby Cloudland Café, and an early gas station on the east side of Main Street. (Courtesy of Heidi Ellis.)

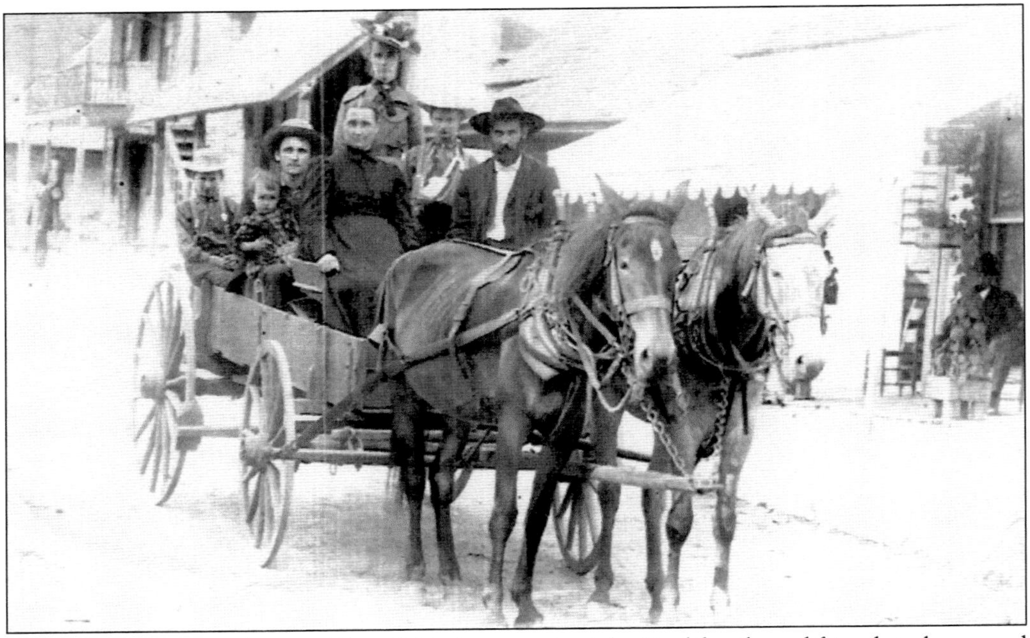

FORDS ON A TRIP TO TOWN. This 1902 photograph of the Ford family and friends in horse and wagon was taken in downtown Blowing Rock. Retail stores can be seen along Main Street. Back then, coming to town was an anticipated event and allowed the exchange of goods, services, and neighborhood news. (Courtesy of Heidi Ellis.)

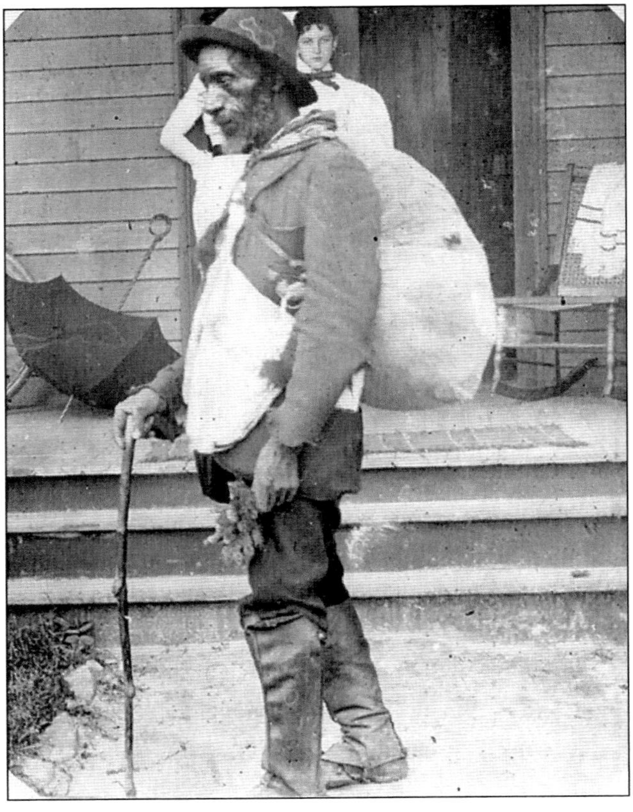

UNCLE HENRY, LATE 1800S. "Uncle" Henry was a well-known African-American man who gathered balsam leaves and sold them along Main Street. Everyone said these leaves made the best pillows. (Courtesy of *The Blowing Rocket*.)

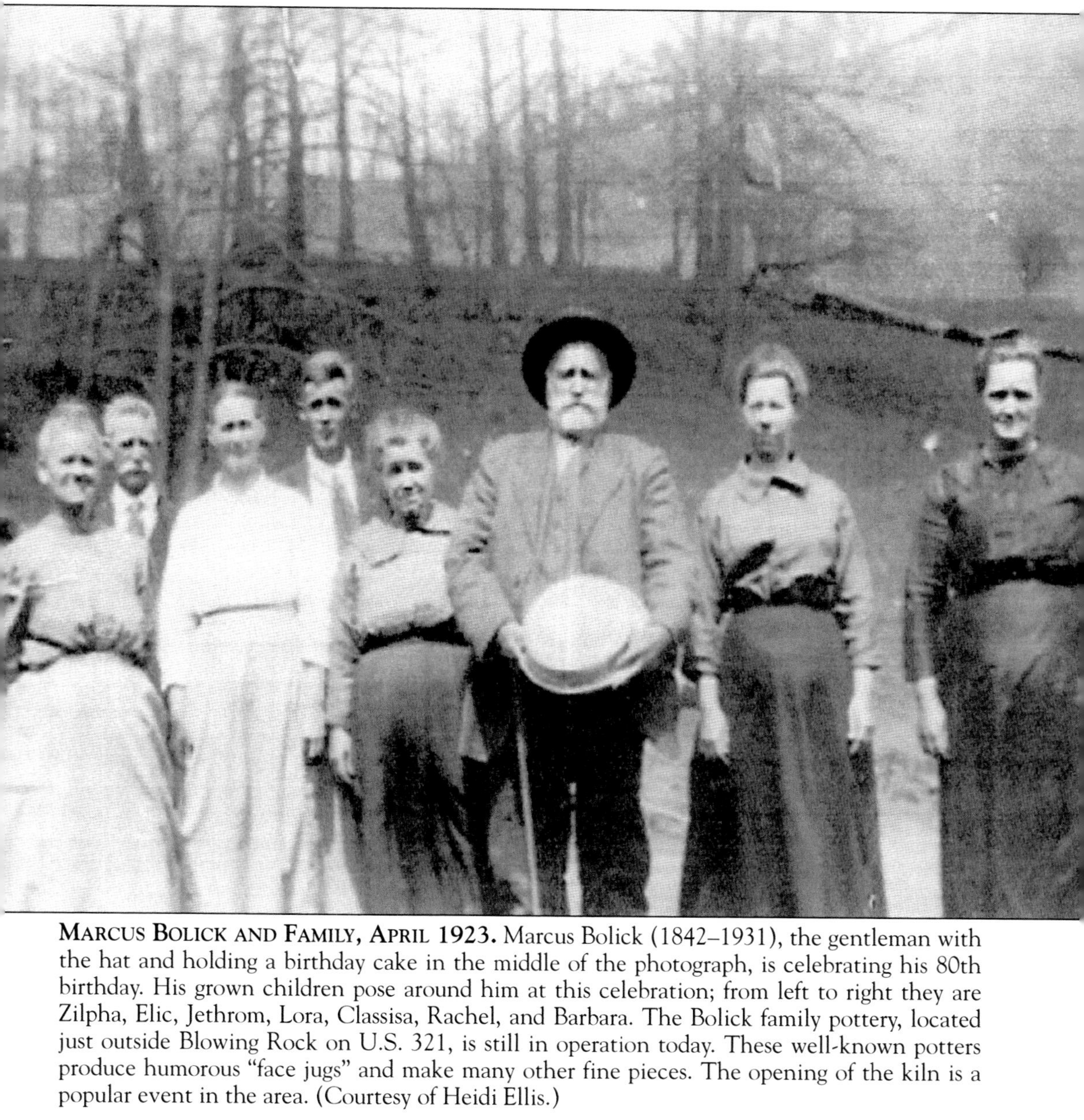

MARCUS BOLICK AND FAMILY, APRIL 1923. Marcus Bolick (1842–1931), the gentleman with the hat and holding a birthday cake in the middle of the photograph, is celebrating his 80th birthday. His grown children pose around him at this celebration; from left to right they are Zilpha, Elic, Jethrom, Lora, Classisa, Rachel, and Barbara. The Bolick family pottery, located just outside Blowing Rock on U.S. 321, is still in operation today. These well-known potters produce humorous "face jugs" and make many other fine pieces. The opening of the kiln is a popular event in the area. (Courtesy of Heidi Ellis.)

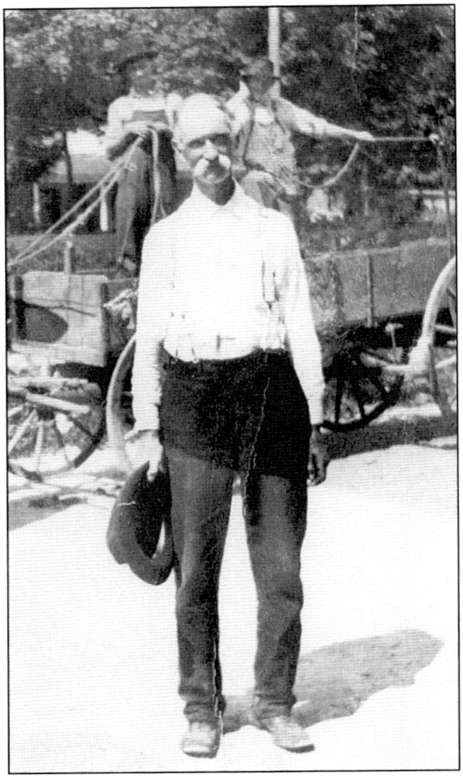

W.P. "DADDY PAT" PENDLEY. "Daddy Pat" Pendley was another popular character from Blowing Rock's early days. This photograph was taken along Main Street, c. 1900. Mr. Pendley was the owner and manager of the Watauga Inn, one of the well-known inns in town. (Courtesy of *The Blowing Rocket*.)

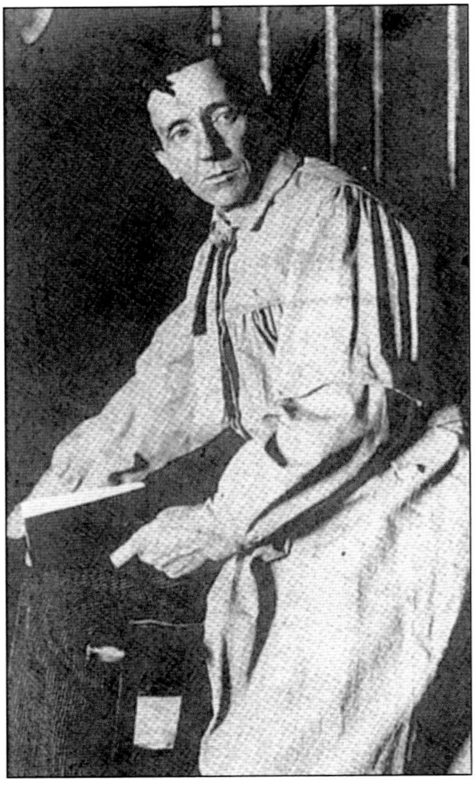

ELLIOTT DAINGERFIELD. Mr. Daingerfield was Blowing Rock's most famous artist. His works are part of the collections of many noted museums, including the National Gallery and the Metropolitan Museum. Mr. Daingerfield donated his masterpiece, *Madonna of the Hills*, to the Stringfellow Memorial Church, which was then renamed St. Mary's of the Hills Episcopal. (Courtesy of *The Blowing Rocket*.)

EMMA AUSTIN GREENE. This lovely young lady is Emma Austin Greene (1875–1967), owner of the Greene Inn on Main Street. She was also a charter member of the First Baptist Church of Blowing Rock. (Courtesy of Pug Greene and Caroline Greene Robbins.)

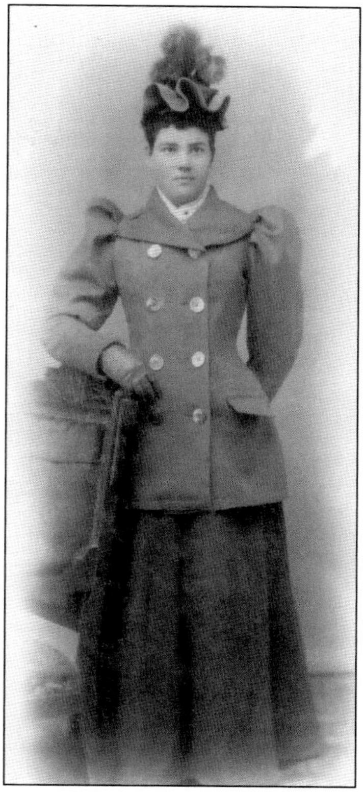

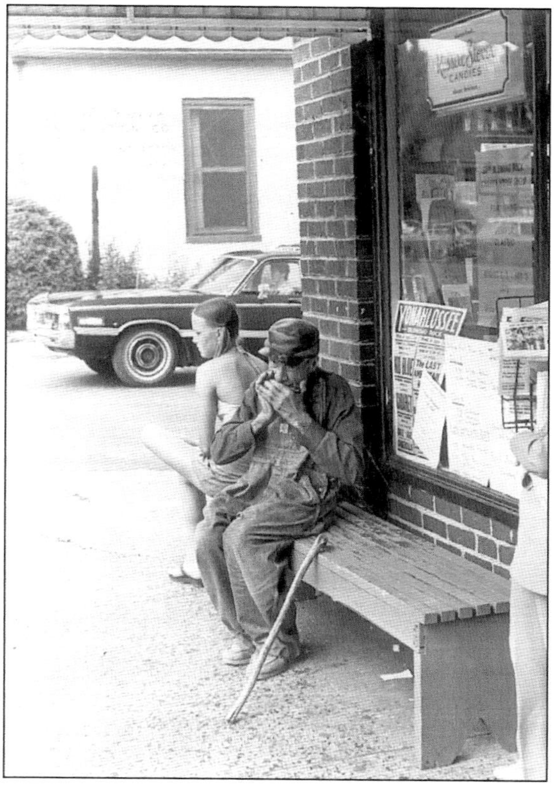

ROB BRADSHAW. Born in 1893, Rob Bradshaw was long a familiar and much loved character in downtown. He sold produce from a wagon and from roadsides for 69 years. Bradshaw sold apples from his pockets and played harmonica for many Blowing Rock residents and tourists until his death in the 1960s. (Courtesy of *The Blowing Rocket*.)

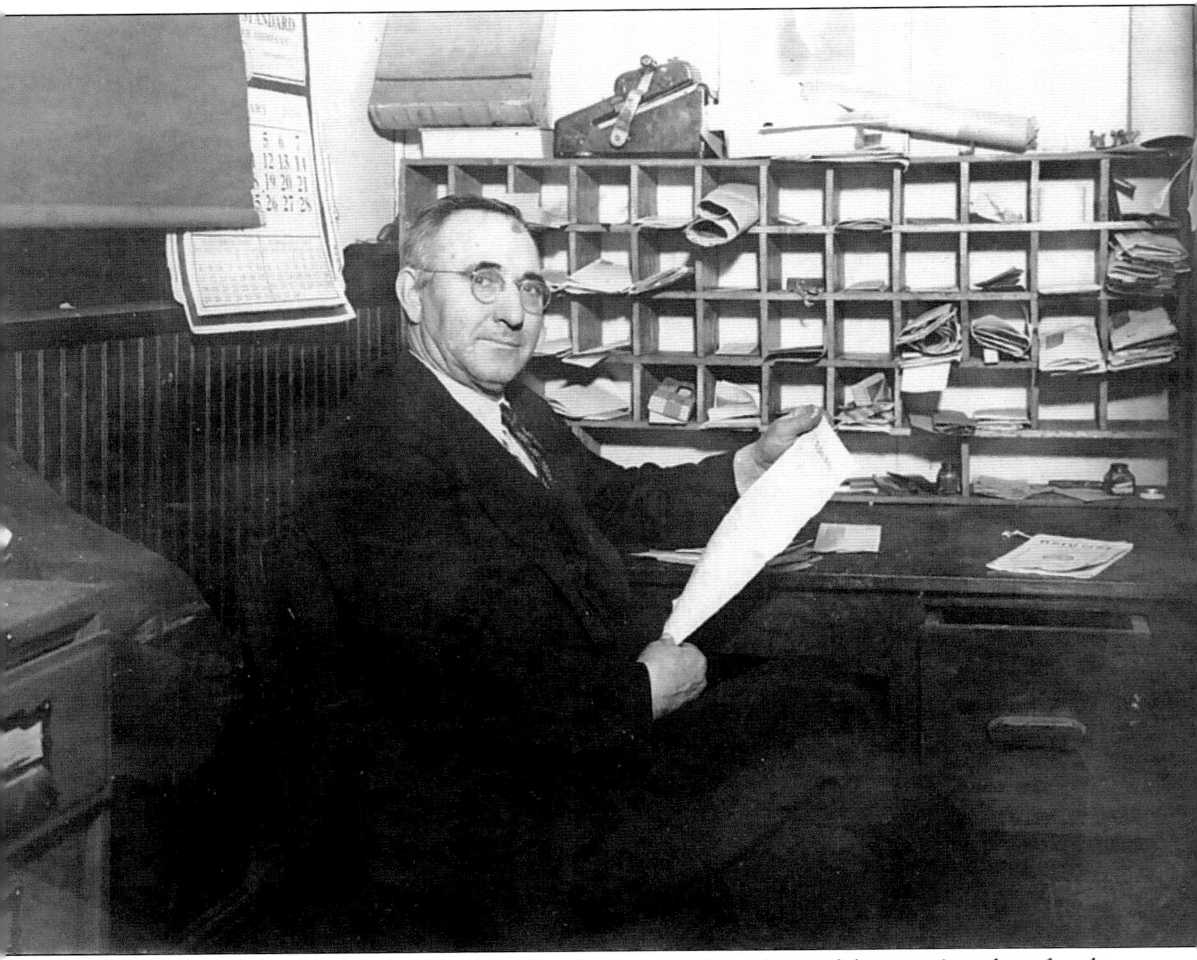

George Murray Sudderth Sr. Mr. Sudderth, a member of one of the town's earliest families, was a man who wore many hats. He was postmaster during the 1930s through the 1950s when the post office was located on Main Street near the corner of U.S. 221. Mr. Sudderth was also a local surveyor, attorney, and served as mayor of Blowing Rock. He is believed to be the first local owner of an automobile in 1913. Mr. Sudderth was also a member of the local Masonic lodge. (Courtesy of Barbara Lentz Wright.)

WILLIAM COUNCIL LENTZ SR. AND FORMER NORTH CAROLINA GOVERNOR TERRY SANFORD. William Council Lentz Sr. (left) is shown shaking hands with a former North Carolina governor, Terry Sanford. Mr. Lentz was active in the community as a business owner, member of the Town Council, and member of the Watauga County Board of Commissioners. (Courtesy of Barbara Lentz Wright.)

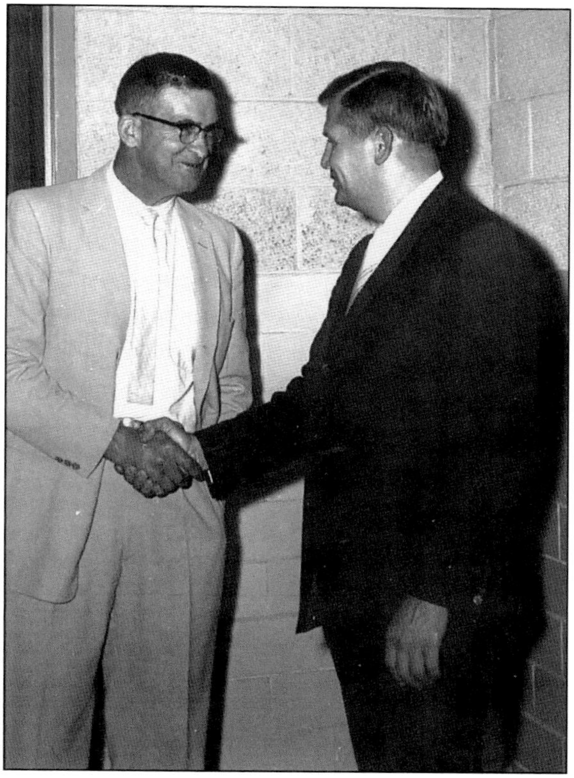

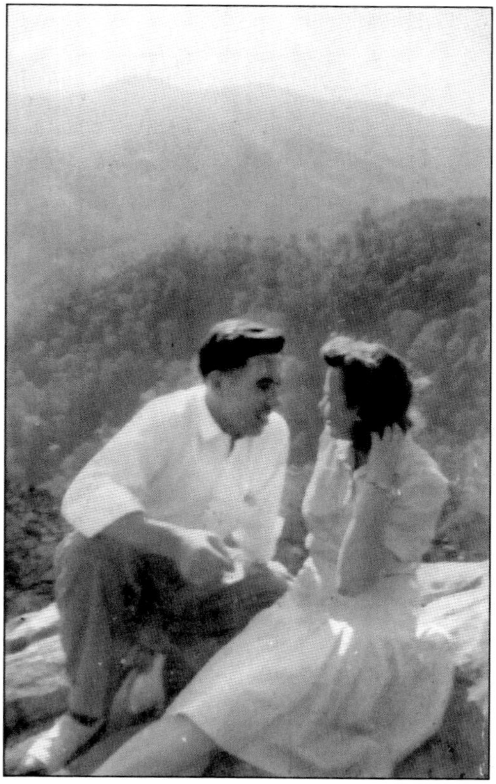

HONEYMOON AT THE BLOWING ROCK. J.H. "Doc" Query of Lenoir and Willie May Self of Hickory made a special trip to the Blowing Rock on June 6, 1942, as newlyweds. After Doc's death in 1977, Willie married Rudolph Jewell and they lived in Blowing Rock for many years. (Courtesy of Willie May Query Jewell and Susan Bratton.)

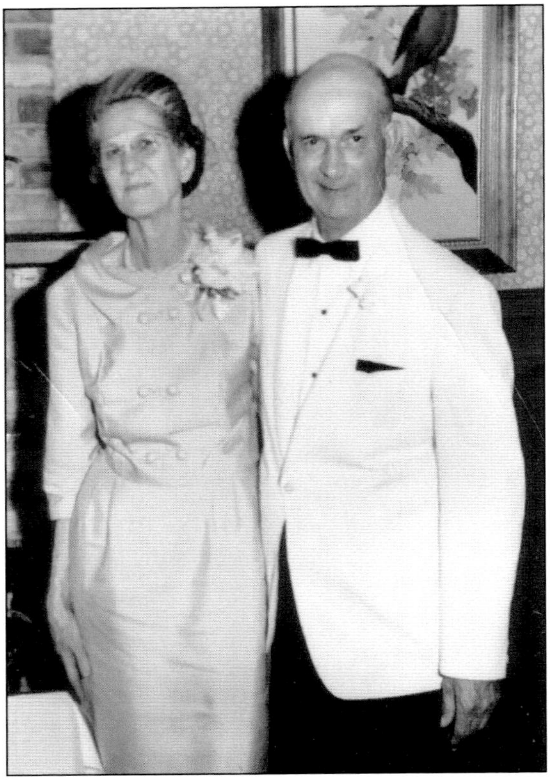

Lloyd Spencer Robbins and Alma Benfield Robbins. Mr. Robbins was well known as a builder who, without a formal education, designed many beautiful houses in the area. Mrs. Robbins helped begin the Reading Room and was involved with the early library in town. She also helped collect clothing for needy children in the local school. (Courtesy of Janie Robbins Campbell.)

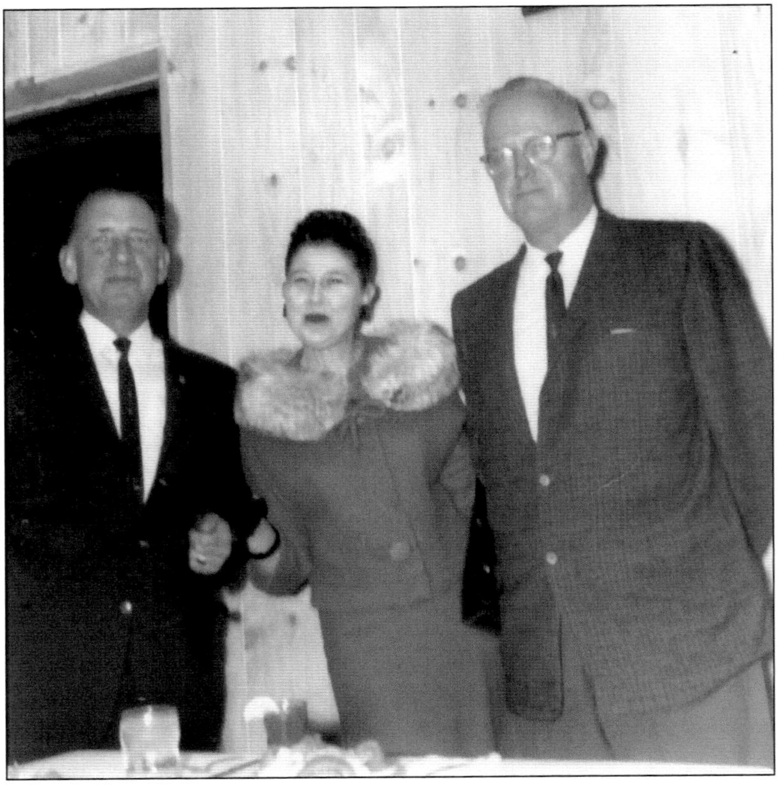

Mr. and Mrs. Cooke and Bob Hardin. From left to right are Council Cooke, Billie Cooke, and Bob Hardin. Mr. Cooke lived in the town and worked at a Boone funeral home. Billie Cooke was a teacher at Blowing Rock Elementary School. Bob Hardin was the longtime mayor of Blowing Rock. He also owned Hardin's Hardware, which was located in the current location of Village Antiques. (Courtesy of Richard Trexler.)

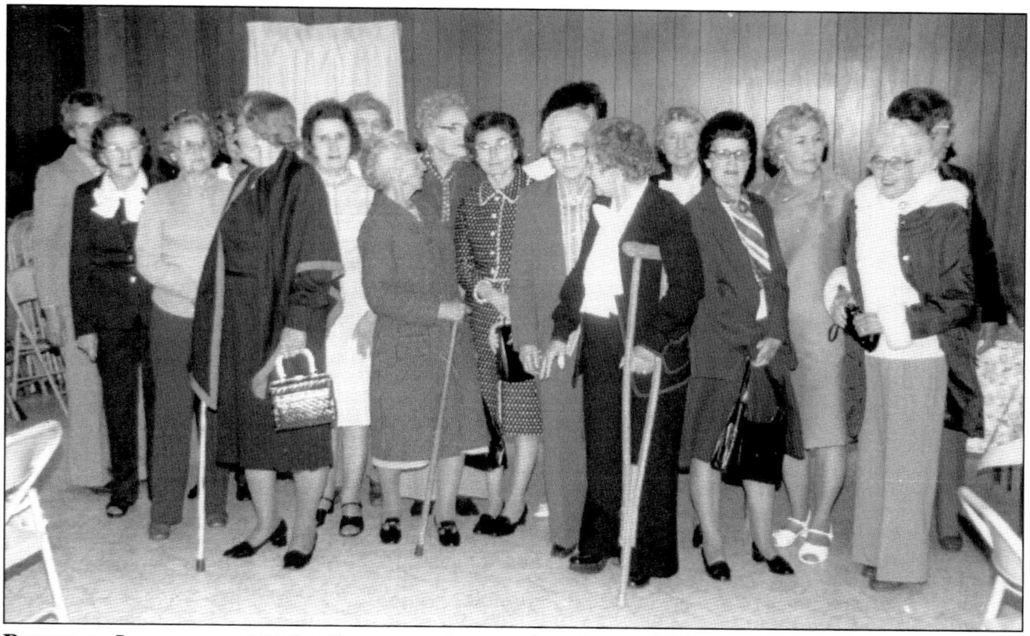

RURITAN LADIES, C. 1972. These members and widows of Blowing Rock Ruritan Club are, from left to right, (front row) Joyce Greene Lentz, Stella Keller, Victoria Sylvia, Lois Greene, Mrs. Ben Moody, four unidentified people, LaVaughn Klutz, Lillian Porter; (back row) two unidentified people, Lois Young, Hattie Brown, unidentified, Mae Coffey, and unidentified. (Courtesy of Stella Greer Dobbins.)

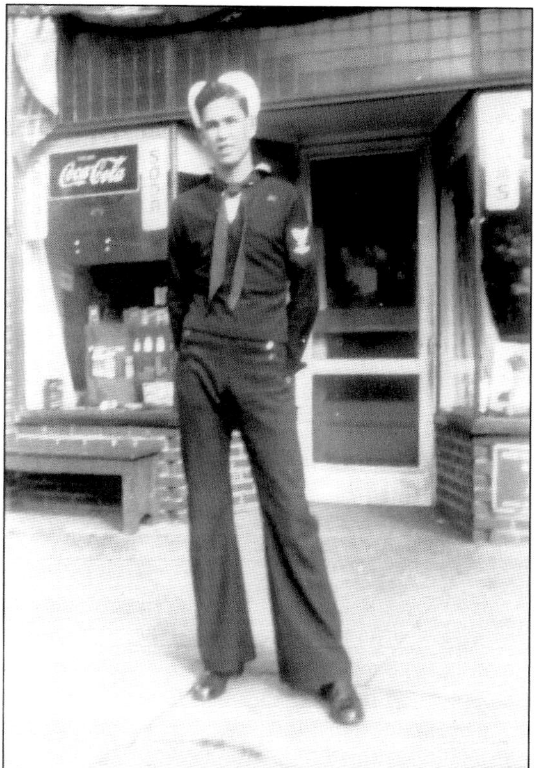

JACK ROBBINS IN THE NAVY. This *c.* 1940 photograph shows Jack Robbins posing proudly in his World War II navy uniform. Mr. Robbins was a contractor and built many houses in the area. He is standing in front of Storie's Soda Shop, a local hangout for the community. (Courtesy of Janie Robbins Campbell.)

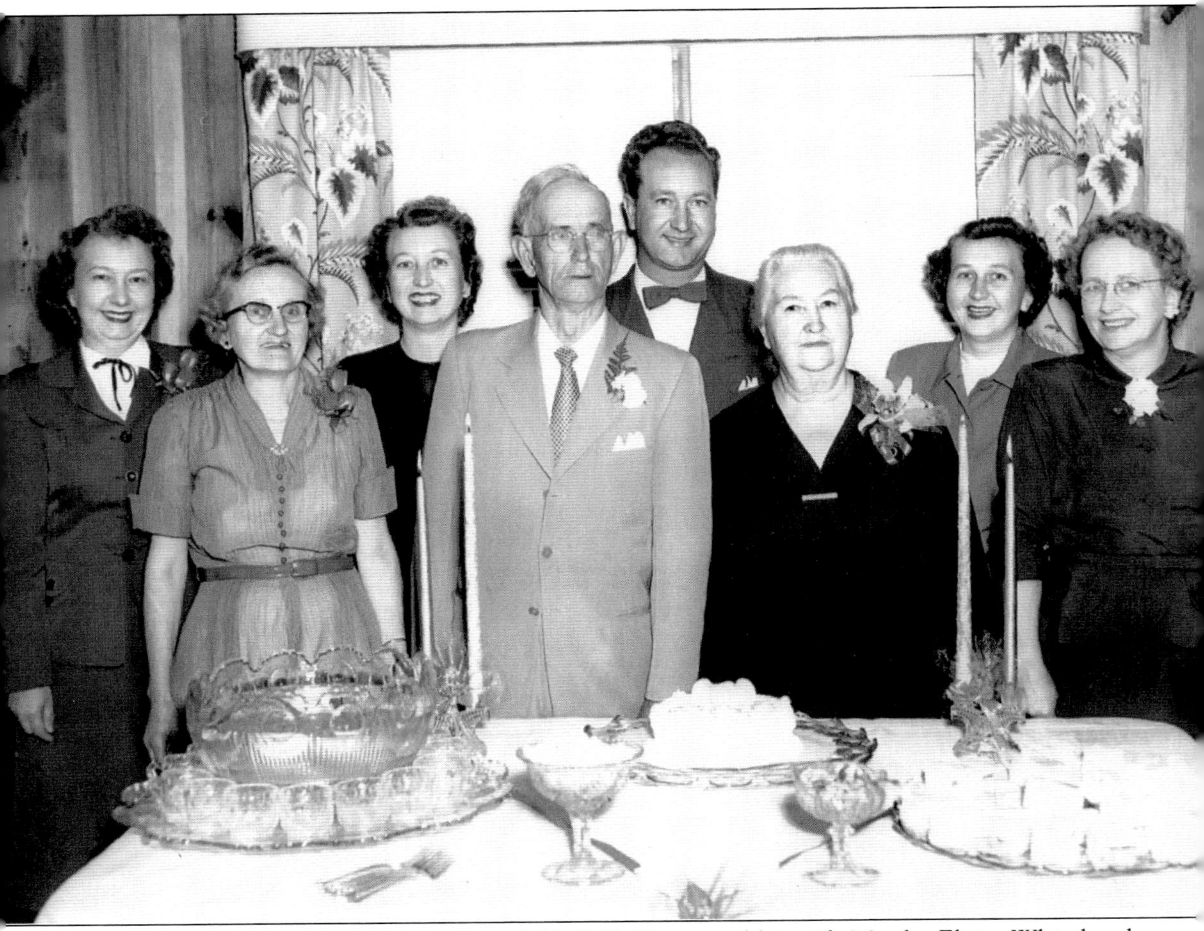

LORENZO DOW TESTER FAMILY IN 1953. L.D. Tester and his wife Martha Elvira Whitehead Tester celebrated their 50th wedding anniversary in 1953. Also in the photograph are six of their eight children; Clyde Tester and Glenn Tester are not pictured. From left to right are Beulah Presnell, Orpha Pitts, Ursula Mae Coffey, L.D. Tester, William Warren Tester, Martha Tester, Gladys Nora Tester, and Velma Greene. L.D. Tester was a master carpenter and contractor, building and renovating many homes in Blowing Rock. He was also involved in the construction of Rumple Memorial Presbyterian Church, the Blowing Rock Clinic, and the office of Dr. Mary Cabell Warfield. Ursula Mae Tester Coffey, one of the daughters in the photo, operated and owned the Blowing Rock Tourist Court on Morris Street from 1947 until 1968 with her husband, Omer R. Coffey. (Courtesy of Janice Coffey Herblin and *The Blowing Rocket*.)

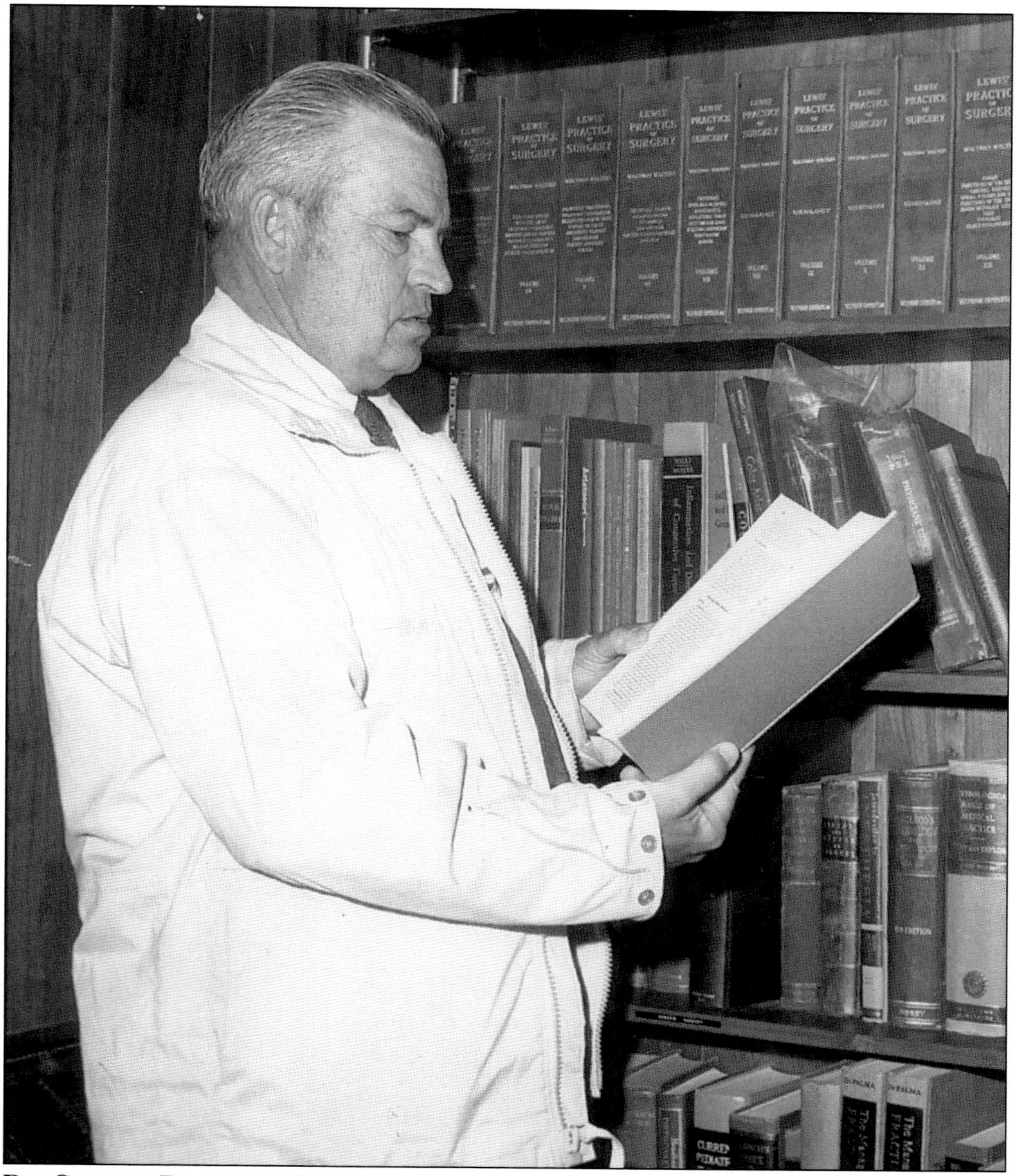

Dr. Charles Davant Jr. Dr. Davant began treating patients in town when he had a practice in Lenoir. As the need for medical care in Blowing Rock increased, Dr. Davant decided to move to the mountains in 1948, and in 1950 he was named director of the Blowing Rock Hospital. "Dr. Charlie" is well-known for his friendly manner and professional skills. His skill and professionalism resulted in the development of the hospital to the state of the art medical facility it is today. (Courtesy of *The Blowing Rocket*.)

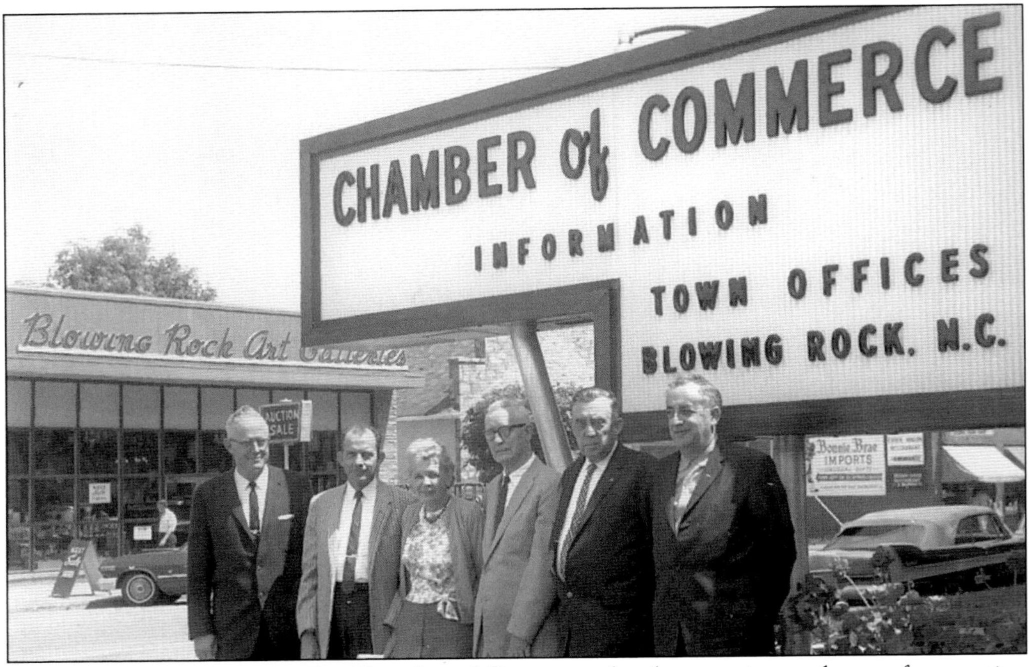

CHAMBER OF COMMERCE. The Chamber of Commerce has been an integral part of promoting the town and increasing its economic diversity. From left to right, these community leaders are Bob Hardin, Howard Barnwell, Mrs. H.F. Custer, John Goodwin, L.H. Smith, and Eli Mattar. (Courtesy of *The Blowing Rocket*.)

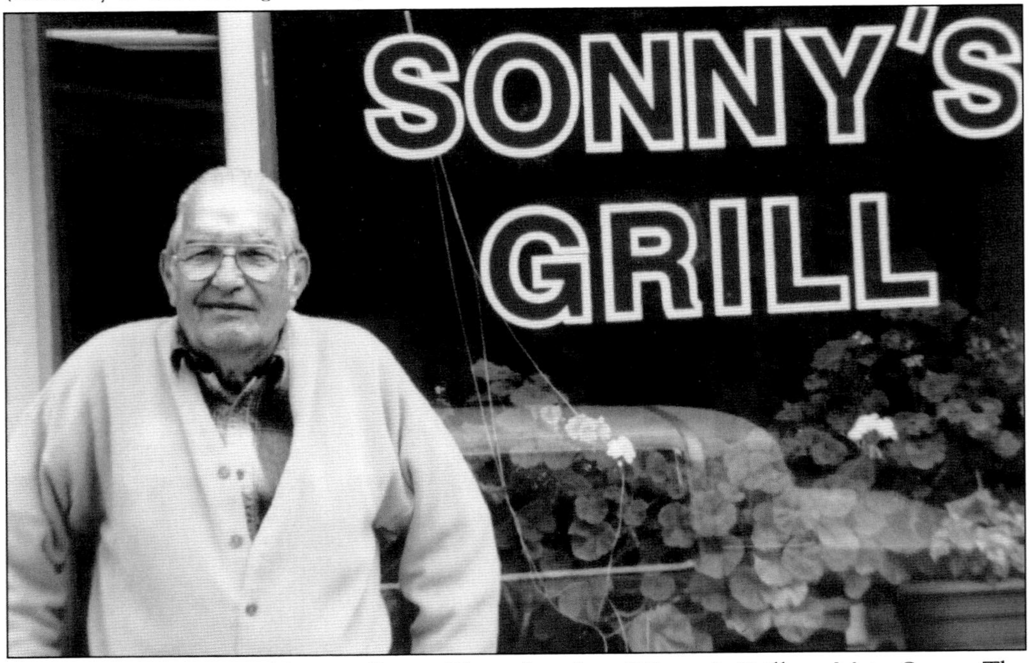

SONNY KLUTZ. Pictured here is Sonny Klutz, founder of Sonny's Grill on Main Street. The restaurant has been open since about 1946. The grill lives on in his memory and is a popular destination for locals and visitors. The restaurant was immortalized in Jan Karon's books on Mitford. (Courtesy of LaVaughn Klutz.)

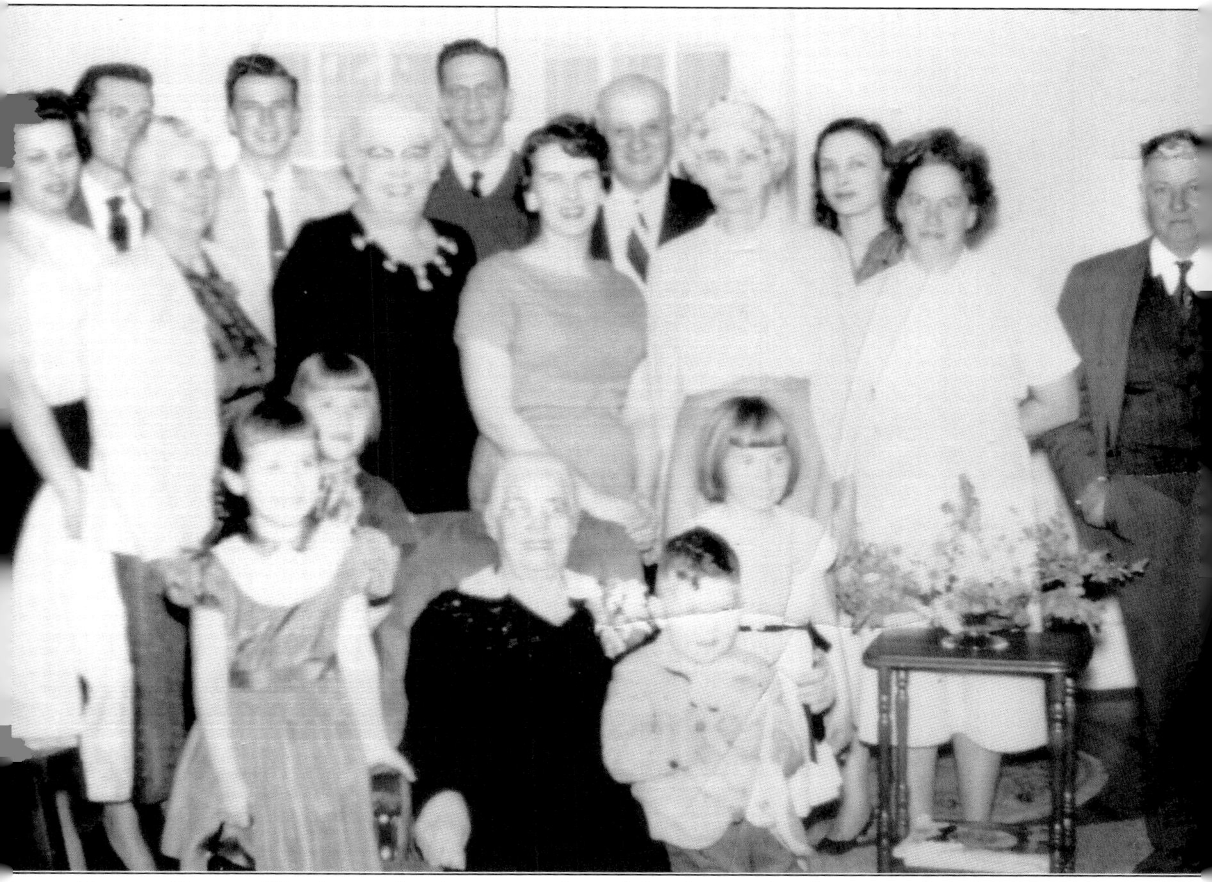

Greene Family. This happy family get-together of the Greene family occurred in about 1956. The Greene family are considered the earliest settlers in Watauga County. This particular branch of the Greenes ran the Greene Inn, located on Main Street. These folks are identified as, left to right, (front row) Ann Frink, Mary Ellen Bowman, Emma Greene, Warren Frink, Emma Jean Bowman; (second row) Nettie Greene, Elizabeth Greene Clubine, Caroline Greene Robbins, Alma Greene Miller, and Frances Puett; (back row) Margaret Miller Frink, Bernard Frink, Ben Greene, Max Robbins, Merlin Clubine, Edith Puett, and Jerome Puett. (Courtesy of Emma Jean Bowman Wynn.)

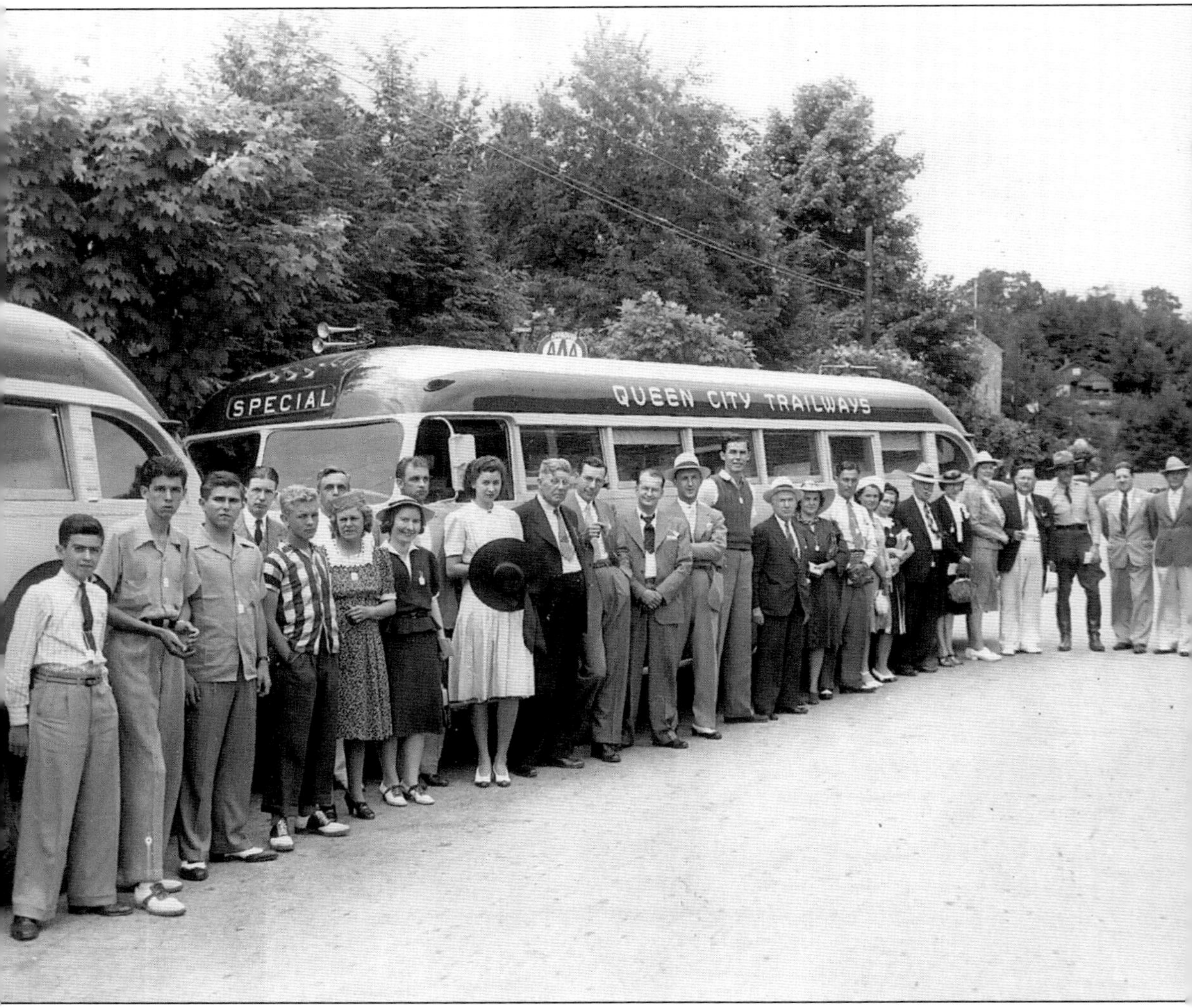

TOURISTS BY THE BUSLOAD. This c. 1940 photograph is proof that full-fledged tourism started in the early years. The Queen City Trailways bus from Charlotte has brought these visitors to the village. Back then, a tourist trip must have been cause to dress up, as they seem to be in their Sunday best. Just after the Civil War, tourists began to visit the High Country. These early summer residents were known as "cottagers" since they built two- and three-story Victorian houses, which they called their cottages. Stagecoaches and then automobiles brought the weary visitors up here to enjoy the scenic splendor. As one slogan went, "there every inspiration of pure air exhilarates the lungs and reddens the blood. There the muscles are quickened and jaded, nerves keyed up by outdoor climbing, walking, trout fishing and sight seeing." (Courtesy of *The Blowing Rocket*.)

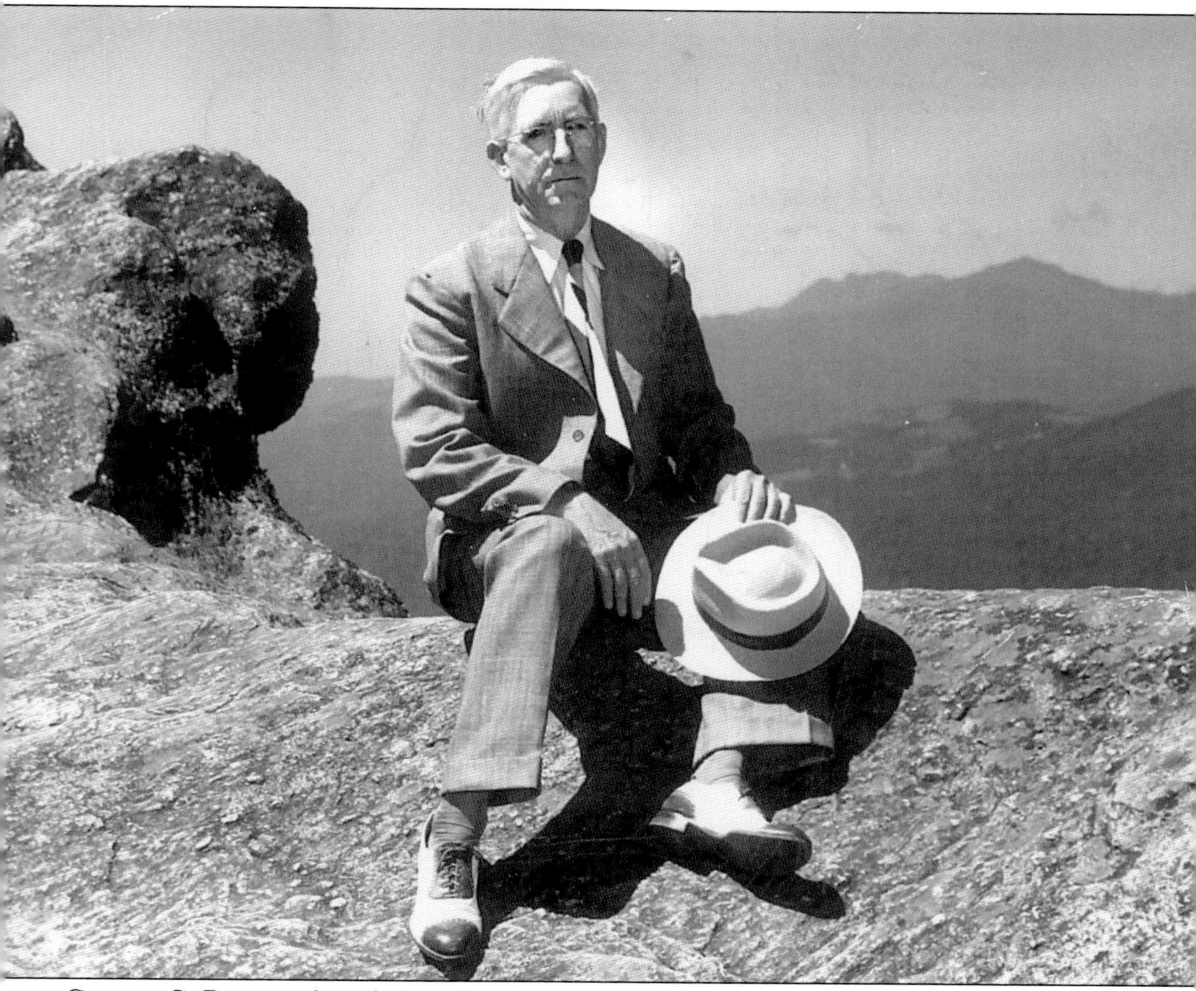

GROVER C. ROBBINS SR. This gentleman was involved in many worthy projects in the area. Beginning as a worker in lumber camps in Shull's Mill, Robbins rose to become a community leader. He served as town mayor for many years and led the town through its growth as a tourist destination. Mr. Robbins was also instrumental in convincing Dr. Davant to come up from Lenoir and provide medical assistance to the town. The Blowing Rock Memorial Park may be his most beloved project. It was his son, Grover Robbins Jr., who began the Tweetsie Railroad amusement park. (Courtesy of *The Blowing Rocket*.)

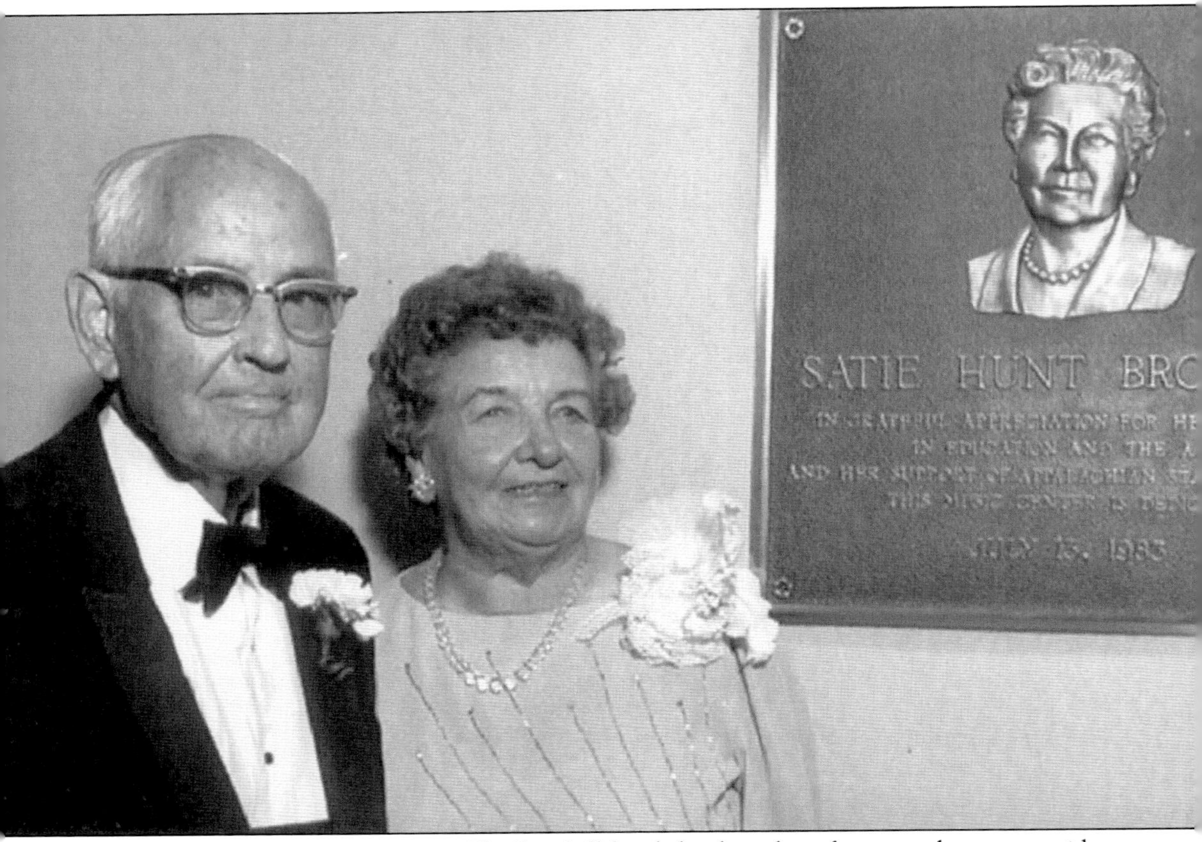

J.E. "ED" AND SATIE BROYHILL. The Broyhill family has been benefactors and summer residents of this area for many years. Ed Broyhill attended Appalachian Training School in Boone and with his brother, Tom, acquired and ran several furniture manufacturing facilities in the Lenoir area. Ed Broyhill also owned the Green Park Hotel after 1952 and sponsored renovations and expansion to the hotel. He also helped with the design of the Blowing Rock Golf Course. The Broyhills contributed to local churches, universities, and hospitals and helped with economic development of the area. (Courtesy of *The Blowing Rocket*.)

Carl Underwood. In this photograph, one can see the extremes that fire crew personnel endure to protect public safety. Carl Underwood, with snow and ice frozen on his uniform and beard, is pausing for a break. The town's public safety personnel have provided protection for residents for many years. (Courtesy of Blowing Rock Fire Department.)

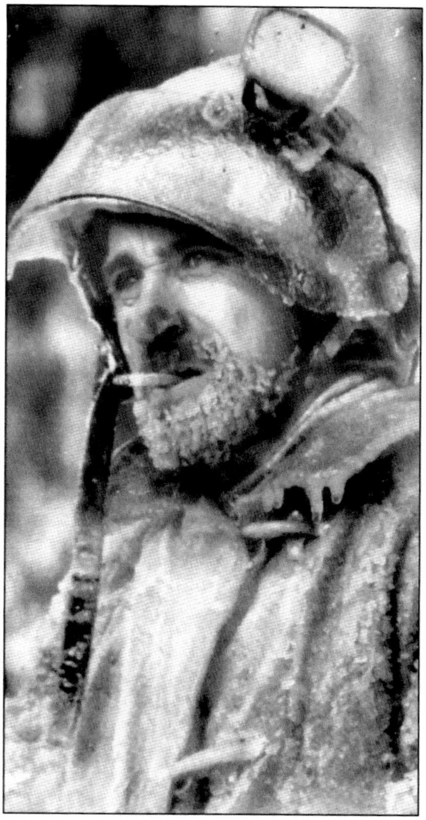

Blowing Rock Police Officers. The town police force also has an important role in public safety. In this c. 1975 photograph, these gentlemen are, from left to right, (front row) Mark "Bush" Lindenmuth and George Kornegay; (second row) Wallace Hardwick and Henry Strahan; (third row) Ray Johnson and Chief Doug Townsend. (Courtesy of Blowing Rock Police Department.)

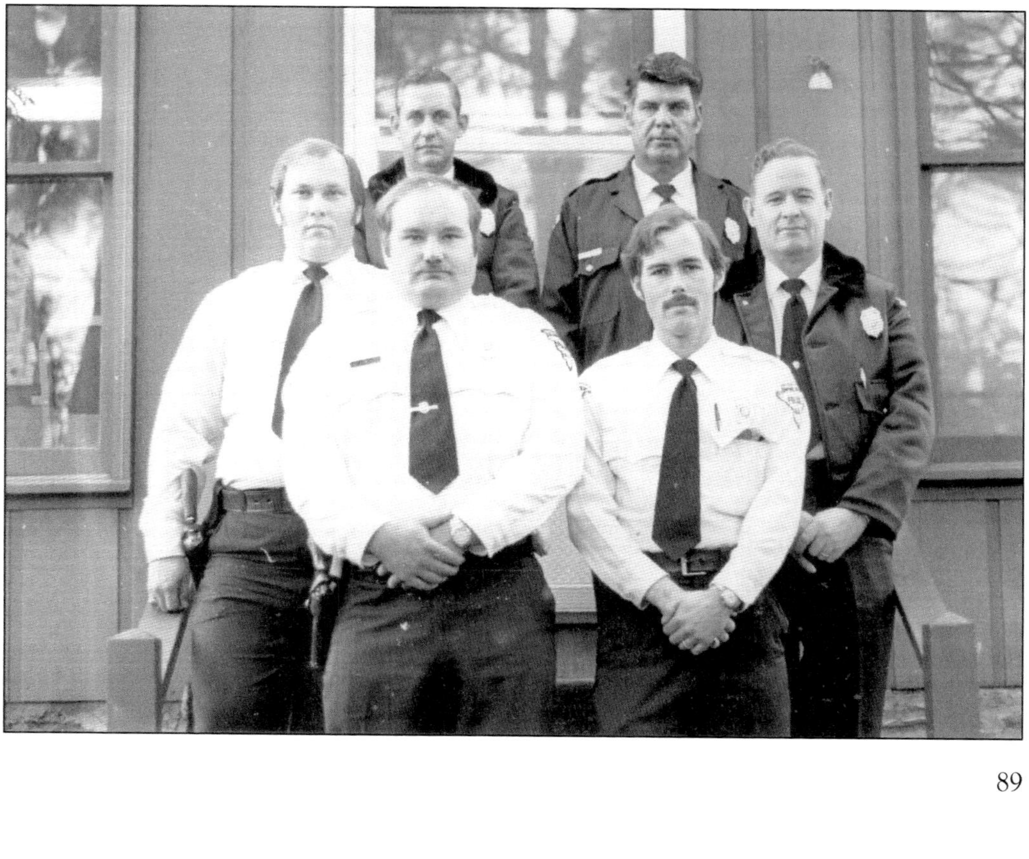

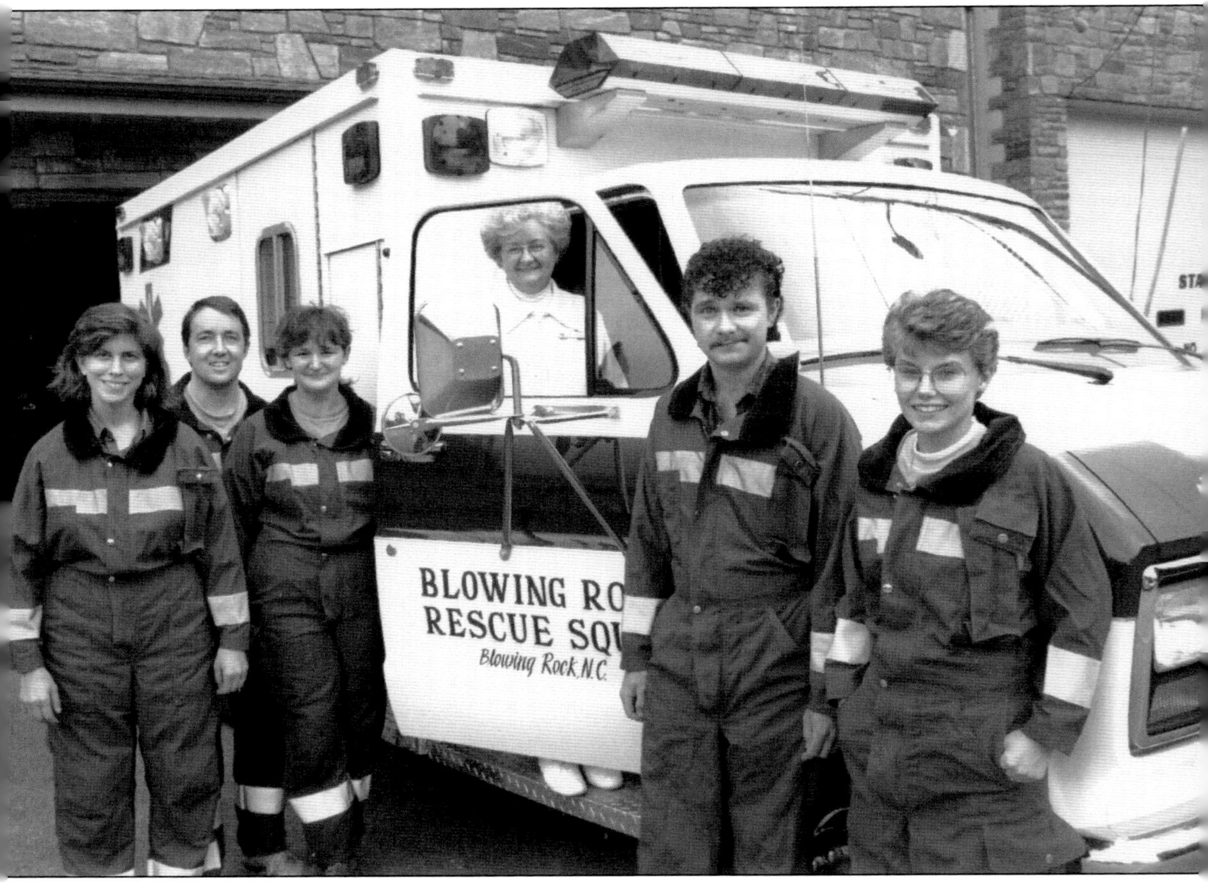

BLOWING ROCK RESCUE SQUAD. This photograph, dating from about 1980, shows just a few of the committed people who worked with the rescue squad. With the influx of visitors in the summer, the demands on the squad increase greatly. From left to right are Jackie Johnston, David Wray, Angie Gregg, Betty Pitts, Mark Cook, and Angie Miller. Volunteers in groups such as these provide emergency assistance in small towns all over the nation. (Courtesy of Blowing Rock Fire Department.)

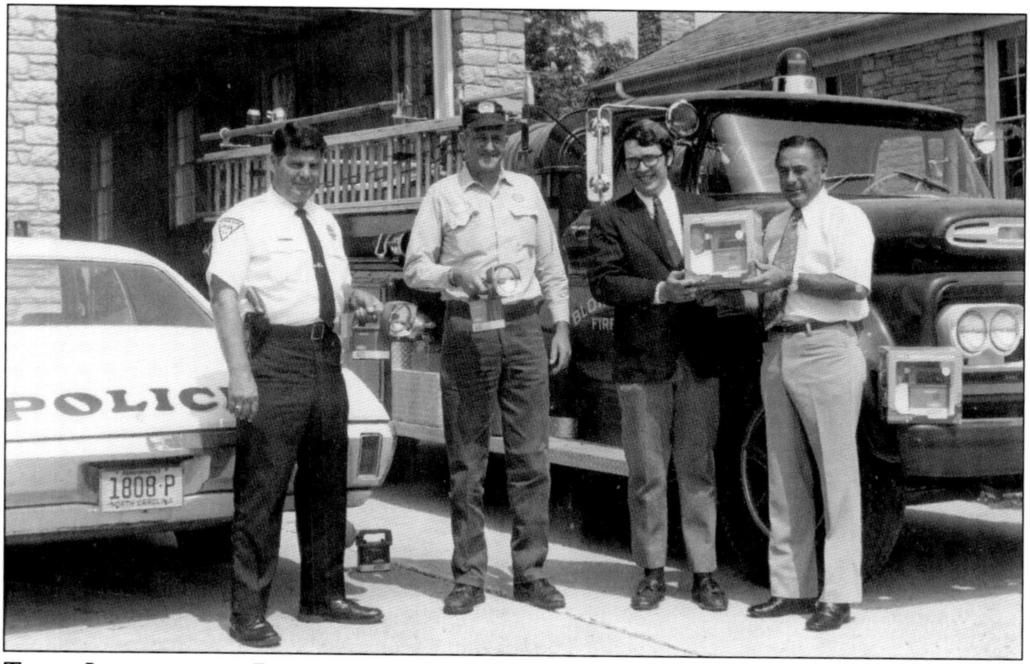

TOWN LEADERS AND POLICE CHIEF. This group is posed in front of town hall, the former location of the fire department. From left to right are Chief Townsend, Hadyn Pitts, Jim Marsh, and Bill Williams, town manager. (Courtesy of Blowing Rock Police Department.)

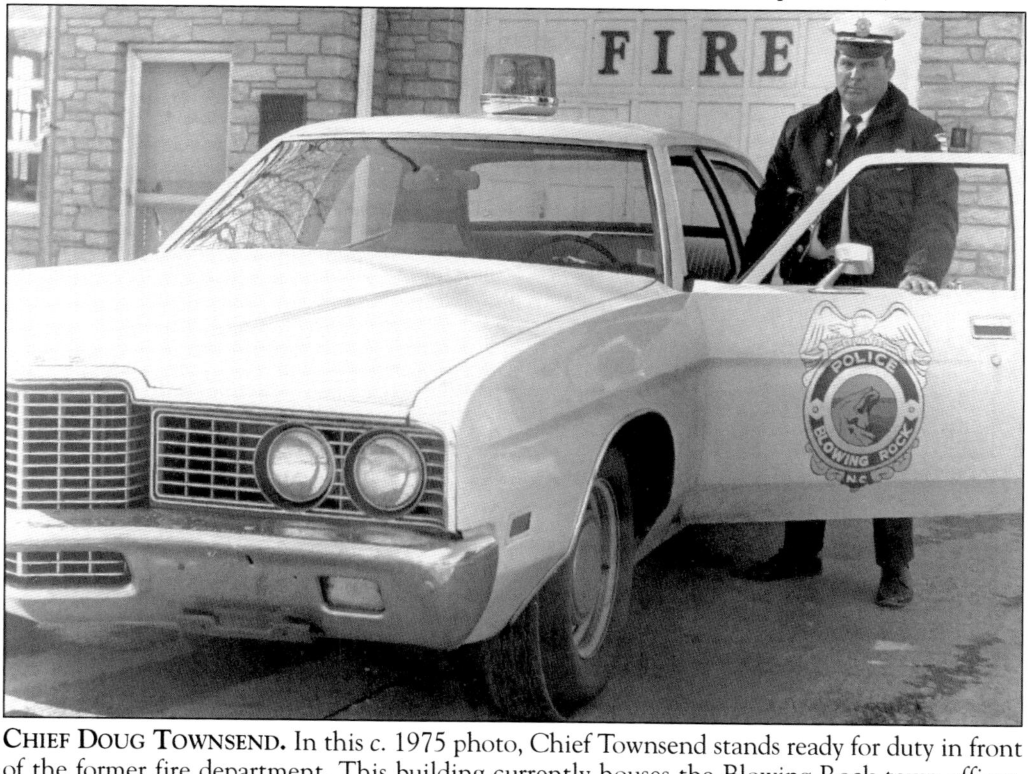

CHIEF DOUG TOWNSEND. In this *c.* 1975 photo, Chief Townsend stands ready for duty in front of the former fire department. This building currently houses the Blowing Rock town offices. (Courtesy of Blowing Rock Police Department.)

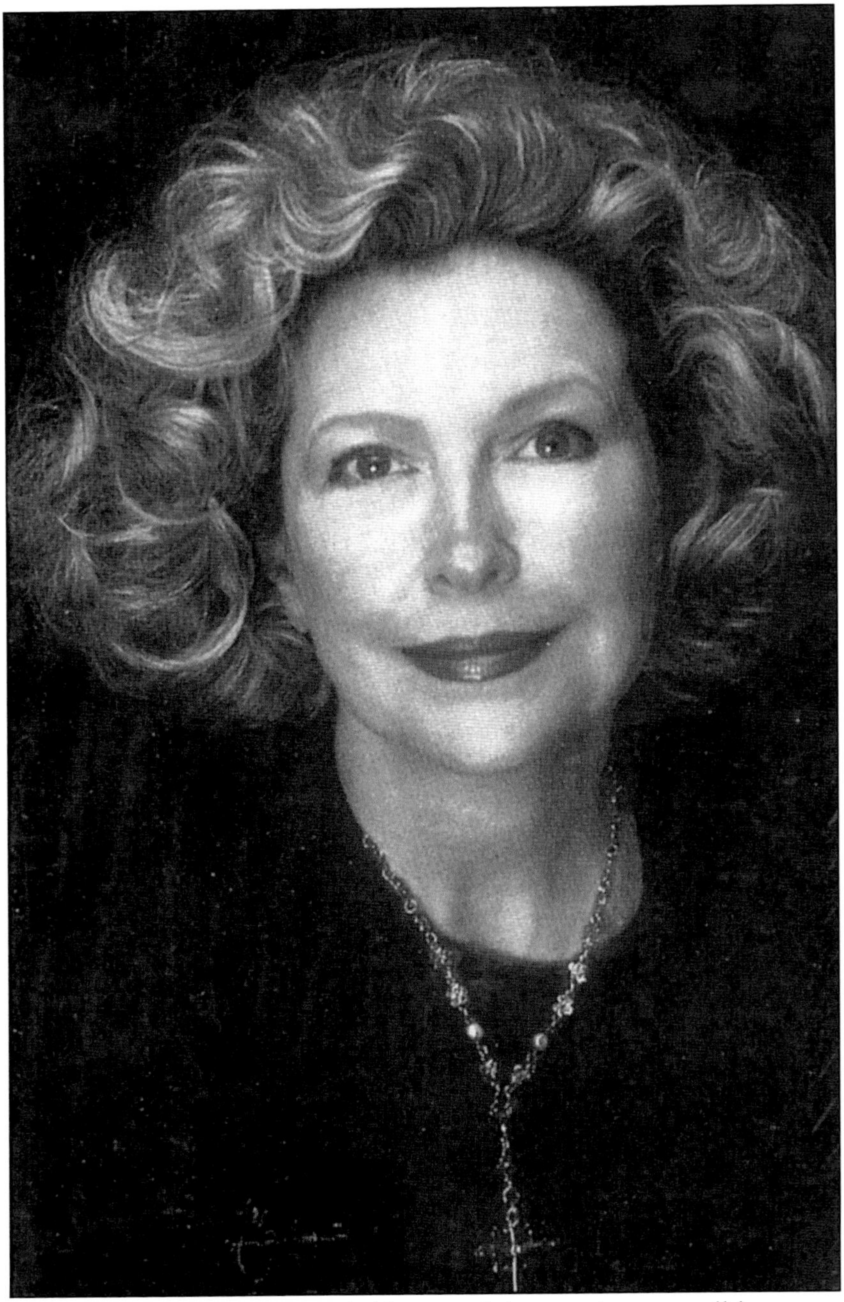

JAN KARON. Author Jan Karon is probably one of the town's most well-known celebrities. Her best-selling series about the fictional town of Mitford is based on Blowing Rock. Her books have been listed on the *New York Times Best Seller* list several times. Ms. Karon no longer lives in the town, but it remains close to her heart. In the forward to the Blowing Rock Historical Society's book, *Post Cards of Historic Blowing Rock*, she writes, "the true building blocks of our village aren't brick and mortar, or even Grandfather stone and chestnut siding. The true building blocks are people; those who give Blowing Rock its incomparable grace, charm and enchantment. . . . whether we live here or come for a visit, Blowing Rock rubs off on us." (Courtesy of *The Blowing Rocket*.)

Six

Recreation and Socializing

Opportunities for recreation abound in the High Country, from fishing, hiking, and horseback riding, to attending a play at the Blowing Rock Stage Company, listening to outdoor concerts, and enjoying ice cream in the park. In the town's early tourism days, activities such as bowling, croquet, dances, and social teas were planned to entertain the summer visitors. Any leisure time the local population may have had would have been enjoyed with families and at church gatherings. Groups of men would gather at the old general stores to play checkers and trade stories. Social clubs such as the Rotary Club, the Garden Club, and the Community Club later developed and brought together many locals and seasonal residents. Festivals such as Art in the Park and Fourth of July parades are events where people get together to celebrate today.

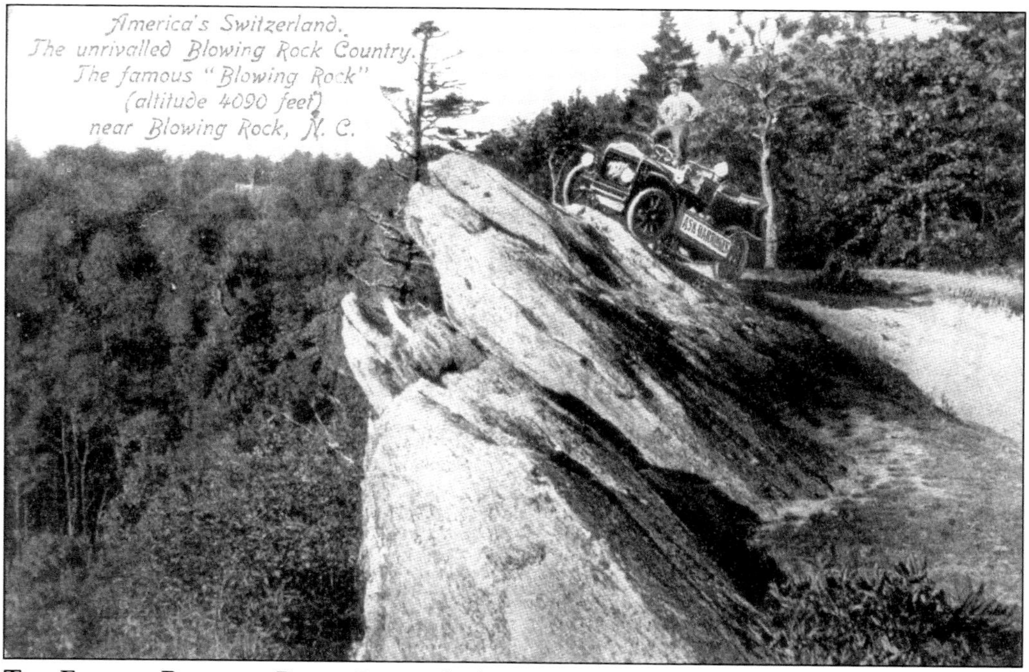

The Famous Blowing Rock. Postmarked 1910, the postcard reads "America's Switzerland. The unrivalled Blowing Rock Country. The famous 'Blowing Rock' (altitude 4090 feet) near Blowing Rock, N.C." The sign on the car reads "Asa Barringer," indicating it may have belonged to Osmond Barringer, who is said to have driven the first automobile to the village in 1908. (Courtesy of Ginny Stevens.)

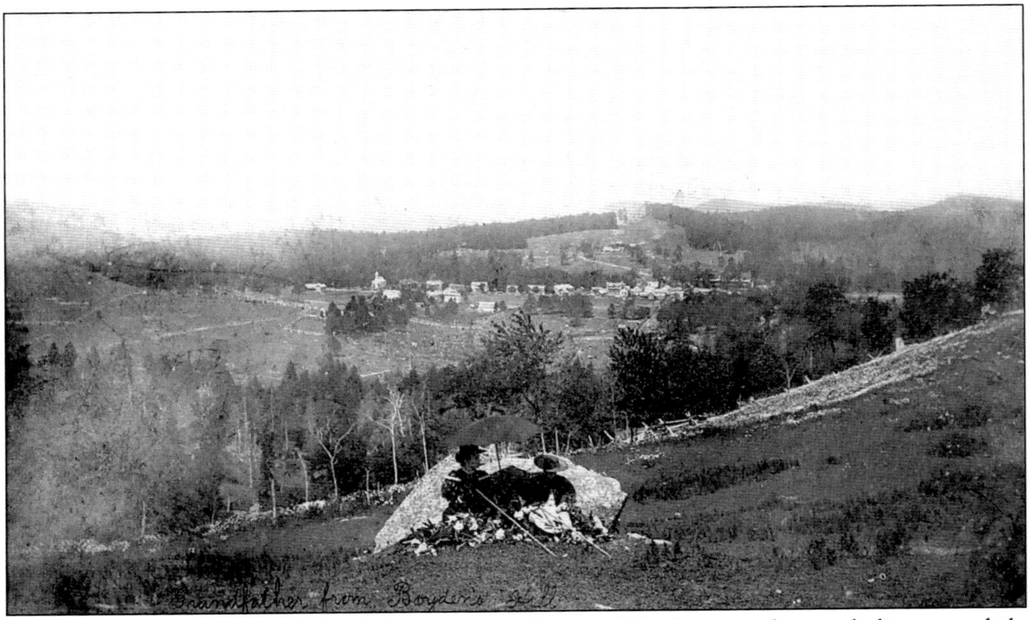

RESTING IN THE SUN ON BOYDEN'S HILL. In this *c.* 1900 photograph, two ladies rest while viewing the village. Their walking sticks and mountain laurel branches show their long skirts have not hampered their travels. Note the extent of logging onto some of the higher ridges. (Courtesy of *The Blowing Rocket.*)

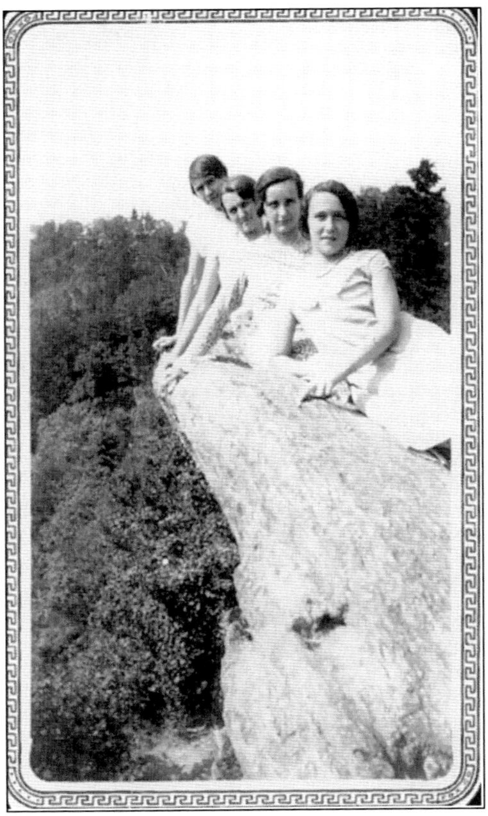

RECLINING ON THE ROCK. These brave girls are relaxing on the edge of the Blowing Rock in the late 1920s. The following are pictured from left to right: Mary Ford (Wood), Pearl Ford (Wood), Lizzie Ford (Teague), and Gracie Bolick (Bradshaw). (Courtesy of Gracie Bradshaw and *The Blowing Rocket.*)

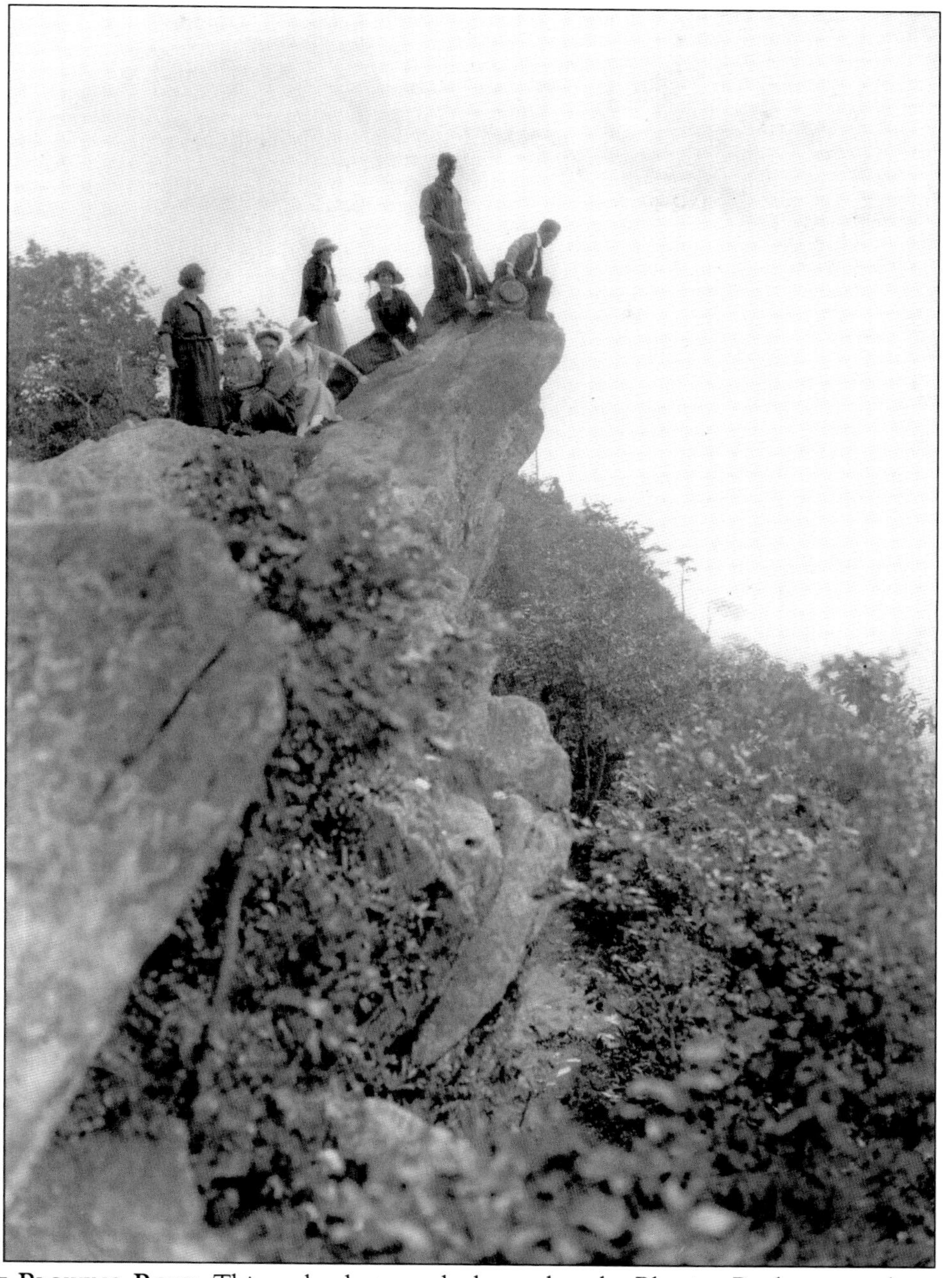

The Blowing Rock. This early photograph shows that the Blowing Rock attracted tourists to admire the views even in the early days. The Rock, located 4,090 feet above sea level, was first owned by J.C. Ford. The Bernhardt family purchased it from him, and it was later owned by the Robbins family. The stone building that currently serves as the gift shop was built by Grover Robbins in the 1930s. Promotion of the rock as a tourist attraction was natural, since the town derived its name from the promontory. The name for the rock is based on the belief that light objects thrown from the rock are blown back up by the winds from the John's River Gorge. In the 1940s, the rock was listed by *Ripley's Believe It or Not* as the place where it snowed upside down. Many postcards and photographs were made of the local landmark. It still holds a fascination for visitors today. (Courtesy of Blowing Rock Historical Society.)

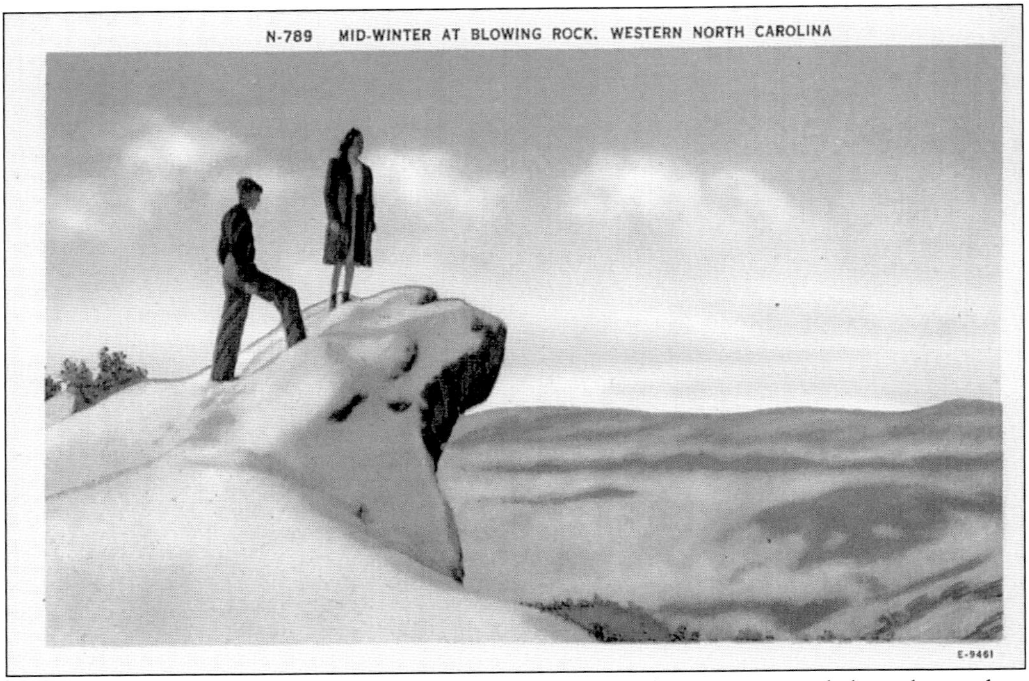

MID-WINTER AT THE BLOWING ROCK. This *c.* 1940 postcard pictures a couple bravely standing on the rock in the colder weather. Mist and clouds often surround the rock and make beautiful photographs. (Courtesy of Ginny Stevens.)

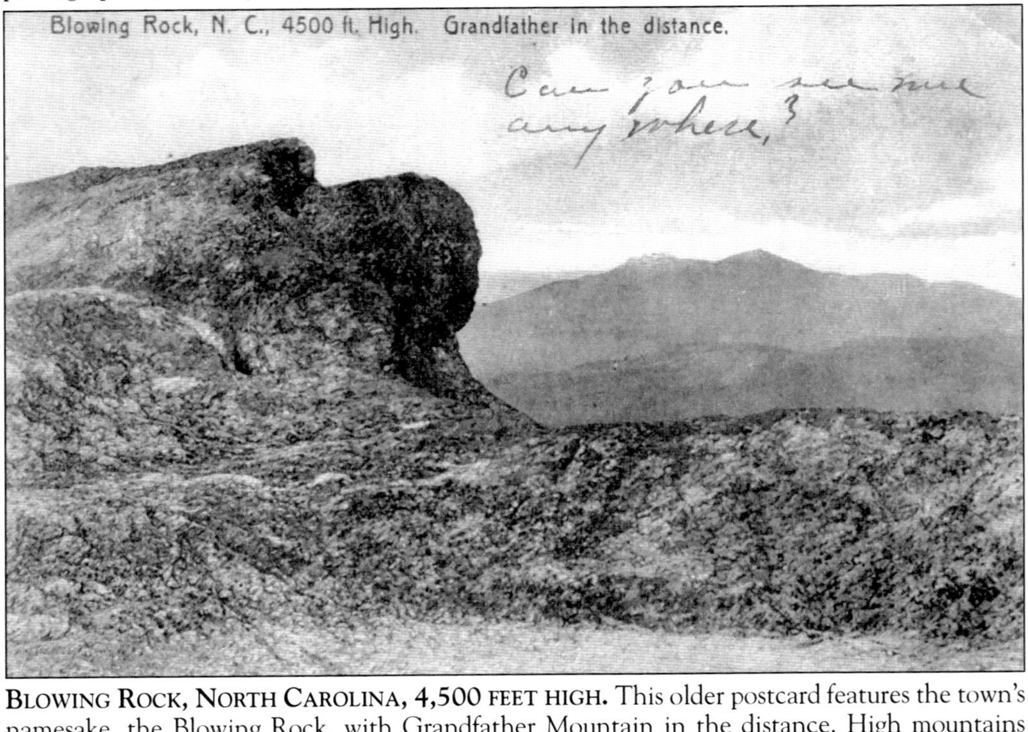

BLOWING ROCK, NORTH CAROLINA, 4,500 FEET HIGH. This older postcard features the town's namesake, the Blowing Rock, with Grandfather Mountain in the distance. High mountains wreathed in clouds provide ample scenic beauty for visitors. Written on the postcard is "Can you see me anywhere?" (Courtesy of Watauga County Public Library.)

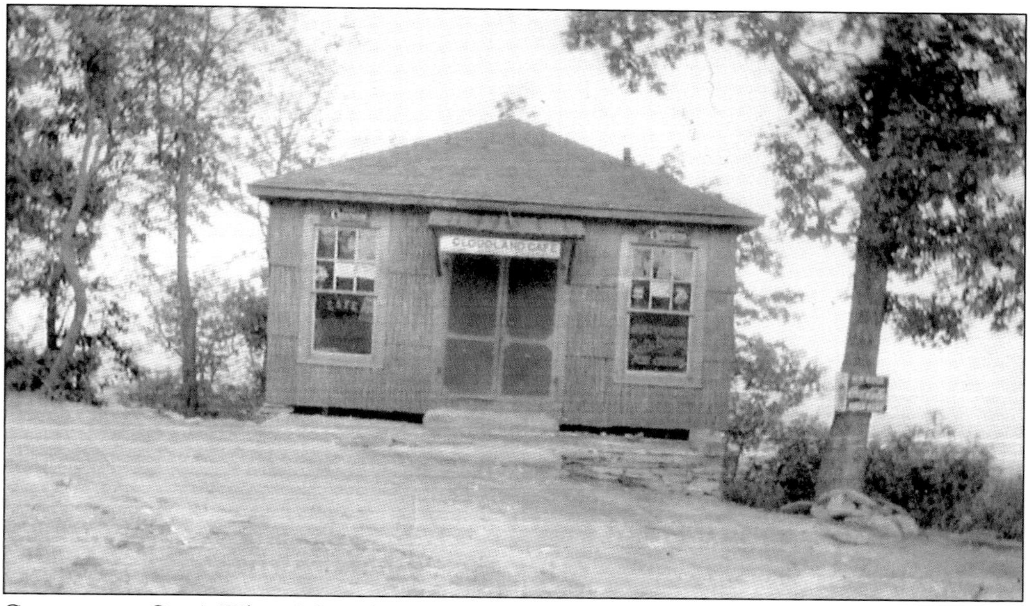

CLOUDLAND CAFÉ. When John Clinton Ford owned the Rock, he installed the Cloudland Café nearby. With such a name, tourists were sure to buy snacks and lunch at this place. (Courtesy of Heidi Ellis.)

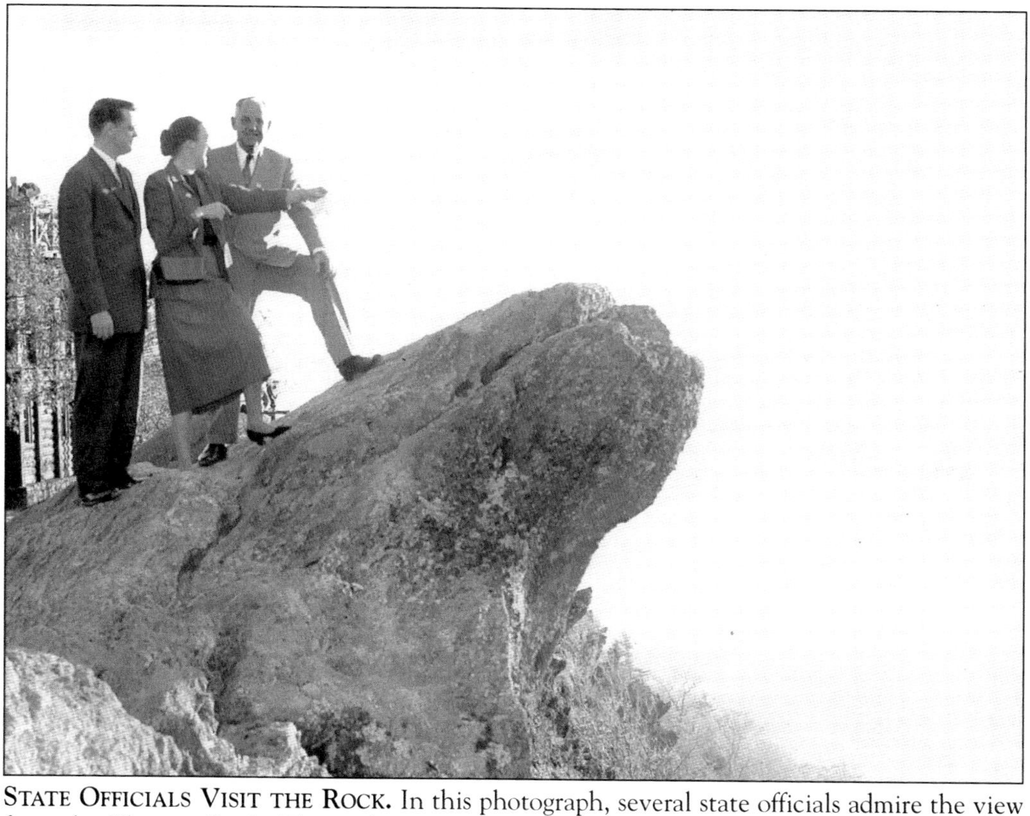

STATE OFFICIALS VISIT THE ROCK. In this photograph, several state officials admire the view from the Blowing Rock. The rocky outcrop has become a widely recognized symbol for the town. (Courtesy of *The Blowing Rocket*.)

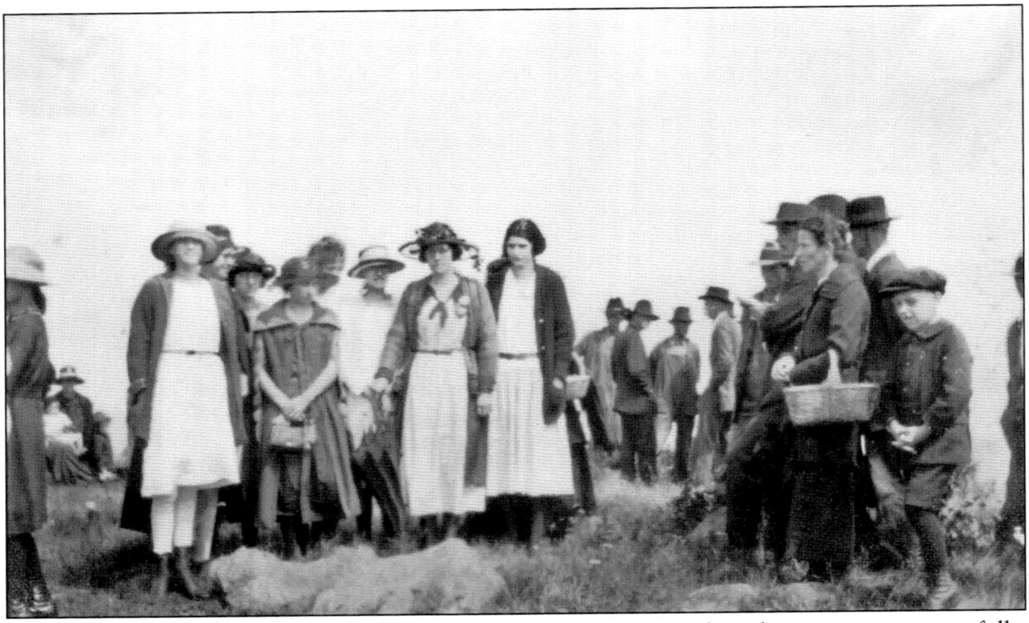

SOCIALIZING ON THE MOUNTAIN, C. 1920. Before television and modern entertainment, folks gathered outdoors and had picnics and "preachings." Because of the white dresses of the group of ladies in the middle of the photo, this picture may have been taken at a church singing. Simple events such as these were the local population's way to get together and socialize. (Courtesy of Joe Dulaney.)

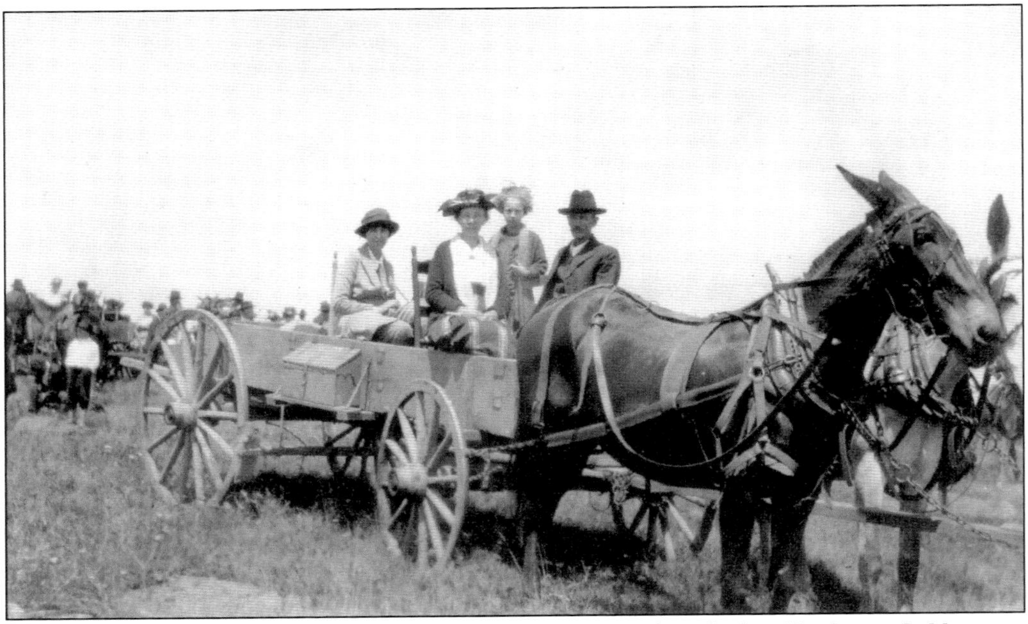

DR. VANCE, A PREACHER, C. 1915. This gentleman is identified as Dr. James I. Vance, a summer visitor who was famous for providing powerful sermons at Rumple Memorial Church. Note the ladder-back chairs serving as extra seating in the wagon bed. (Courtesy of Joe Dulaney.)

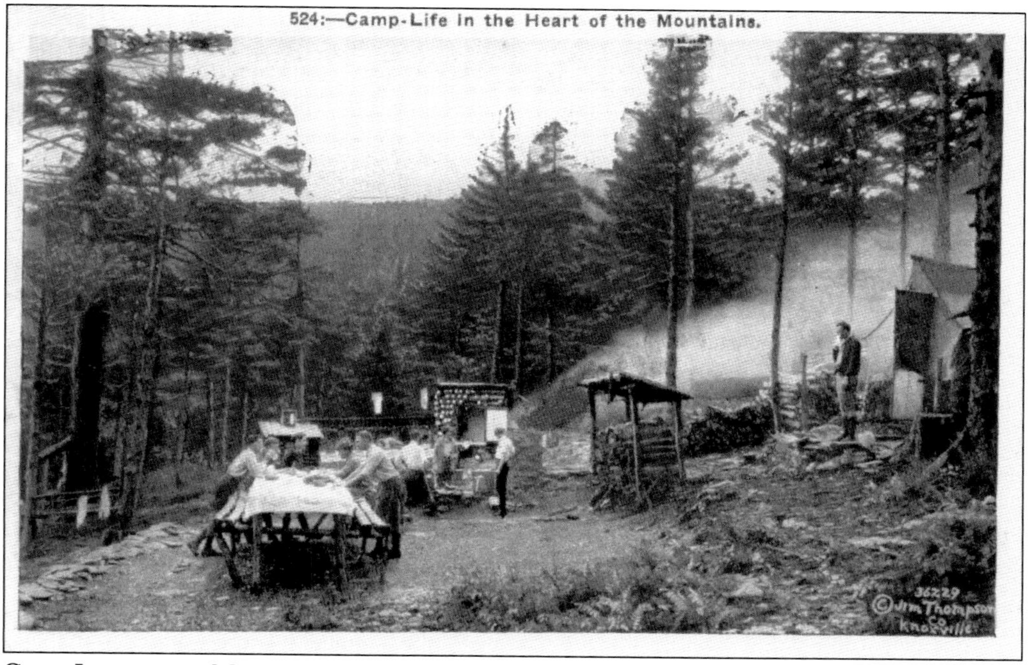

CAMP LIFE IN THE MOUNTAINS. Camping was a favorite pastime for visitors to the mountains, especially when the local inns were full. The early tourists who arrived after the Civil War did not have many other choices for lodging while visiting. (Courtesy of Stella Greer Dobbins.)

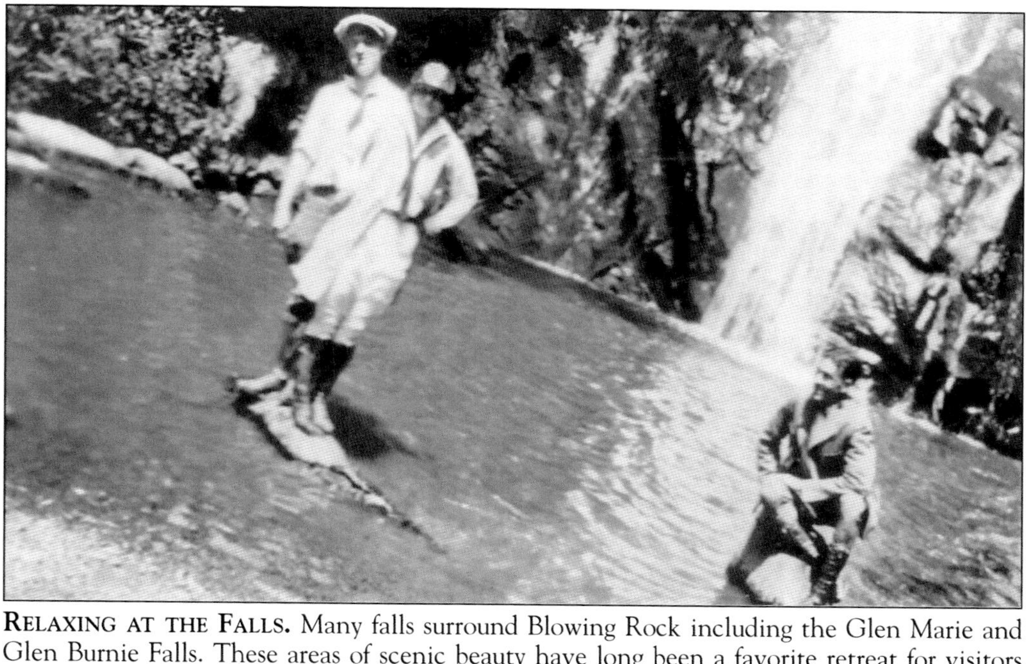

RELAXING AT THE FALLS. Many falls surround Blowing Rock including the Glen Marie and Glen Burnie Falls. These areas of scenic beauty have long been a favorite retreat for visitors from "off the mountain." (Courtesy of Joe Dulaney.)

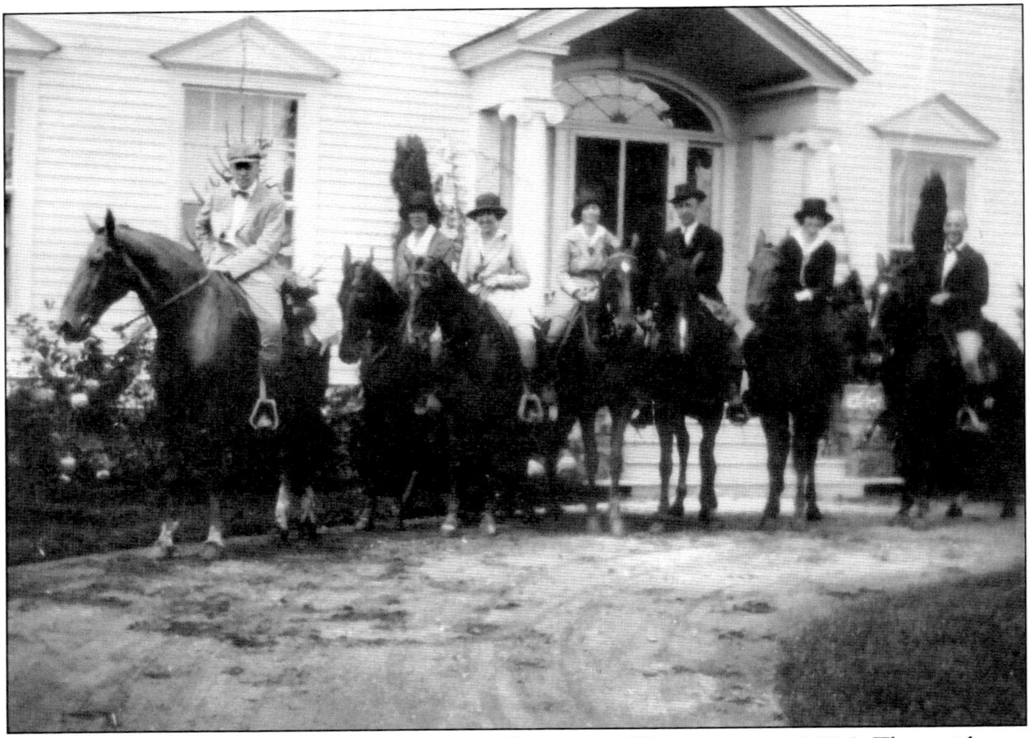

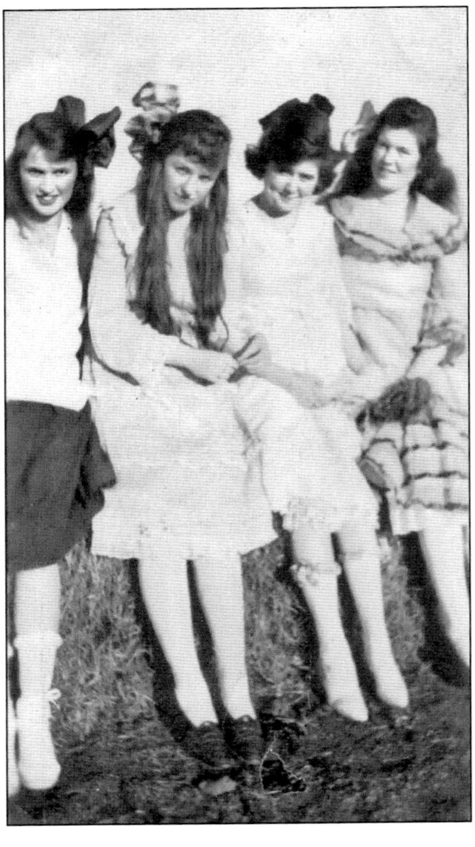

Riders at Westglow, c. 1915. These riders, including members of the Elliott Daingerfield family and friends, are posed in front of the grand home, Westglow. Horseback riding was a popular recreational activity for Blowing Rock visitors; there were several stables in town. (Courtesy of Joe Dulaney.)

Four Young Beauties, c. 1915. Although perched on hay, these four young women visiting Blowing Rock are clearly dressed up for the occasion. (Courtesy of Joe Dulaney.)

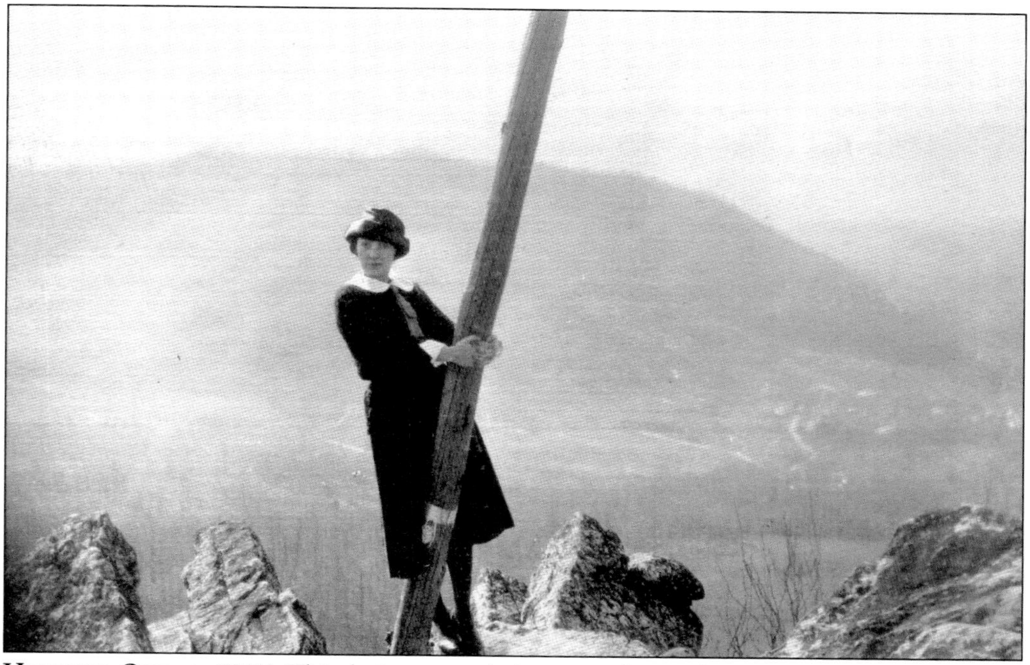

HANGING OUT, C. 1915. This daring young lady tempts fate as she poses on an outcropping in the mountains here. Still, the views are worth the risks. (Courtesy of Joe Dulaney.)

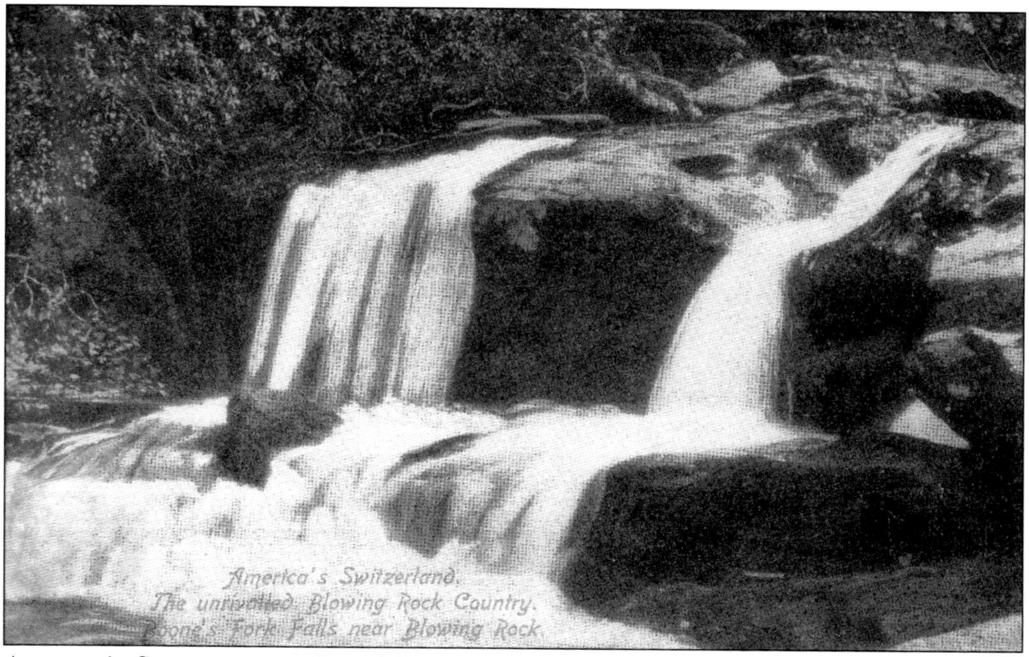

AMERICA'S SWITZERLAND. Waterfalls in the area were the subject of many older postcards. These beauties of nature held a special attraction for visitors. The card advertised it as the "unrivalled Blowing Rock Country." (Courtesy of Web Alexander.)

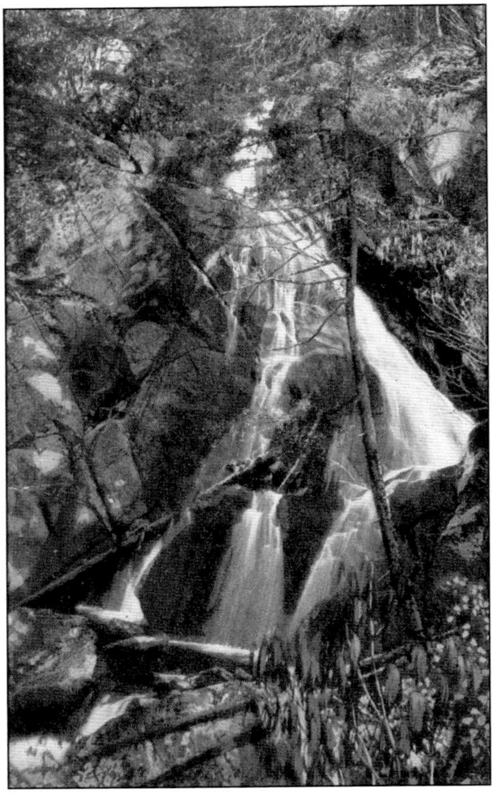

GLEN MARIA FALLS. These falls are located in the John's River Gorge and cascade down hundreds of feet. It may be a challenging hike to see these falls, but it is well worth the trip. (Courtesy of Web Alexander.)

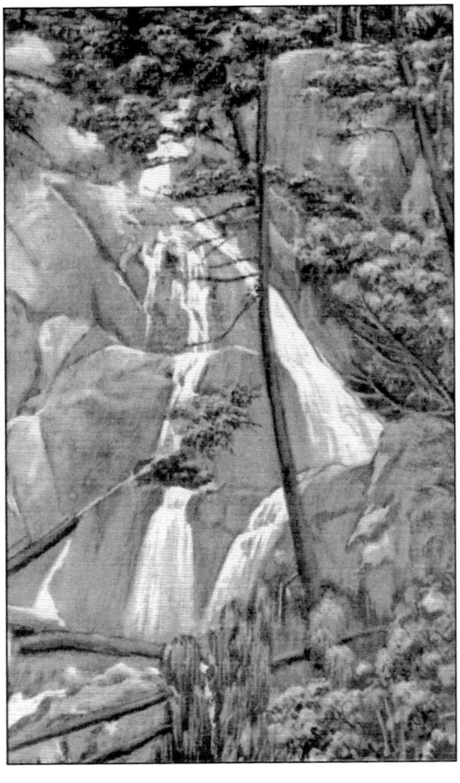

GLEN BURNIA FALLS. The Glen Burnie (or Glen Burney or Glen Burnia) falls, near downtown, have long been a popular recreation spot. Waterfalls in the mountains fascinated visitors and these postcards were popular keepsakes. (Courtesy of Cullie Tarleton.)

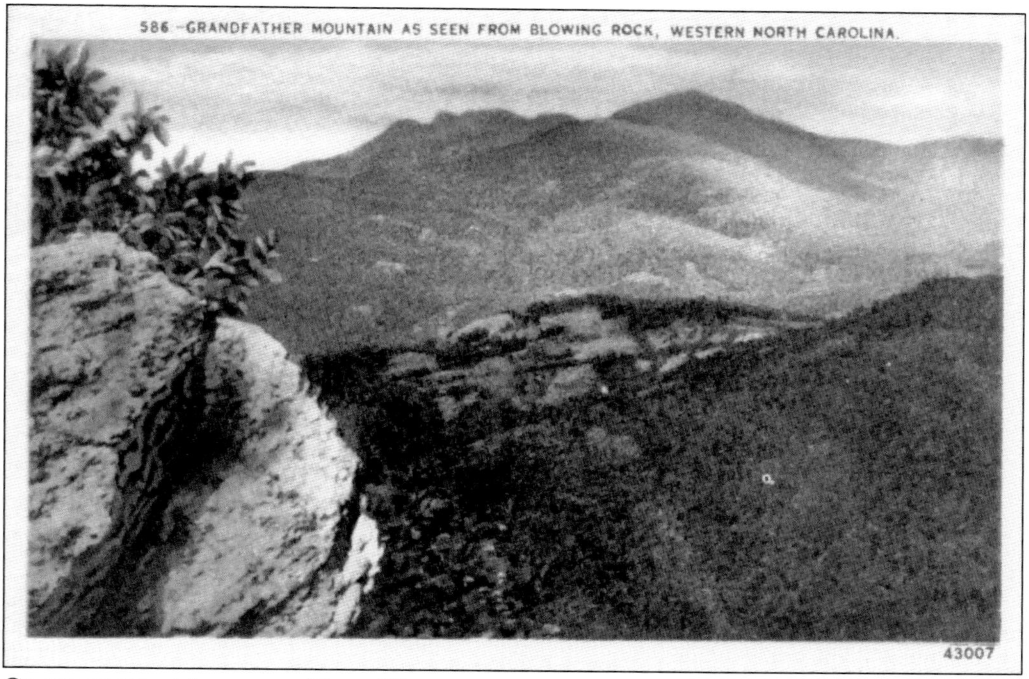

GRANDFATHER MOUNTAIN VIEW. The postcard reads, "Grandfather Mt. On Blue Ridge Parkway is one of the most rugged mountains east of the Rockies. A scenic road enables driving up to its peak." The mountains drew visitors to this high place, even when the roads were not in the safest condition. (Courtesy of Cullie Tarleton.)

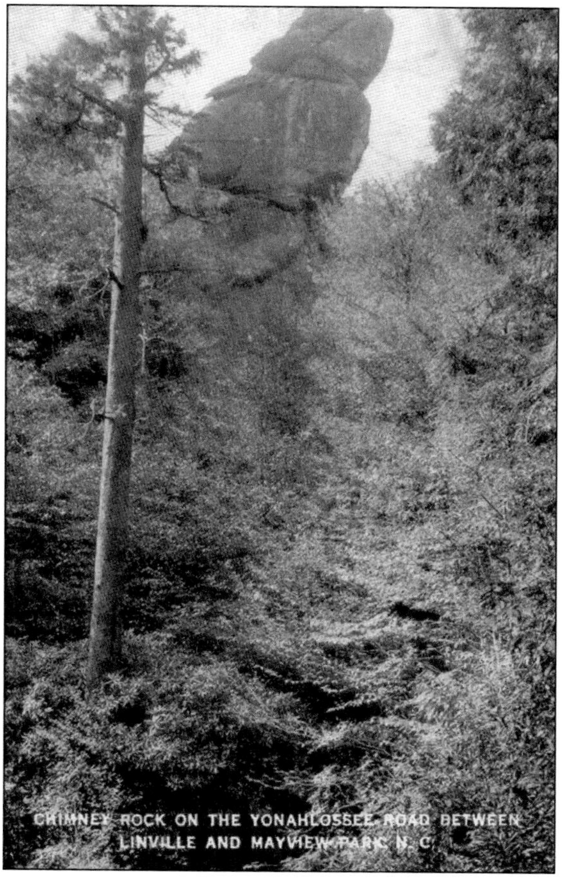

CHIMNEY ROCK ON YONAHLOSSEE ROAD. The Yonahlossee Road was one of the most scenic and popular drives in the High Country. Rock outcroppings were often named after familiar objects. Landscape postcards were quite popular in the early days. (Courtesy of Web Alexander.)

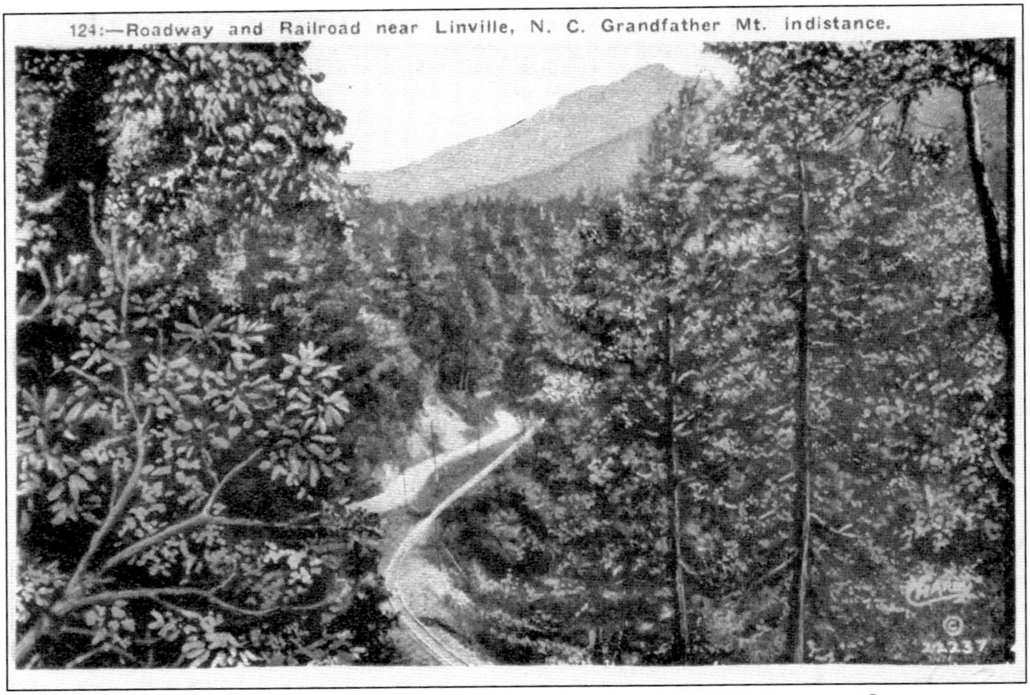

ROADWAY AND RAILROAD NEAR LINVILLE, NORTH CAROLINA, WITH GRANDFATHER MOUNTAIN IN THE DISTANCE. The steep winding road and railroad bed can be seen climbing through these majestic mountains. The journey up to Blowing Rock in the past was even more of a challenge than it is today, but many summer visitors trusted their early automobiles to make the climb safely. (Courtesy of Richard Trexler.)

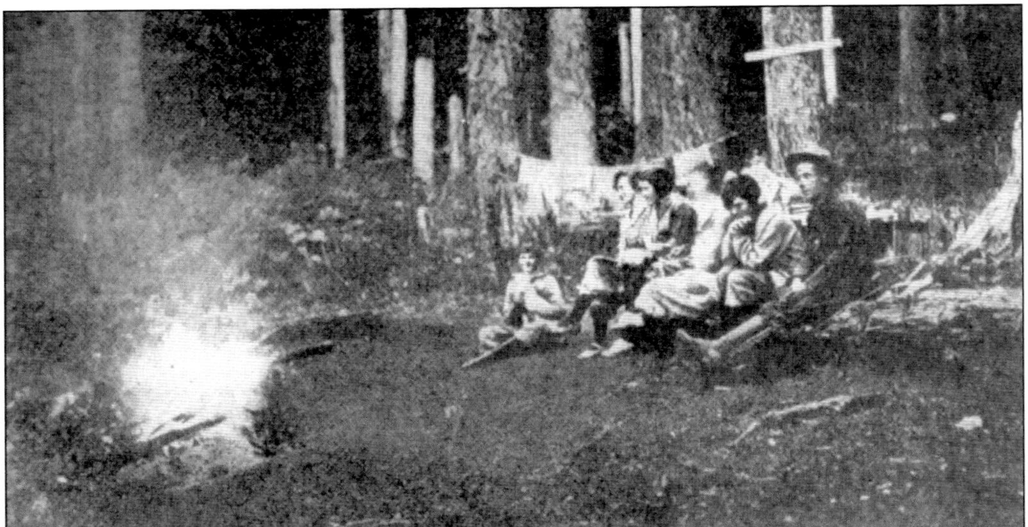

CAMP YONAHLOSSEE. This photograph from an early brochure shows several campers lounging outside. This girls' camp offered typical camp activities and encouraged campers to become respectful and considerate of others. The community was very proud of the camp. (Courtesy of Richard Trexler.)

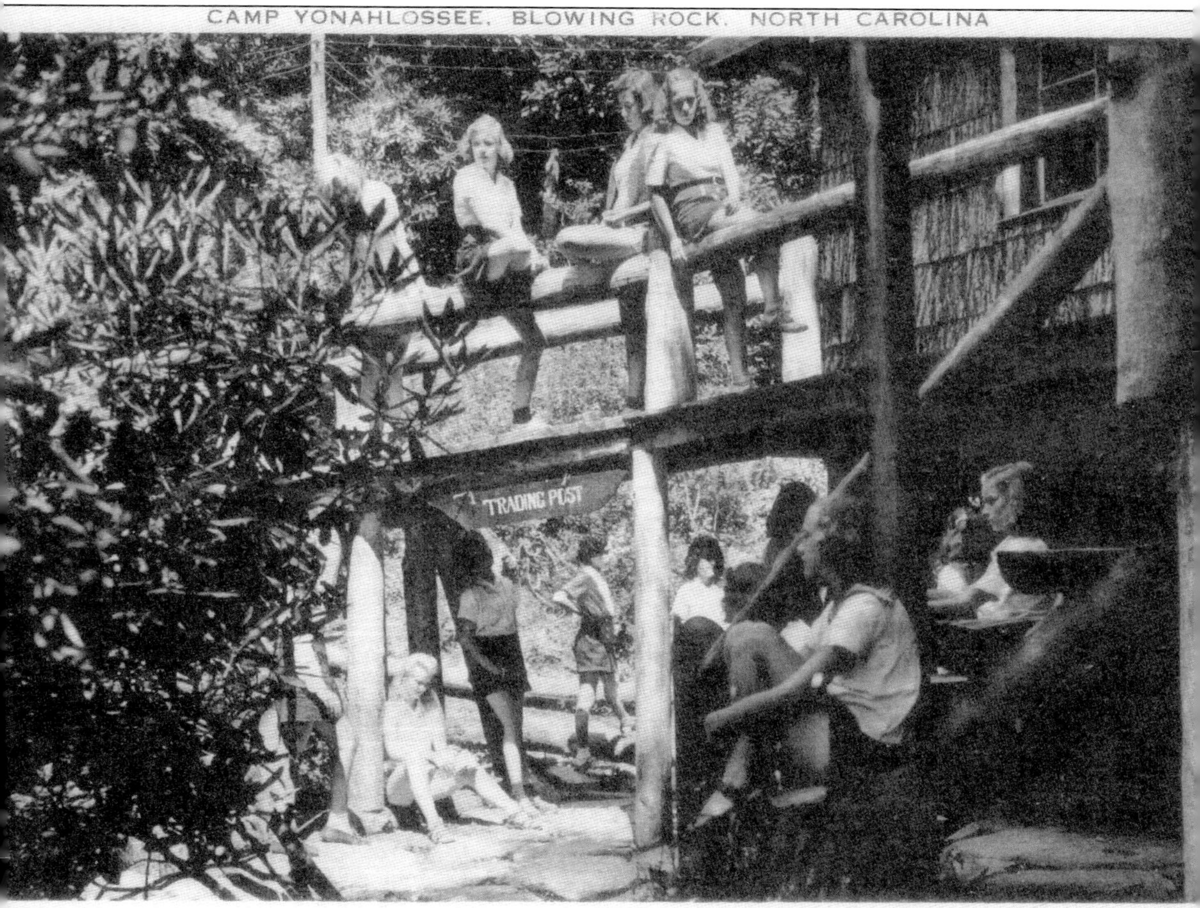

CAMP YONAHLOSSEE. This summer camp for girls was conducted by Mr. and Mrs. A.P. Kephart of Greensboro, North Carolina. The Kepharts were pioneers in planning summer camps in the south. The program included activities in outdoor life, arts and crafts, and camp government. Next to the camp was the W.L. Winkler farm, which produced food, milk, and meat for camp residents. The tuition for the season was $250, which included transportation from Lenoir or Shull's Mill. Attributes such as independence, respect for others, and appreciation of nature were encouraged in the girls. By 1938, the camp included stables, a farm house, sleeping quarters, an infirmary, office, crafts cabin, nature cabin, weaving room, dining hall, recreational hall, indoor plumbing at shower houses, and a lighting plant. Camp Yonahlossee was located on Shull's Mill Road at Poplar Grove. The area is now the Yonahlossee Saddle Club. (Courtesy of David Harwood.)

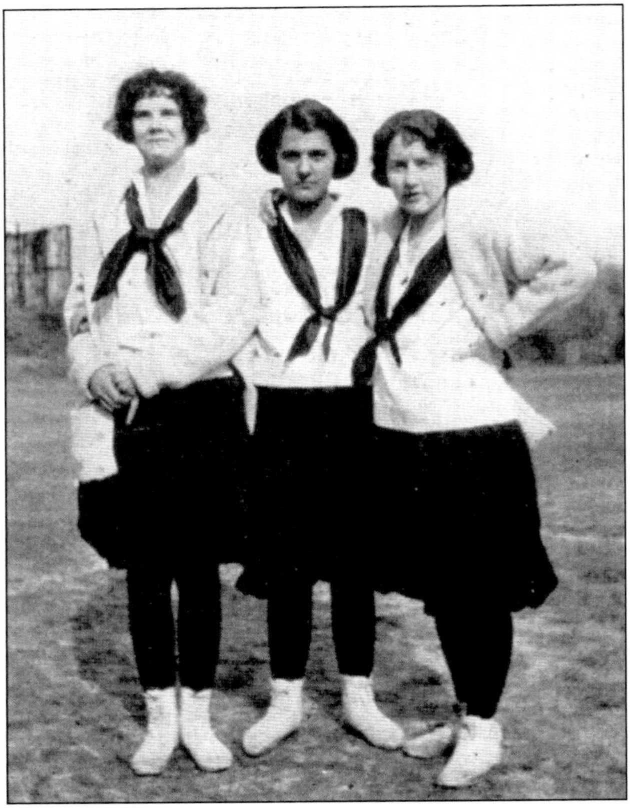

OUTFITS FOR YONAHLOSSEE CAMPERS. These girls are outfitted according to the day's fashions and the strict specifications given in the 1922 brochure. Their recommended clothing included 2 pairs serge or poplin bloomers (preferably black), 4 white middies, 1 middy tie (preferably maroon), 6 pairs heavy hose (black), and 1 pair high white sneakers. (Courtesy of Richard Trexler.)

MASKED BALL AT MAYVIEW MANOR. Mayview Manor was the perfect location for parties and get-togethers. This Halloween masked ball took place in the basement of the Manor and was well-attended by these merry-makers. (Courtesy of Ann Allison Kincaid.)

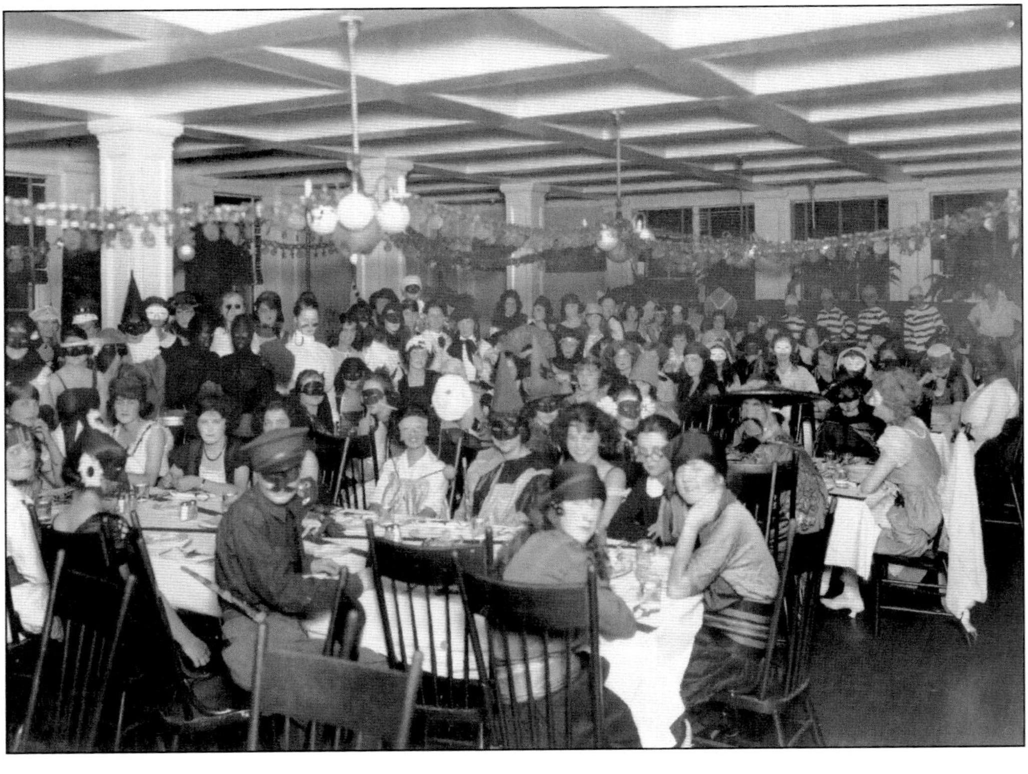

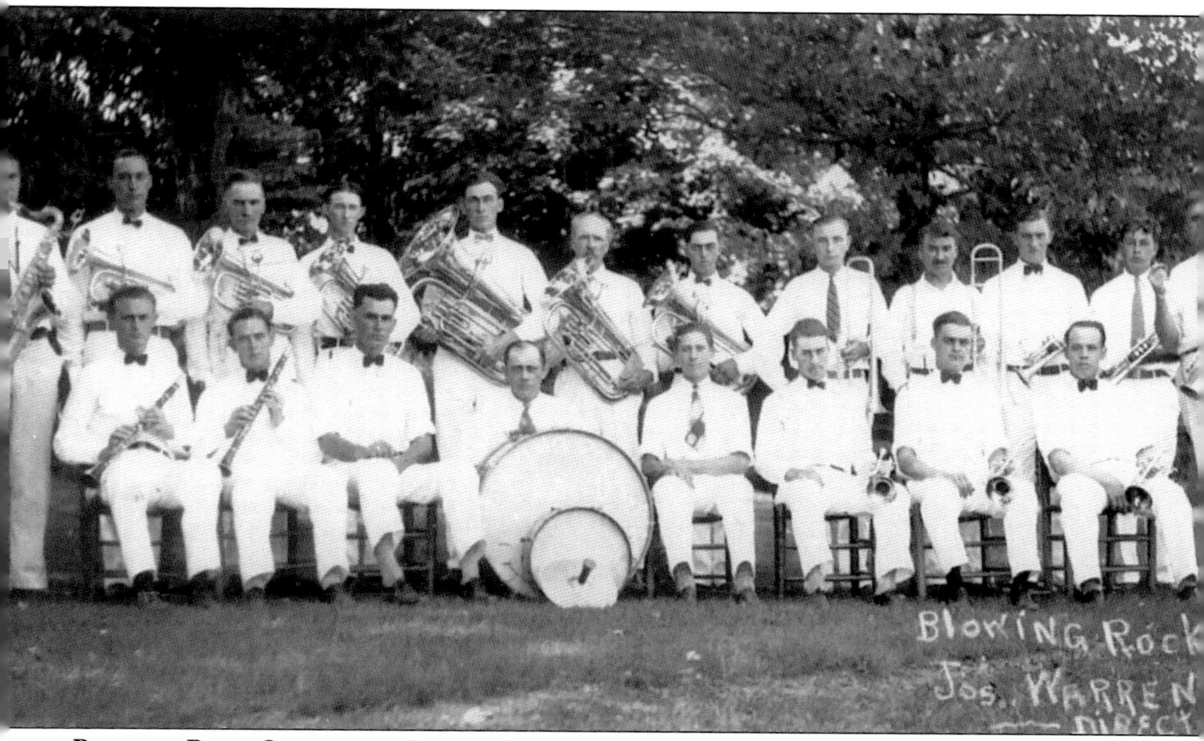

Blowing Rock Community Band. This photograph of the community band was taken July 4, 1927. Bands were an important social group. The activity appears to be male dominated in this time period. Pictured from left to right are (front row) Don Johnson, Spencer Greene, Max Cannon, Bud Bolick, Joe Panella, Bynum Crisp, Ronda Foster, Randal Foster, Stewart Cannon, and Jos Warren (director); (back row) Earl Coffey, W.C. Knight, W.B. Castle, T.A. Weaver, John Clure, A.B. Craig, Howard Coffey, J.M. Foster, Don Greene, and Paul Foster. Band members not in the photograph included B.K. Jenkins, Jay Knight, Kermit Bolick, Don Reid, and Parks Knight. (Courtesy of *The Blowing Rocket*.)

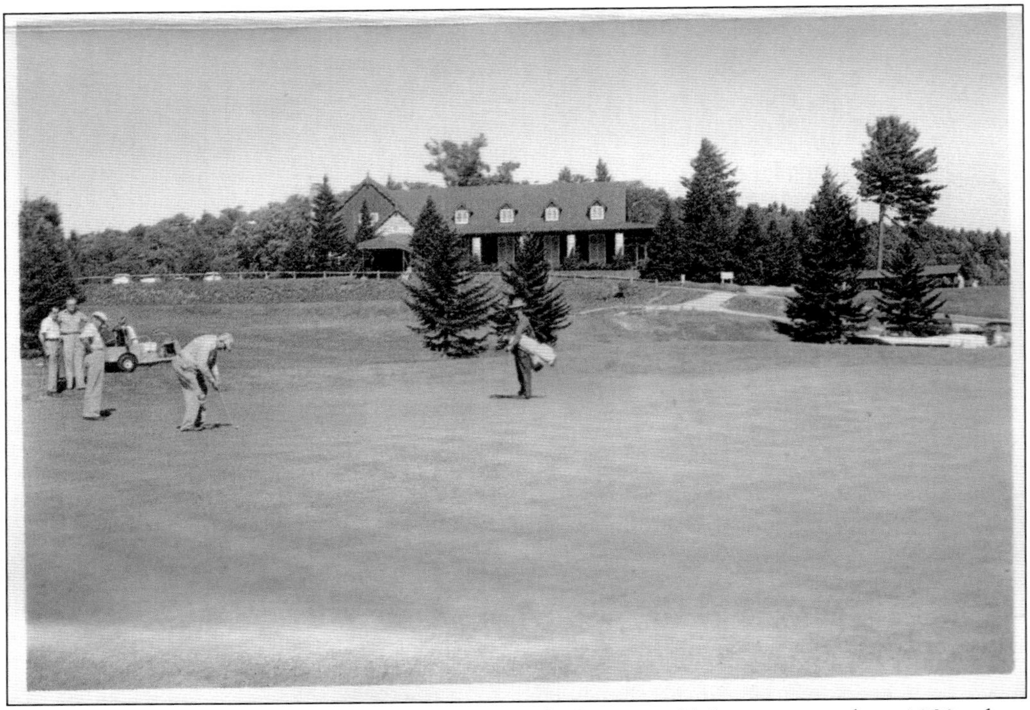

Blowing Rock Country Club. Blowing Rock Country Club was started in 1939 when several cottage owners purchased land next to the Green Park–Norwood Golf Course. The club officially opened in 1941. This building burned in 1974, and a new club house was built. The course continues to attract discriminating golfers and is considered to be at the highest elevation of any golf course in Eastern America. (Courtesy of Brian Lambeth.)

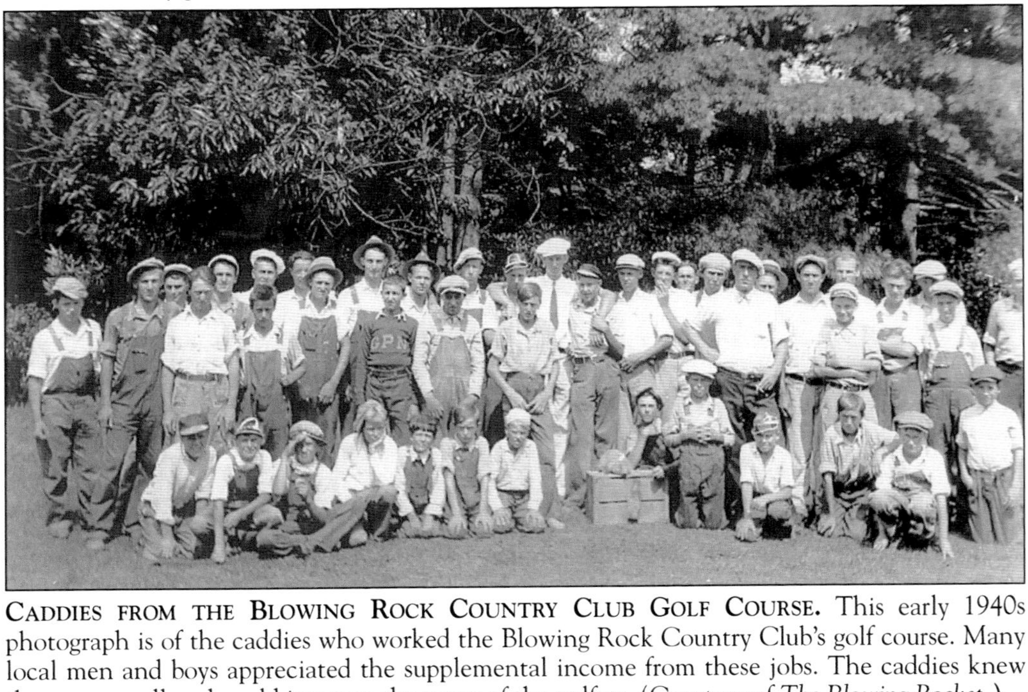

Caddies from the Blowing Rock Country Club Golf Course. This early 1940s photograph is of the caddies who worked the Blowing Rock Country Club's golf course. Many local men and boys appreciated the supplemental income from these jobs. The caddies knew the course well and could improve the game of the golfers. (Courtesy of *The Blowing Rocket*.)

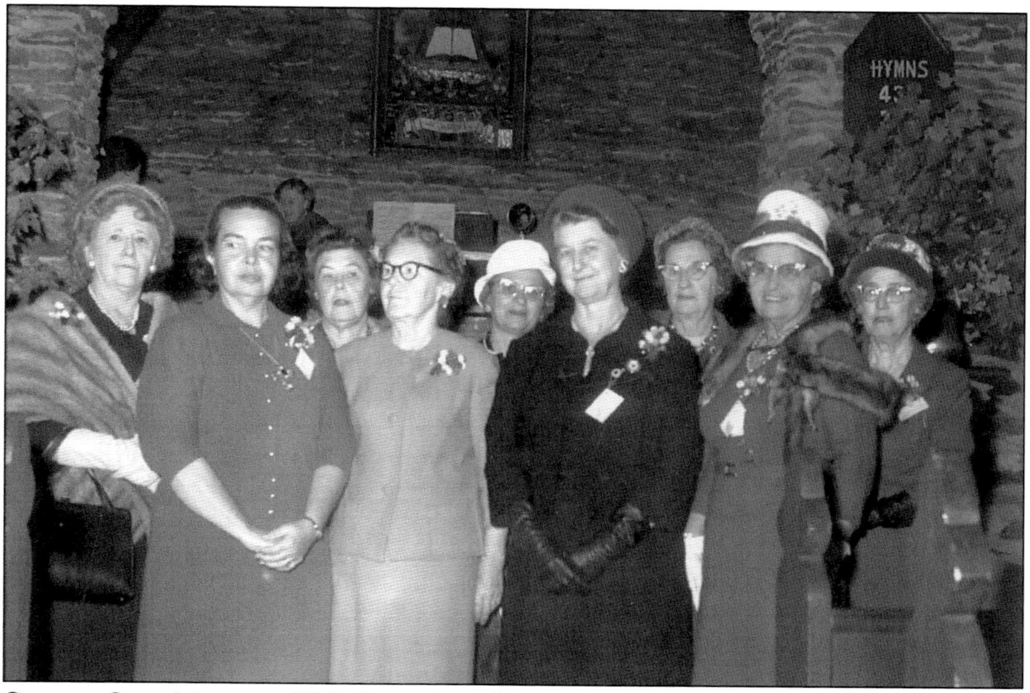

GARDEN CLUB MEETING. Clubs have always been an important part of the social fabric of the town. In this *c.* 1940 Garden Club photograph, the ladies are well-dressed and coifed for the event. (Courtesy of *The Blowing Rocket*.)

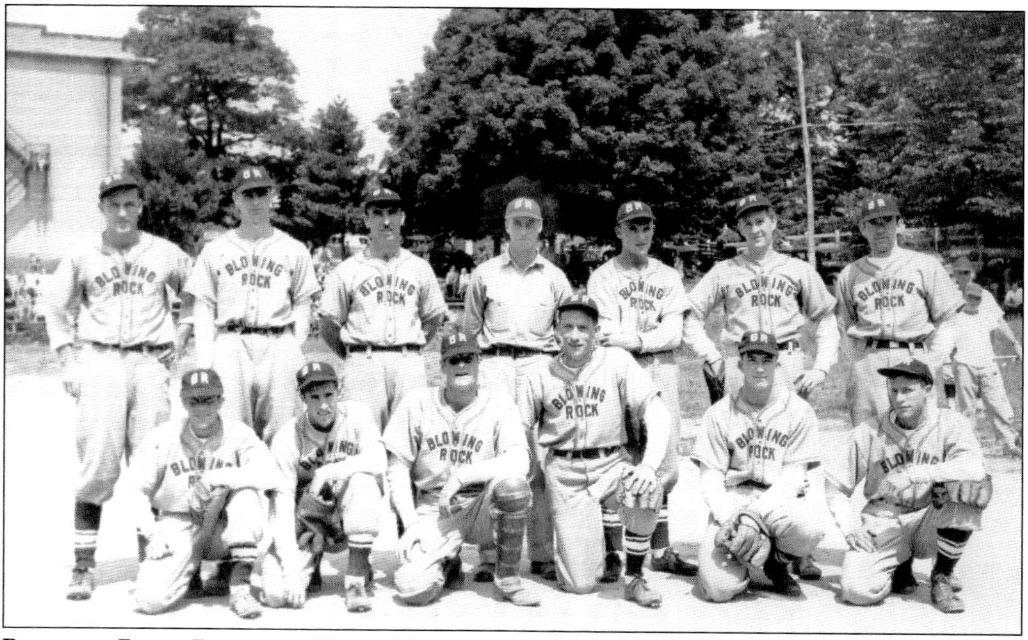

BLOWING ROCK BASEBALL TEAM. The team played on fields located near the town's water treatment facility on U.S. 321. The players are, from left to right, (front row) Johnny Brooks, "Pete" Lentz, Carter Lentz, Perry Ashley, Shuford Edmisten, Perry Lentz, and Lewis Lentz; (back row) Rudolph Greene, Frank Jestus, Coy Estep, Eugene Lentz, Bruce Greene, Ernest Hayes, and Clarence Berryman. (Courtesy of Ralph E. Lentz II.)

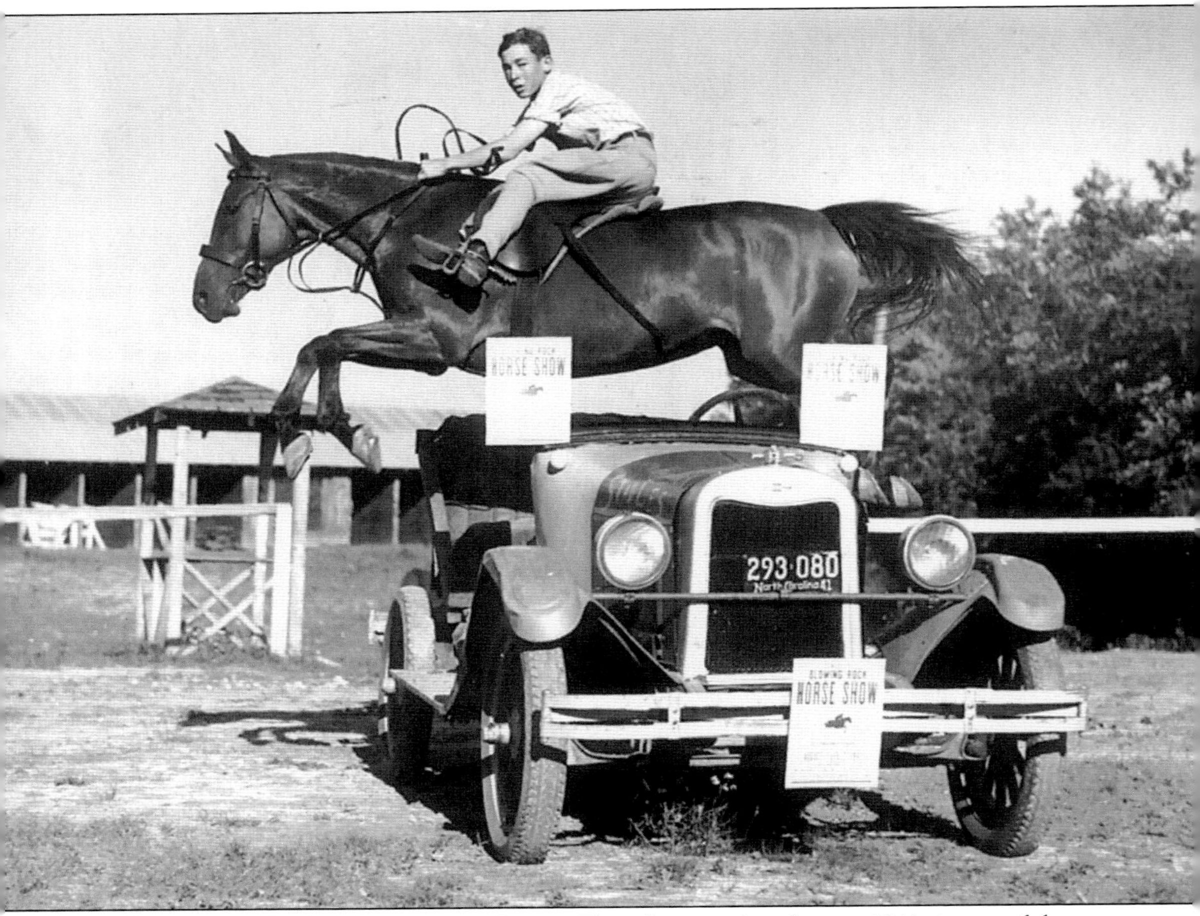

"June Bug" Tate at the Horse Show. This photograph, taken in 1941, is one of the most famous advertisements for the Blowing Rock Charity Horse Show. June Bug's father, L.M. Tate, is credited for beginning and developing the horse show. The horse show began in 1923 and was mainly a social event for local riders. In 1928, the show moved to its present location on the old Mayview Golf Course and appealed mainly to the summer residents. Lunches, dances, and parties preceded the event, and it truly became the social event of the summer for the summer dwellers. Today, the three-week event attracts the highest levels of equine competitors from all over to the small village of Blowing Rock. The show is the oldest continuous horse show in the nation. (Courtesy of *The Blowing Rocket*.)

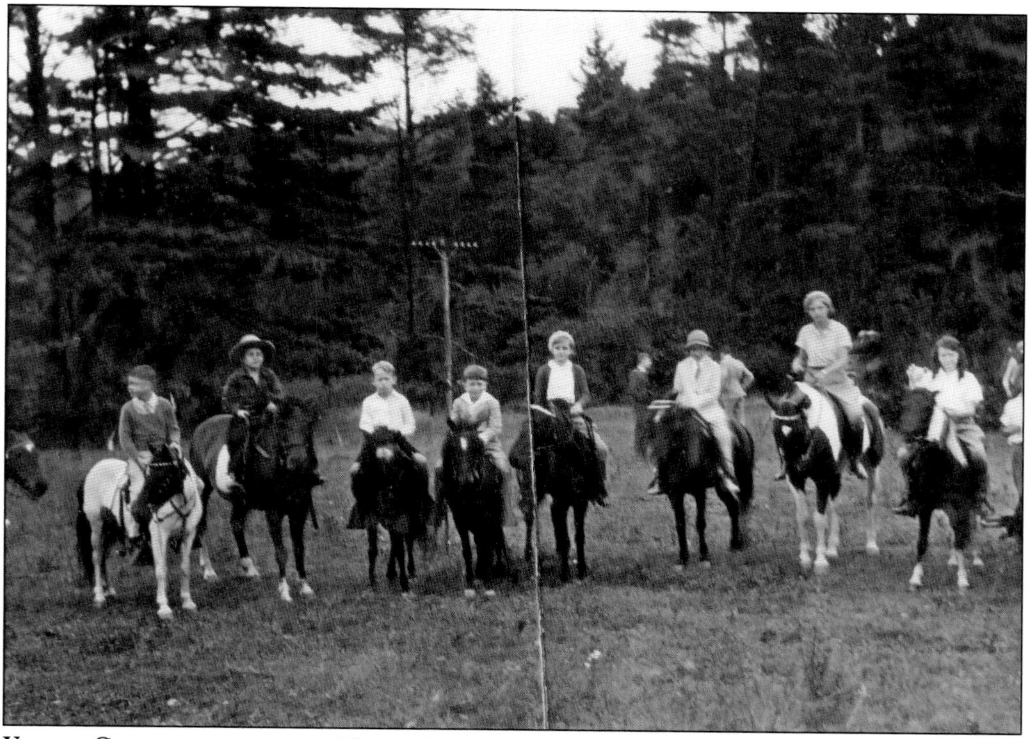

Young Competitors in the Horse Show. These children are proudly posing on ponies for the Blowing Rock Charity Horse Show. The boy with the hat on, second from the left, is "June Bug" Tate, son of L.M. Tate who started the show. This photograph was taken when the show was held on a vacant lot on Ransom Street. (Courtesy of Stella Greer Dobbins.)

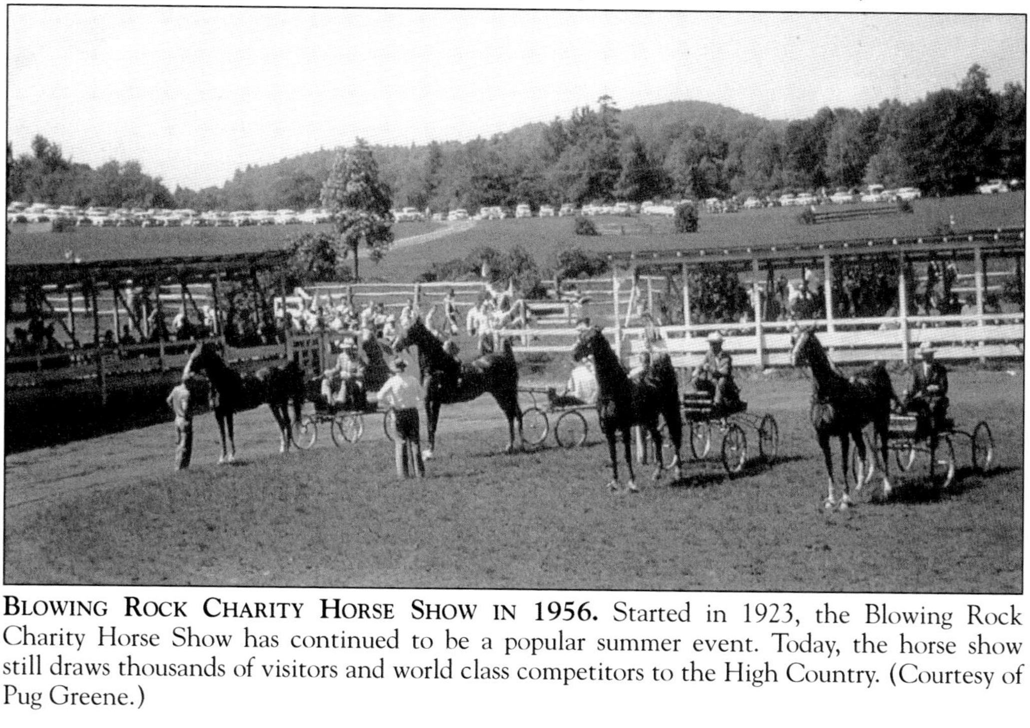

Blowing Rock Charity Horse Show in 1956. Started in 1923, the Blowing Rock Charity Horse Show has continued to be a popular summer event. Today, the horse show still draws thousands of visitors and world class competitors to the High Country. (Courtesy of Pug Greene.)

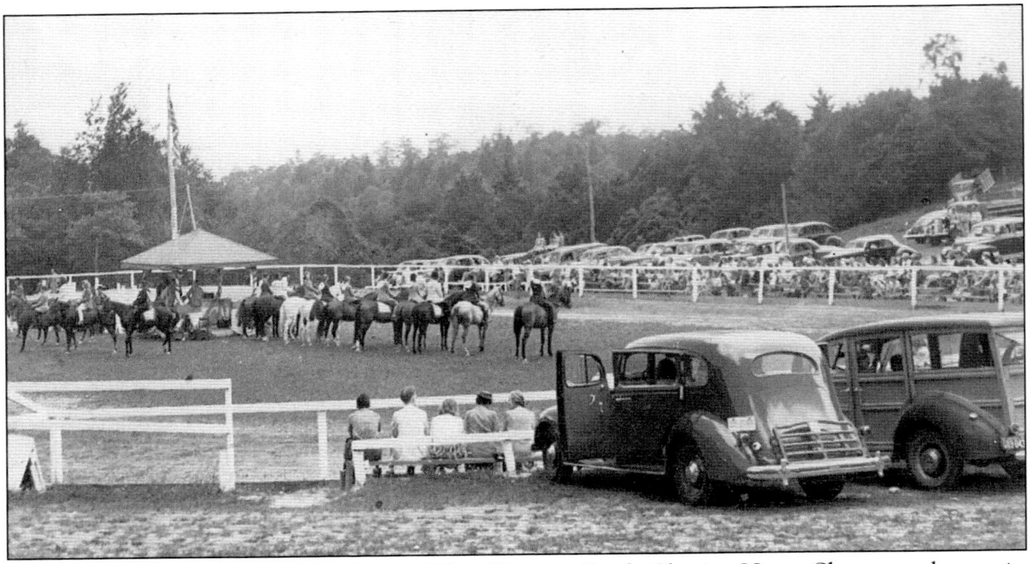

COMPETITION AT THE HORSE SHOW. The Blowing Rock Charity Horse Show was begun in 1923 and is considered the oldest continuous horse show in the nation. Fancy dinners and parties often accompanied the event. Even today, the horse show brings in thousands of visitors and is known as one of the better horse shows in the nation. (Courtesy of *The Blowing Rocket*.)

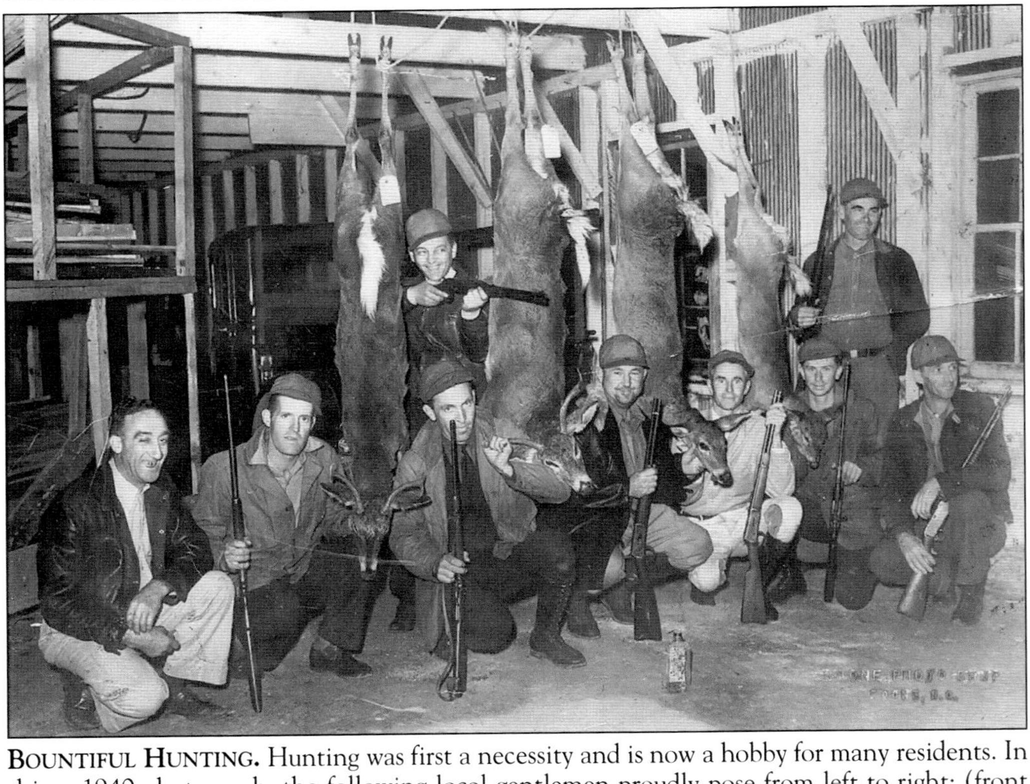

BOUNTIFUL HUNTING. Hunting was first a necessity and is now a hobby for many residents. In this c. 1940 photograph, the following local gentlemen proudly pose from left to right: (front row) Eugene Storie, Paul Coffey, Dan Johnson, Cecil Critcher, Cameron Williams, Stewart Winkler, and Fred Hartley; (back row) Howard Holshouser and William "Bud" Bolick. (Courtesy of *The Blowing Rocket*.)

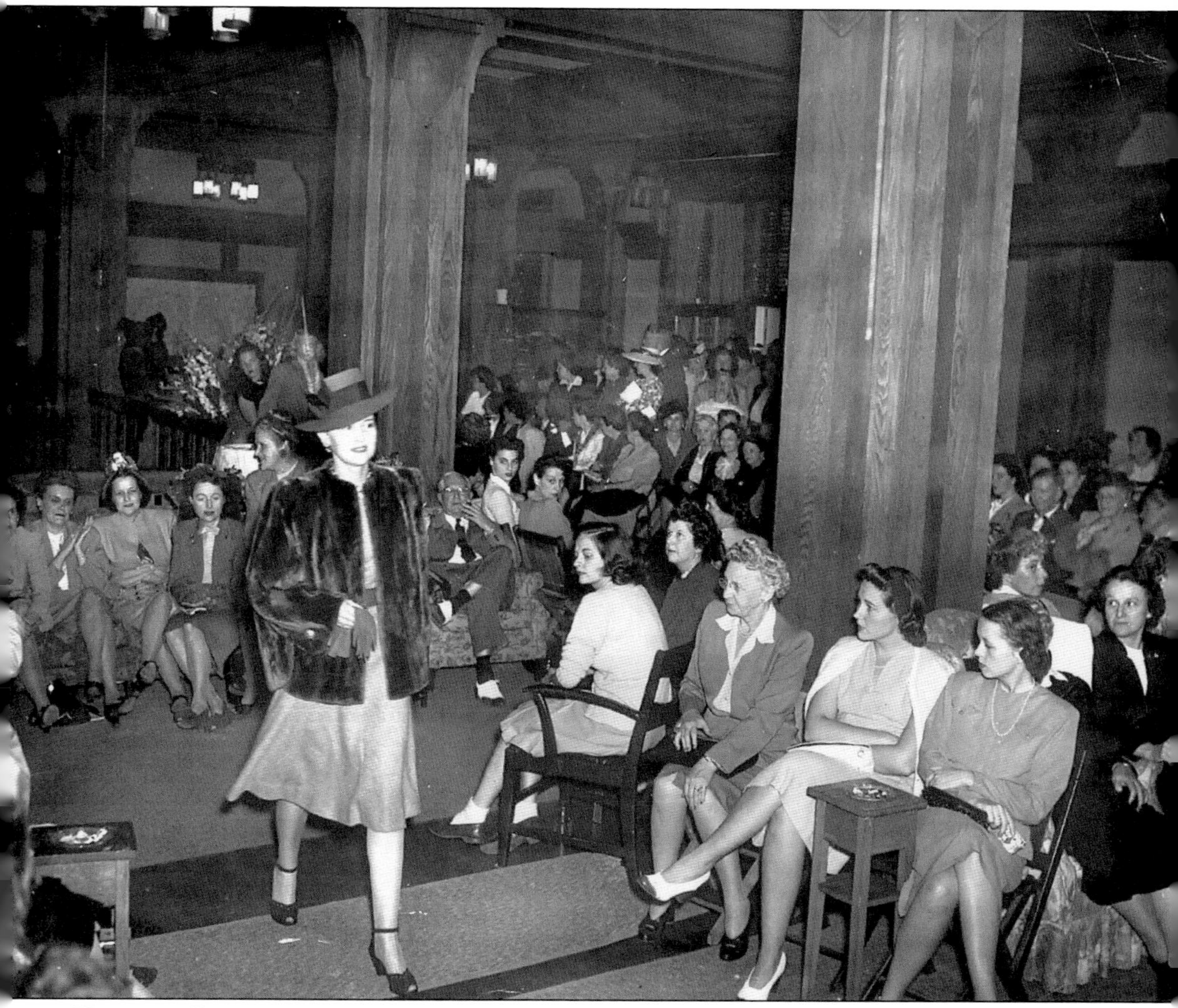

Hospital Benefit Fashion Show. The Hospital Benefit Fashion Show was quite popular and helped assist development of the Blowing Rock Hospital. It was held at Mayview Manor. Judging by the dress styles, this photograph appears to have been taken in the 1940s. Mayview Manor was a marvelous hotel built in Blowing Rock's heyday; it hosted both ordinary folks and celebrities such as Annie Oakley. The grand hotel was opened in 1922 with a total of 138 rooms and had a rustic, not fancy, mountain charm. Social events, fine entertainment, and wonderful food drew visitors and locals. The hotel closed in 1966 and, sadly, in 1978 the manor was demolished. Condominiums now occupy the manor's former location. (Courtesy of *The Blowing Rocket*.)

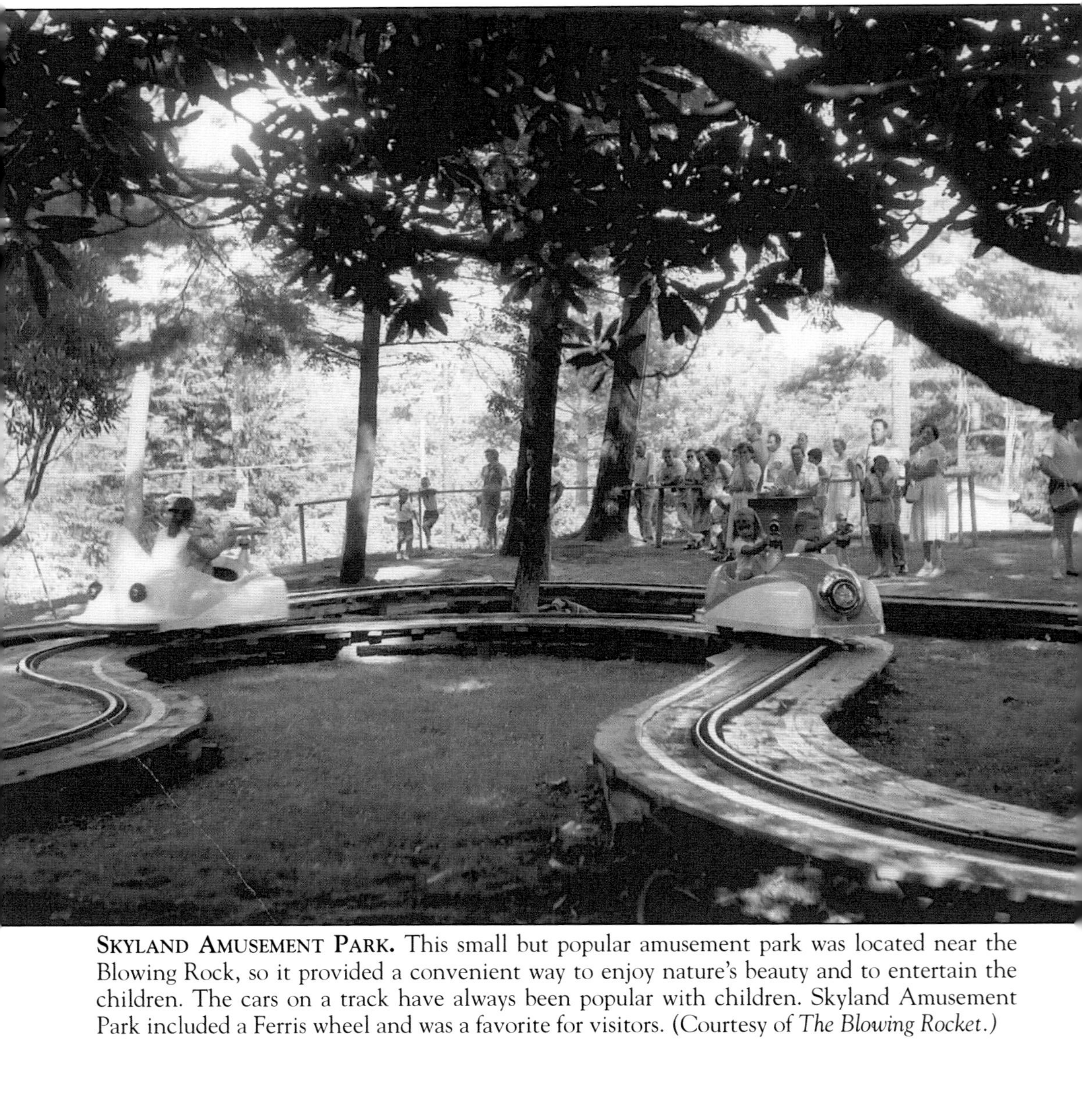

SKYLAND AMUSEMENT PARK. This small but popular amusement park was located near the Blowing Rock, so it provided a convenient way to enjoy nature's beauty and to entertain the children. The cars on a track have always been popular with children. Skyland Amusement Park included a Ferris wheel and was a favorite for visitors. (Courtesy of *The Blowing Rocket*.)

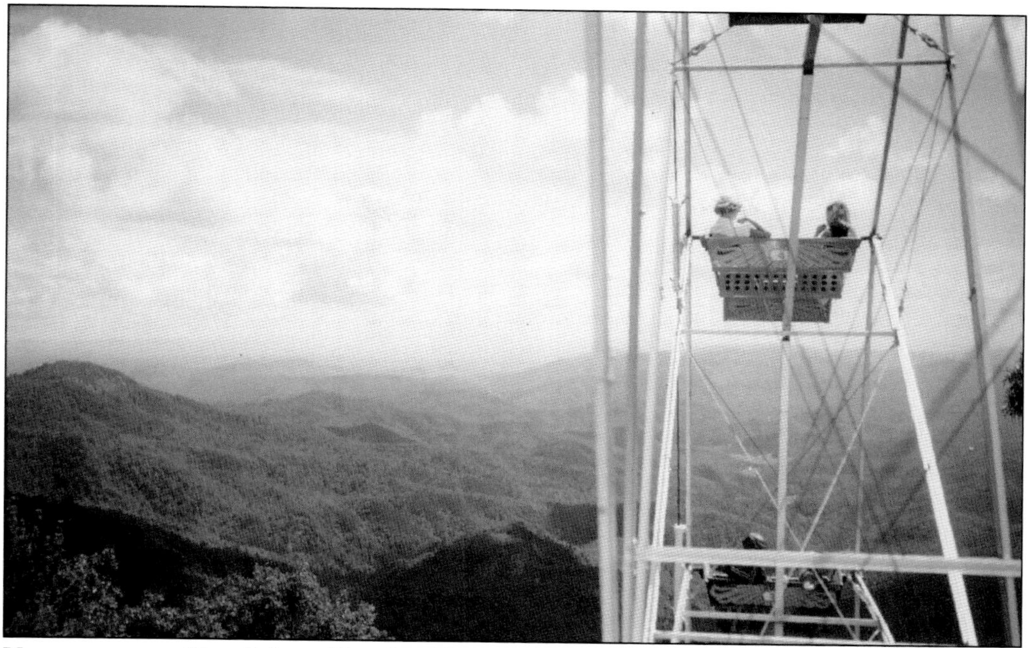

VIEW FROM THE TOP. Palmer Blair, local Boone photographer for many years, took this amazing photograph of the Ferris wheel at the Skyland Amusement Park. The park, although short-lived, was an added attraction while visiting the Rock. This photograph won an award for Palmer Blair at the North Carolina Photographers Association in 1957. (Courtesy of Sarah Blair Spencer.)

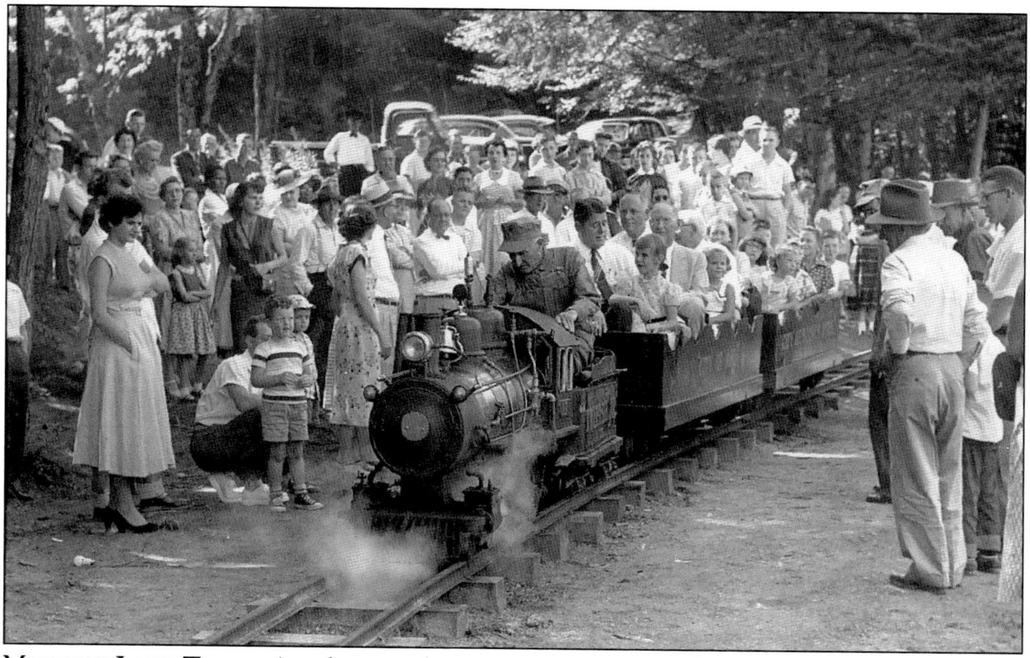

MAYVIEW LAKE TRAIN. Another popular summer pastime was the Tweetsie Jr. train. The train ran around the shores of Mayview Lake, now Broyhill Lake. The train only ran for a few years, but it appealed to many visitors. The walkway around the Broyhill Park runs along the old train bed. (Courtesy of *The Blowing Rocket.*)

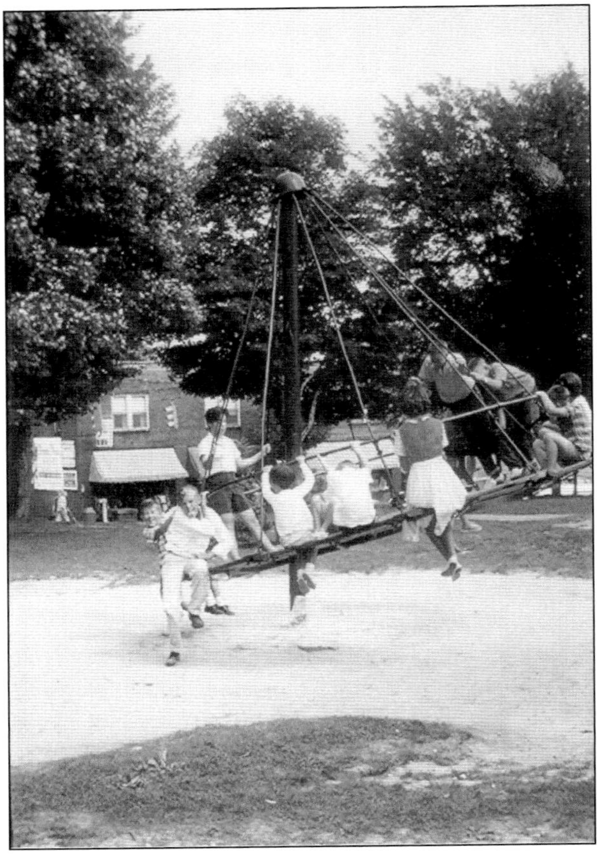

Blowing Rock Town Park. Children and adults alike have enjoyed the green space in the center of downtown. The park property was acquired by the town in 1945 and was built as a memorial to those soldiers who served during World War II. This land was the former site of the ill-fated Watauga Inn. Today, the park is a popular place to eat ice cream cones downtown and let the children unwind. (Courtesy of Pug Greene.)

Broyhill Park. The Broyhill family has given much to the town, so this park was dedicated to them. The lake was originally Mayview Lake, and in the 1950s the Tweetsie Jr. train took children on rides around the lake. The attractive walking path around the lake was once the track for the train. (Courtesy of Donna Warmuth.)

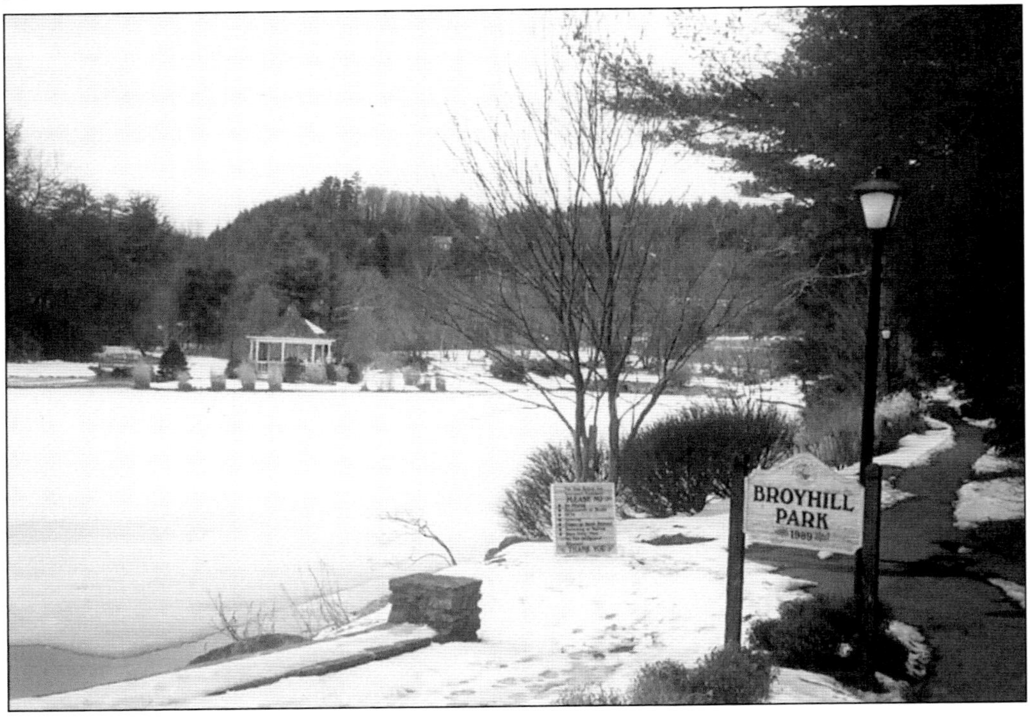

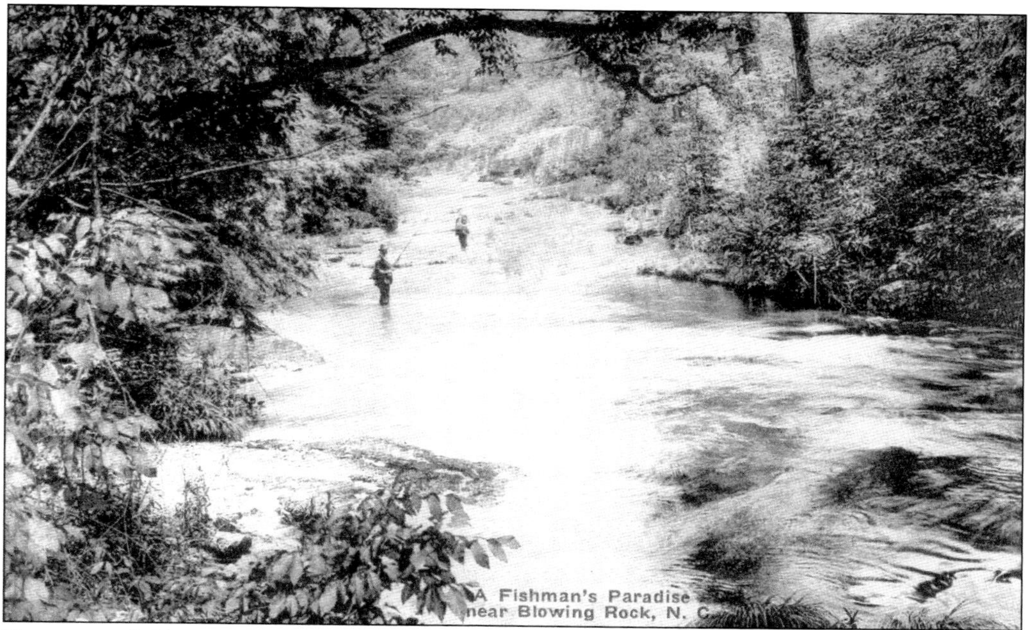

FISHERMAN'S PARADISE. Outdoor sports and activities were a draw for even the earliest visitors and continue to draw people today. The mountain streams and lakes hold an abundance of fish for every skill level of fisherman. (Courtesy of Web Alexander.)

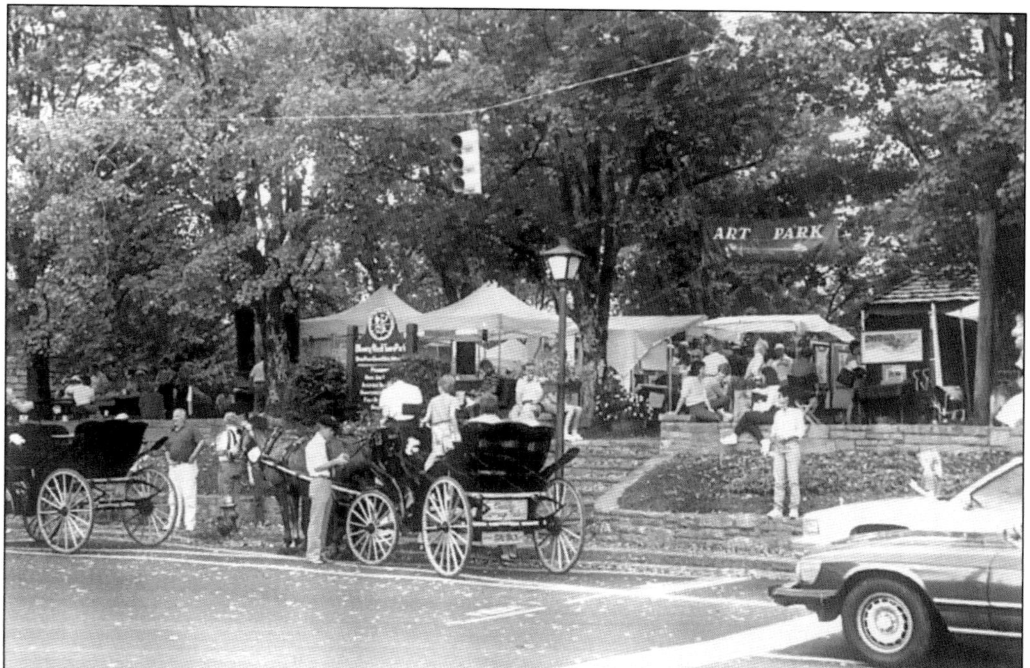

ART IN THE PARK. This highly regarded art show in Blowing Rock has been named among the top 20 events by the Southeast Tourism Society several times. The show had a small beginning in 1962 and has since grown and is now is operated by the Chamber of Commerce. This photograph dates from 1988, when this juried arts and fine handcrafts show was located in Memorial Park. (Courtesy of *The Blowing Rocket*.)

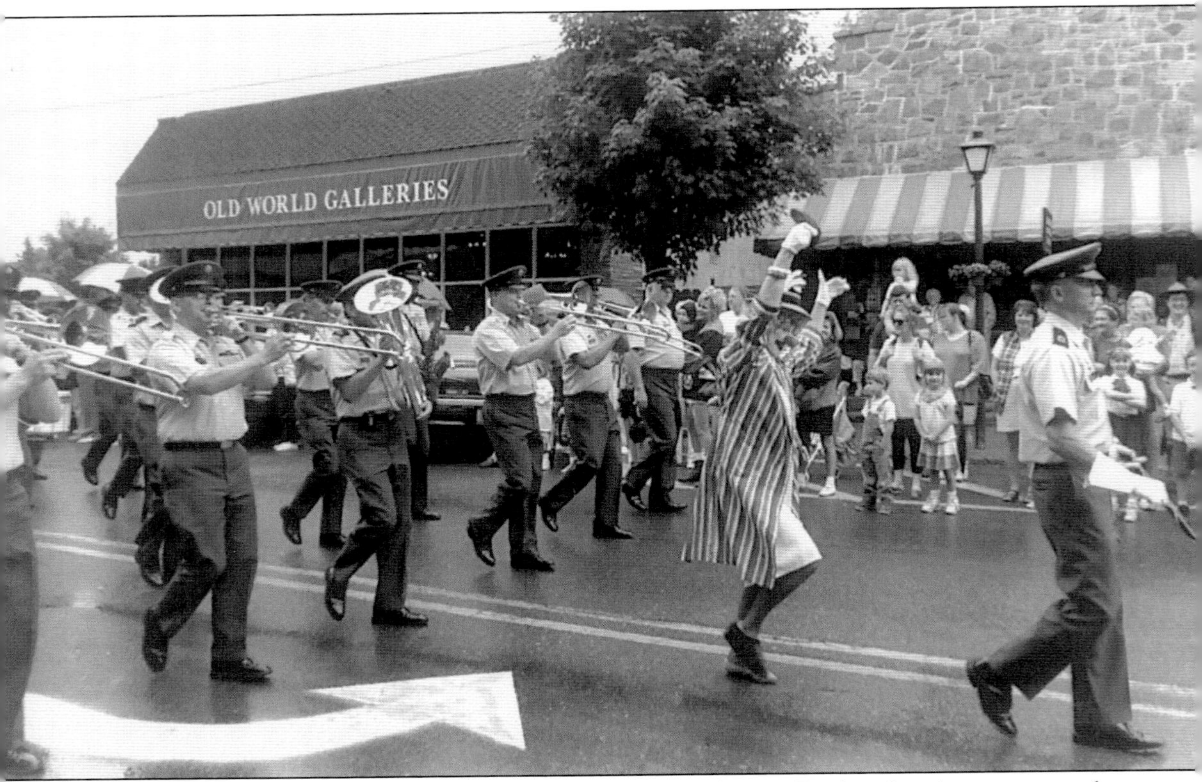

TOWN PARADE. Parades have long been popular in Blowing Rock, often bringing together locals, summer residents, and visitors. This Fourth of July parade features a military band and clown. (Courtesy of *The Blowing Rocket*.)

Seven

HIGH COUNTRY ATTRACTIONS

Many attractions are available in the High Country region and offer something for everyone. Tourism and the service industry have become major components of the economy. From Grandfather Mountain to Tweetsie Railroad, activities are plenty. Opportunities to simply enjoy the outdoor scenery are plentiful, too, with hiking, biking, and riding trails surrounding the town. In the winter, skiing, snow boarding, and ice skating are the major sports. In such communities, there is always the problem of balancing land use and access with environmental and scenic protection, similar to the problem of the goose who laid the golden egg. The town of Blowing Rock has been proactive in preserving its historic heritage and environmental quality, and these resources will hopefully be saved for future generations of residents and visitors to appreciate and enjoy.

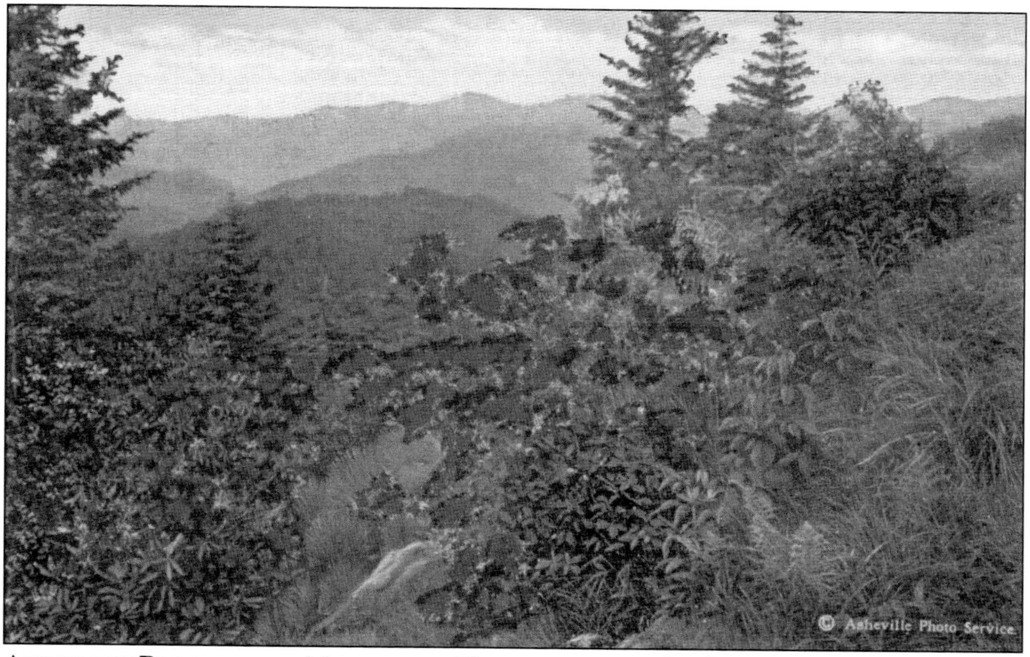

AZALEAS IN BLOOM IN THE MOUNTAINS. This scenic postcard reflects the natural beauty of the mountains, a continuing draw to the area. Promotional materials for the area in the early 1900s touted the clean air, water, and inspiring views as food for the soul. Today's visitors would agree, too. (Courtesy of Richard Trexler.)

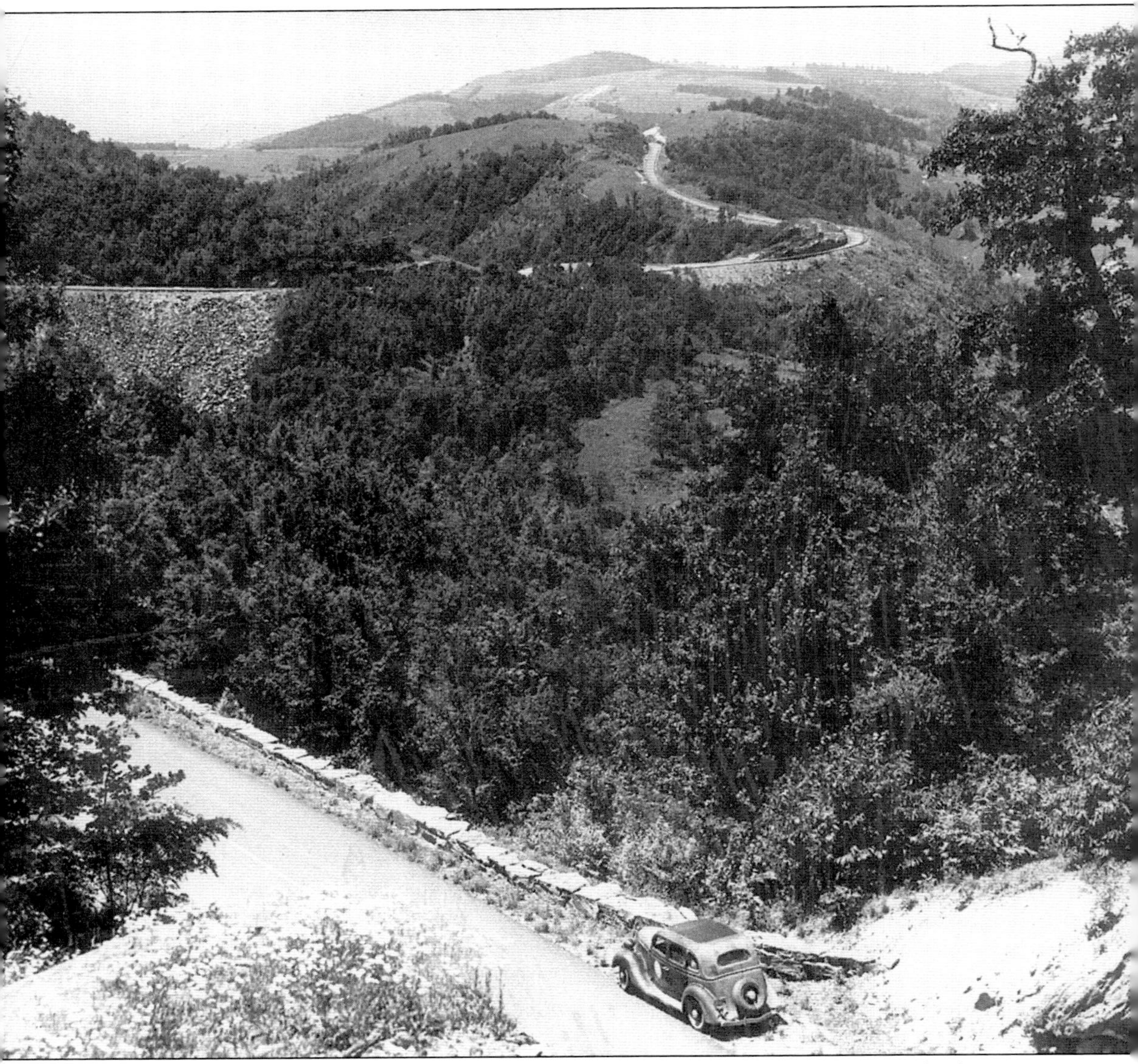

BLUE RIDGE PARKWAY. A major asset to the region is the Blue Ridge Parkway, which runs near Blowing Rock. Although the town was active in supporting construction of the parkway from its beginnings, nobody could have estimated its impact on the area. The Blue Ridge Parkway is a link between the Shenandoah and the Great Smoky Mountains National Park systems. In 1933, President Franklin D. Roosevelt approved construction of the parkway. Some displaced families from the parkway construction regret being forced to sell their land to the government. However, this linear green space is an irreplaceable treasure and shows much foresight from the politicians. The parkway attracts thousands of visitors and offers camping, hiking, and nature programs. (Courtesy of *The Blowing Rocket*.)

Leaning Rock on Yonahlossee Road. The Leaning Rock rises majestically from the mountains along Yonahlossee Road. Walking, riding along, and then driving the mountain roads was and still is a favorite past time of visitors to the area. (Courtesy of Stella Greer Dobbins.)

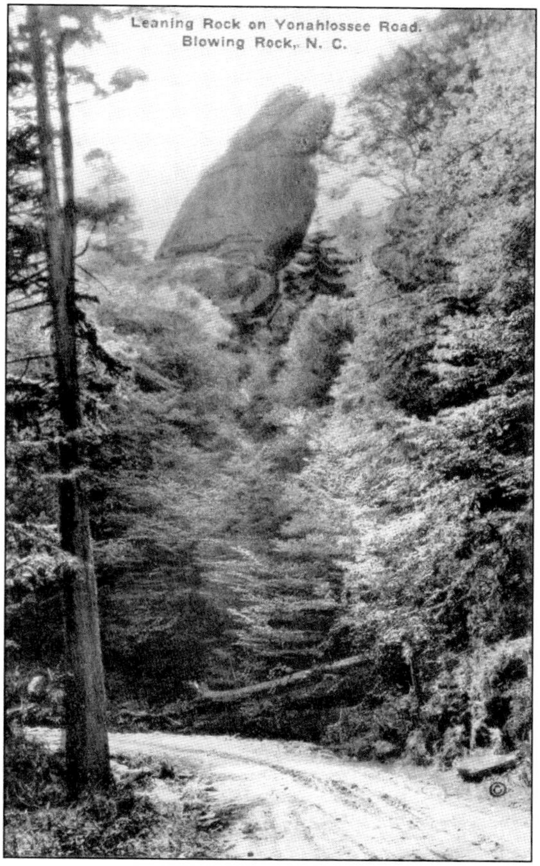

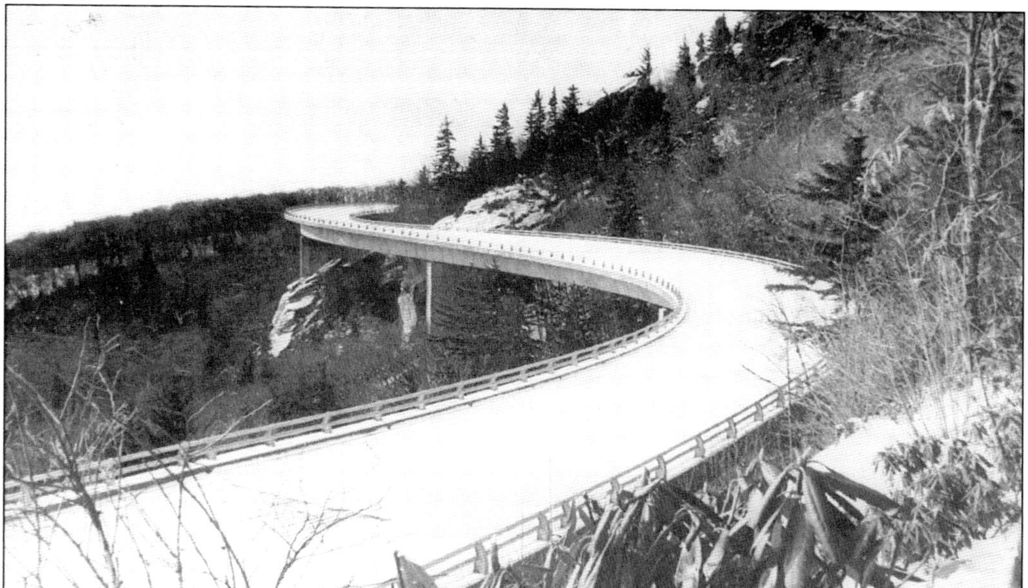

Linn Cove Viaduct in Winter. This section of the Blue Ridge Parkway is still considered to be an engineering marvel. The road arches out over thin air and winds around the Blue Ridge approaching Grandfather Mountain. (Courtesy of *The Blowing Rocket.*)

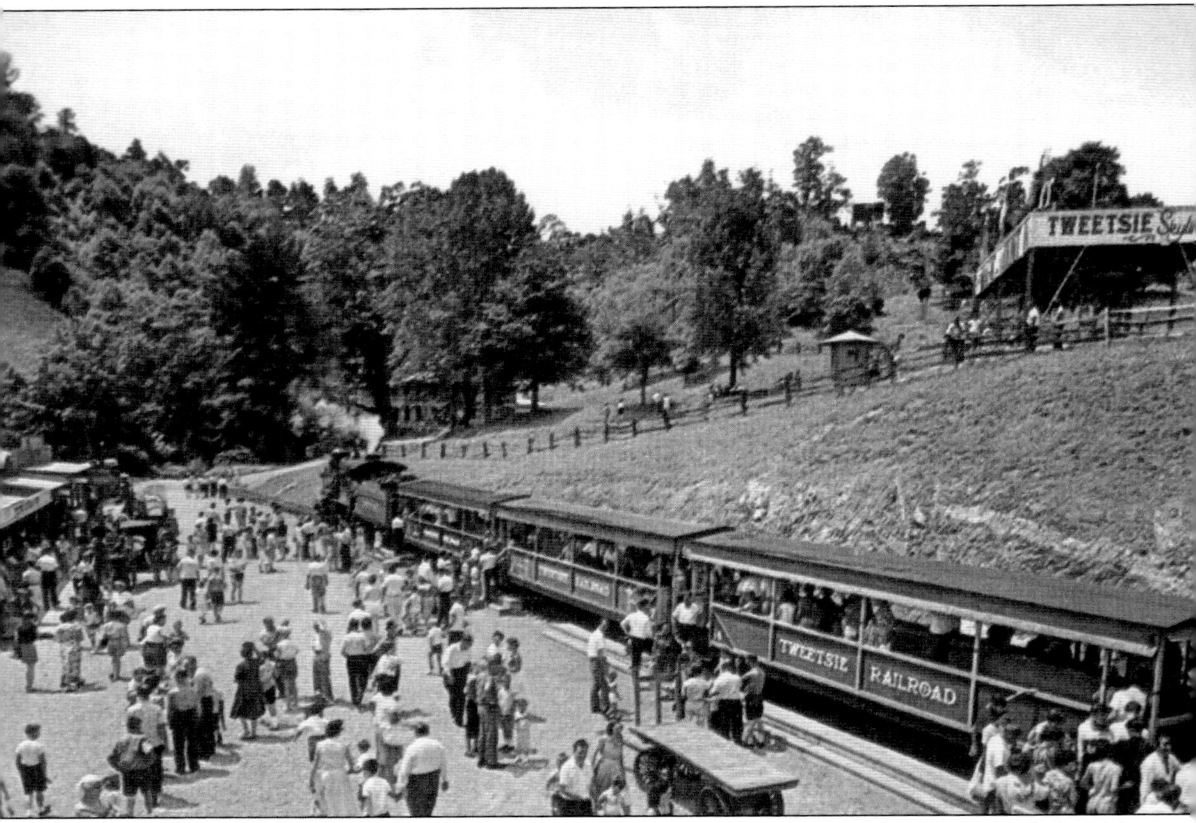

Tweetsie Railroad. This theme park has been around since 1957 and has provided Wild West fun for millions of visitors. Tweetsie was the affectionate nickname for the East Tennessee & Western North Carolina Railroad, which ran through Boone to Tennessee. After a major flood in 1940, most of the tracks were washed away and the tracks to Boone were abandoned. Gene Autry, famous singing cowboy, planned to purchase the train to use in filming westerns. To its rescue came Grover Robbins Jr., who bought the option on Tweetsie locomotive #12 from Autry in 1955. The train was transported from Virginia to Hickory by train flat car. The Tweetsie train was restored in Hickory, and then the engine and three cars were slowly pulled by truck and trailer up the steep mountain to Blowing Rock. Mr. Robbins had a vision of a frontier village and museum—the area's first theme park. A three-mile section of track was reconstructed around the park to provided visitors with a short ride through the wilderness. The park has been a major addition to the tourism industry and is also a symbol of the area's past. The author will always remember her first visit as a child to Tweetsie, as do many others. (Courtesy of Richard Trexler.)

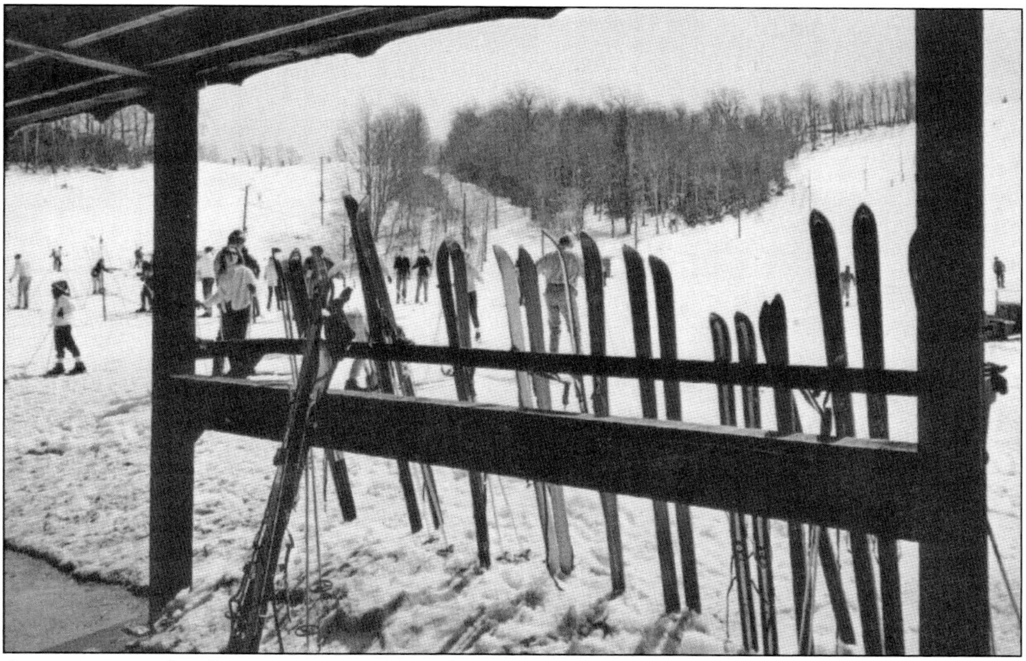

APPALACHIAN SKI MOUNTAIN. In 1962, the Blowing Rock Ski Lodge opened on a mountaintop near Blowing Rock, which later became known as Appalachian Ski Mountain. The snow-making technology enabled numerous other ski resorts to open near Banner Elk. The economic importance of skiing and winter sports to the area is tremendous and makes the High County a full season resort. (Courtesy of Richard Trexler.)

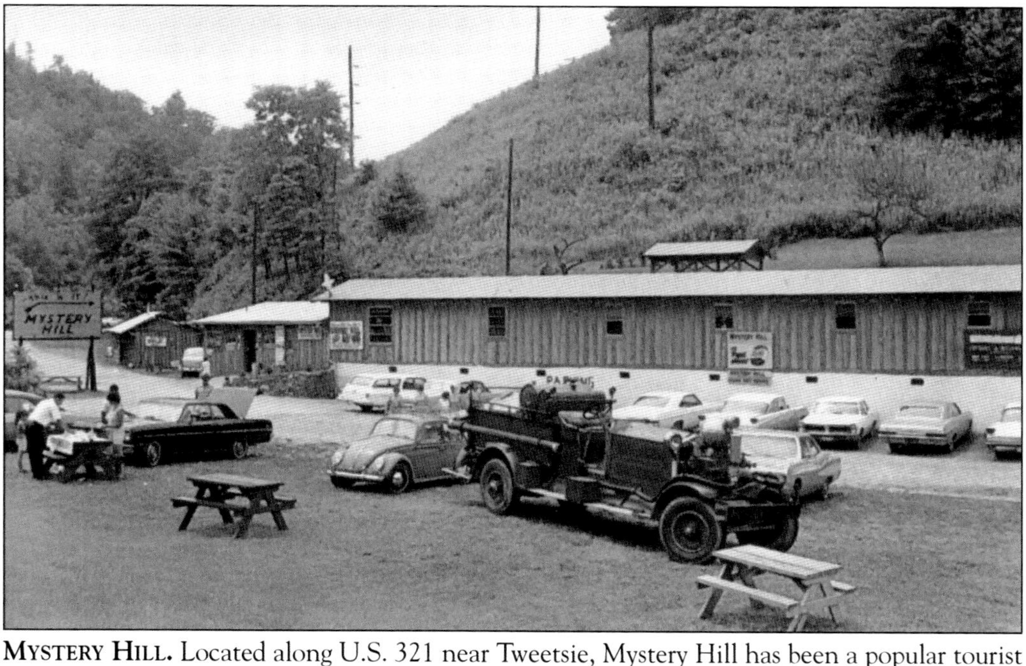

MYSTERY HILL. Located along U.S. 321 near Tweetsie, Mystery Hill has been a popular tourist stop for many years with its gravity-defying exhibits. The Dougherty House (home of the founders of Appalachian State University) is also located adjacent to Mystery Hill. (Courtesy of Richard Trexler.)

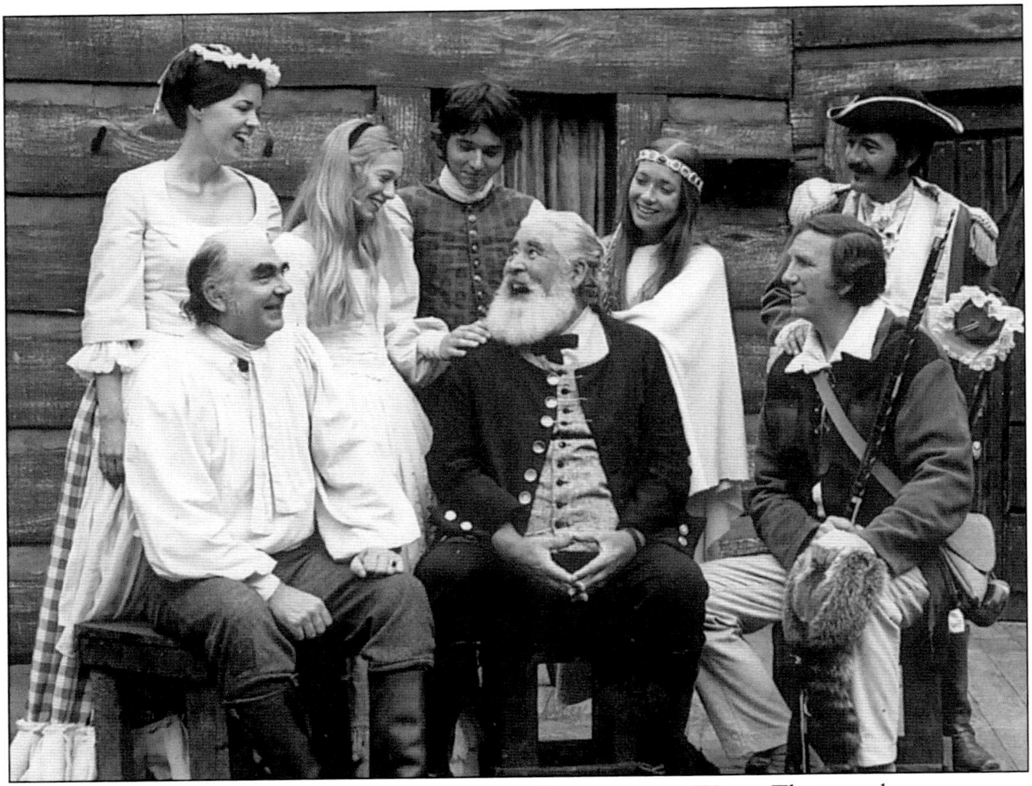

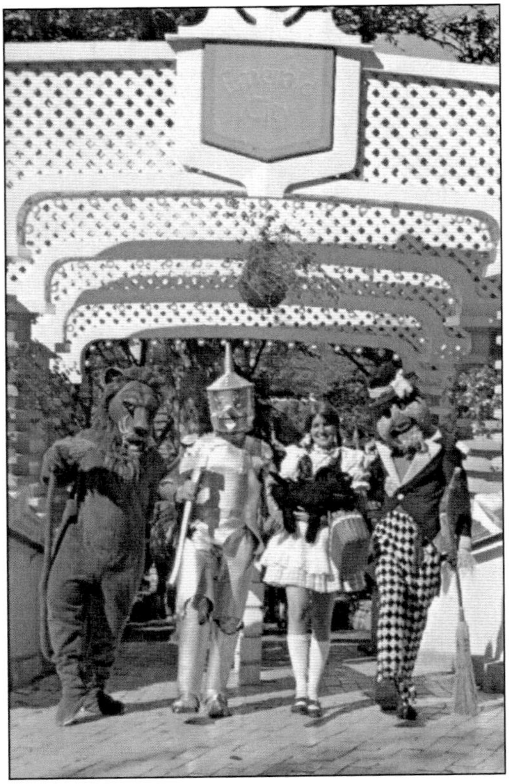

Horn in the West. This popular summer drama staged in Boone tells the story of Daniel Boone and the pioneers. The long-running outdoor drama has been staged since 1952 at the Hickory Ridge Homestead. The homestead includes restored log cabins and exhibits of frontier life in the mountains. (Courtesy of *The Blowing Rocket*.)

Land of Oz. Grover and Harry Robbins also developed the Land of Oz on top of Beech Mountain. The park was closed in 1980, but parts of the park still remain above Ski Beech resort. Recent plans by the Emerald Mountain Development include home sites and some restoration of Dorothy's farm and other park elements. (Courtesy of Richard Trexler.)

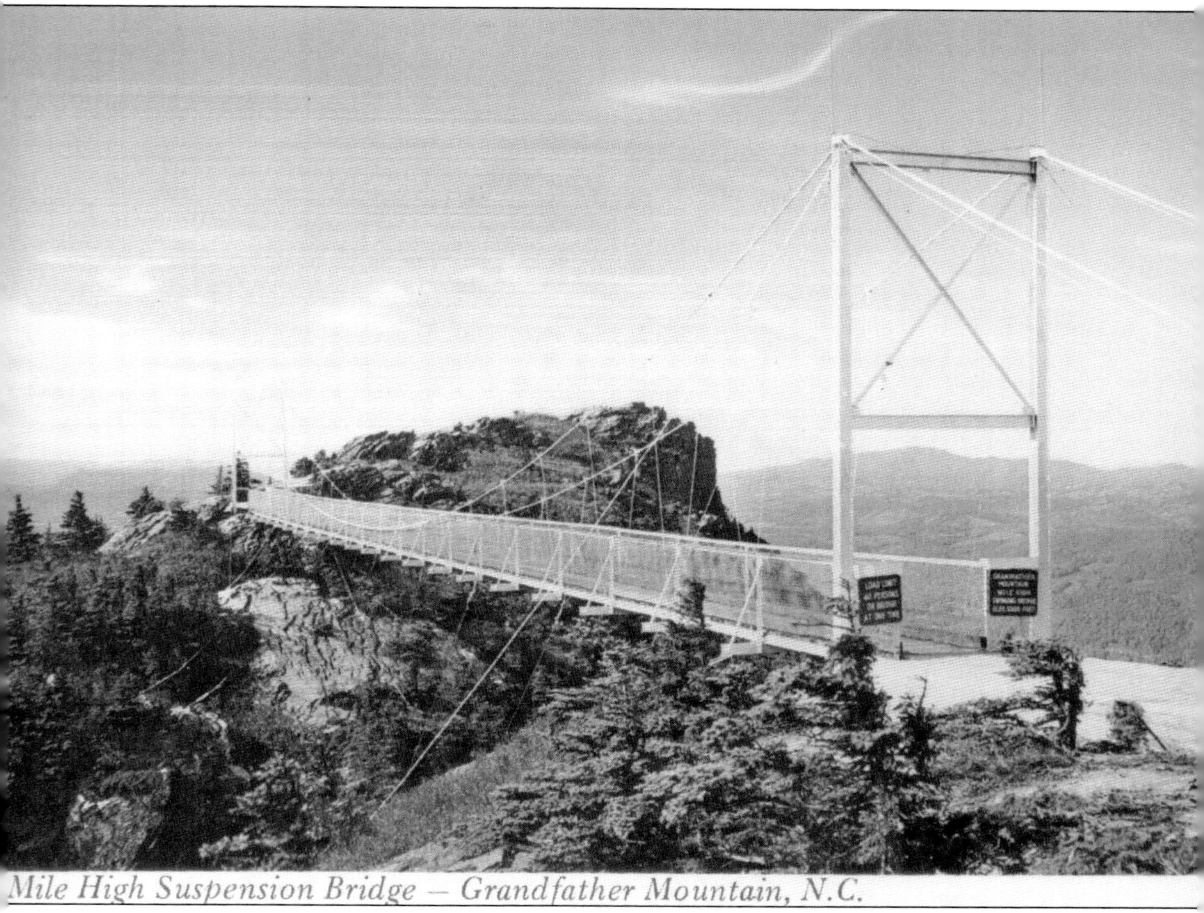

MILE HIGH SWINGING BRIDGE. The swinging bridge has become a landmark on top of famous Grandfather Mountain in nearby Linville. Hugh MacRae was the first owner of the mountain. Efforts were made to have the mountain become a national or state park, but these were unsuccessful. MacRae's grandson, Hugh Morton, a well-known photographer, currently owns and operates the mountain preserve. Morton has been able to encourage new forest growth on the peak and to promote it as a tourist attraction and biopreserve. The first approach to the mountain was the old Native American trail. As early as the 1890s, a rough road had been in place, but thankfully, it was improved and extended in 1935. The mile high swinging bridge, a challenge for the bravest, opened in 1952. Hiking trails, picnic areas, a zoo, and mineral museum attract visitors from far and wide. The mountain is open year-round, depending on weather conditions. The Highland Games take place in the summer in MacRae Meadows. The popular gospel event, Singing on the Mountain, also takes place in the same meadow near Grandfather. The mountain is a recognizable and memorable symbol of the High Country. This photograph was taken by Walter Cline. (Courtesy of Richard Trexler.)

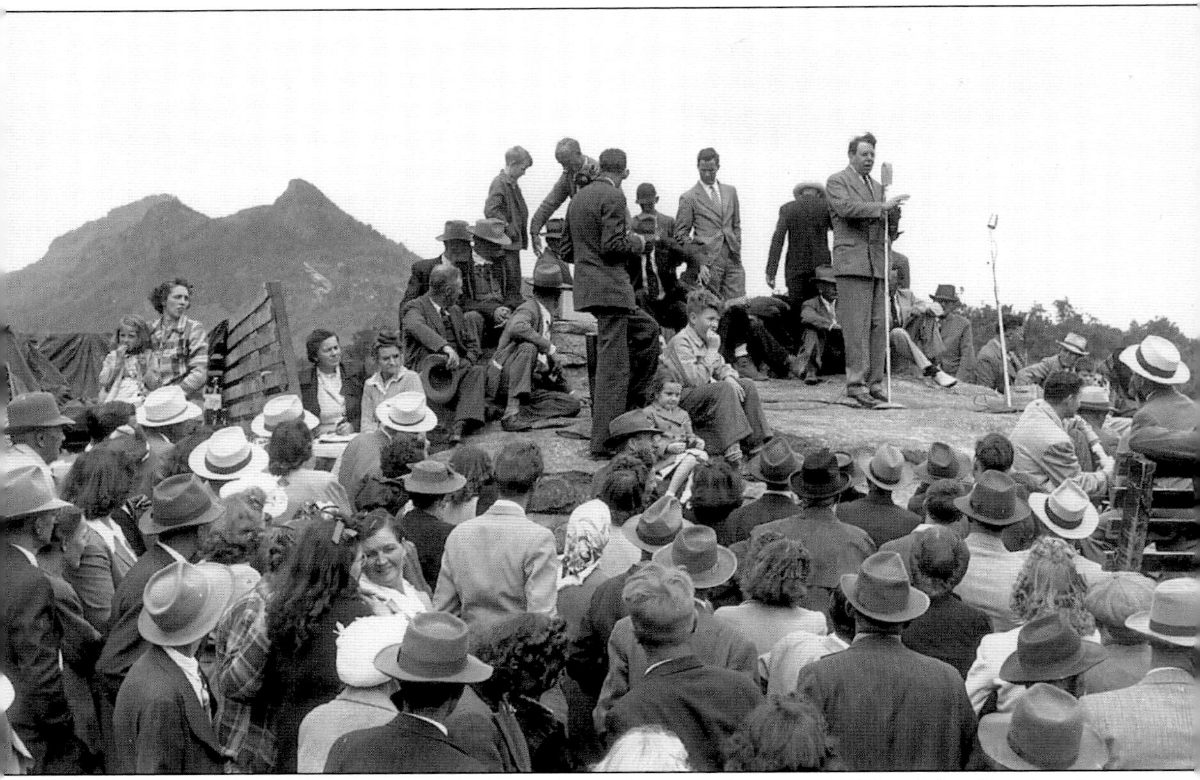

SINGING ON THE MOUNTAIN. This annual gospel singing began in 1926 with Joe Hartley. From a family gathering, it has grown to an event that attracts thousands from all over to hear gospel music beneath the profile of the Grandfather. Hosts for the event have included Billy Graham, Bob Hope, and other entertainers, politicians, and athletes. The all-day event is still held with no charge for admission and thousands attend. The event is known as the oldest and largest old-time singing convention in the nation. (Courtesy of *The Blowing Rocket*.)

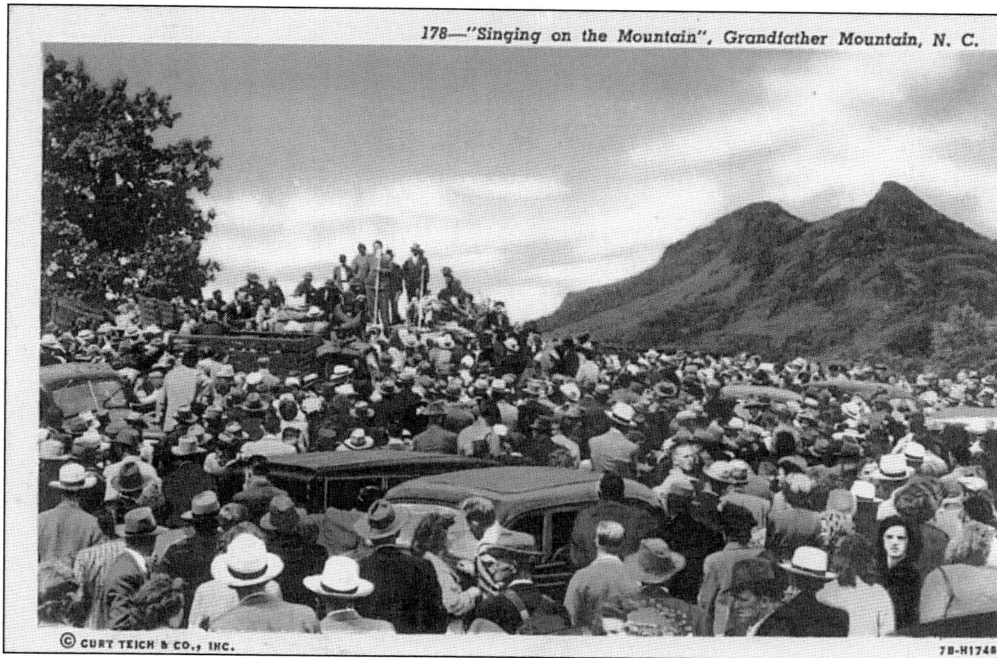

SINGING ON THE MOUNTAIN. This postcard shows the annual gospel singing that began in 1926 with Joe Hartley. The show has grown tremendously and thousands now gather to hear gospel music beneath Grandfather Mountain. (Courtesy of Ginny Stevens.)

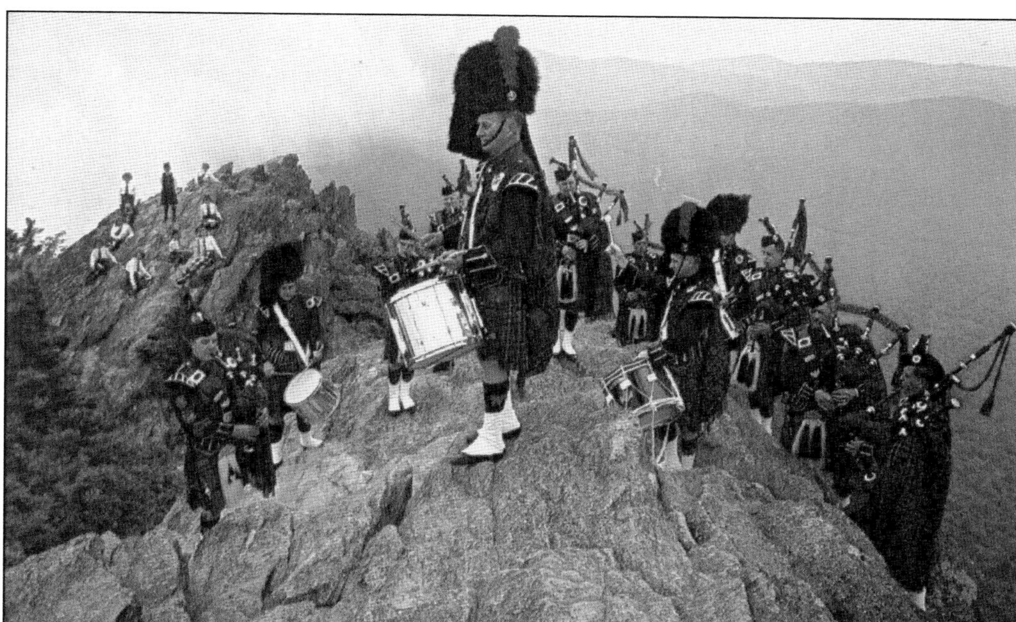

HIGHLAND GAMES AND GATHERING OF CLANS. This event was begun in 1956 and has grown to attract thousands of visitors and competitors. It is one of the largest clan gatherings in the world. Traditional athletic events, dancing, and gatherings of the clans make it a fascinating and colorful event. (Courtesy of Stella Greer Dobbins.)

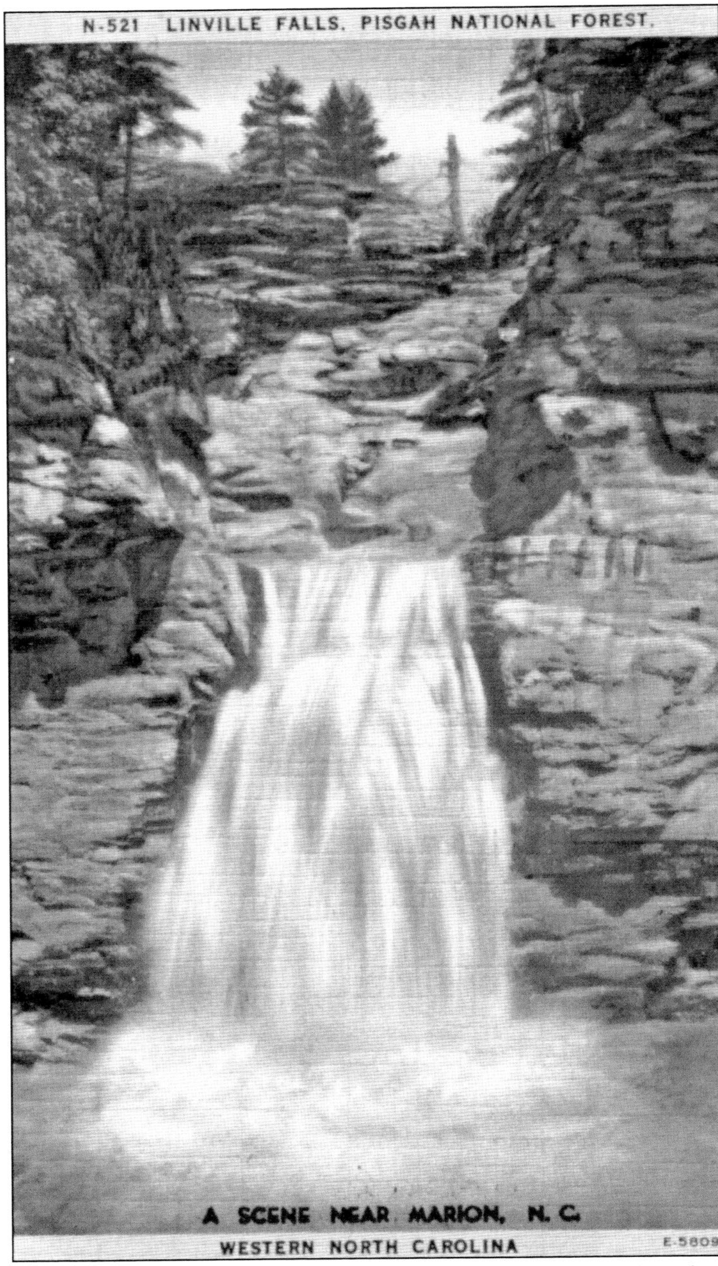

LINVILLE FALLS. This postcard dated 1946 shows some of the area's best known waterfalls, near Linville. The hiking areas to overlook the falls and the trail down to the bottom are truly breathtaking. These early postcards were popular with visitors to show the folks back home the splendors of the mountains. This attraction continues to bring hikers and outdoor enthusiasts to the area. One of the greatest assets of the region is its wonderful scenic beauty, which may be at risk due to poor land management practices, development, and environmental pollution. Views from the Blue Ridge Parkway could be seen to Charlotte just a few years ago, but now smog and air pollution cuts visibility even on low humidity days. This land truly is "God's Country," requiring that we, the caretakers, provide careful management and protection. (Courtesy of Richard Trexler.)